PHYSIQUE and
DELINQUENCY

by Sheldon and Eleanor Glueck

Five Hundred Criminal Careers, 1930
One Thousand Juvenile Delinquents, 1934
Five Hundred Delinquent Women, 1934
Preventing Crime (Editors), 1936
Later Criminal Careers, 1937
Juvenile Delinquents Grown Up, 1940
Criminal Careers in Retrospect, 1943
After-conduct of Discharged Offenders, 1945
Unraveling Juvenile Delinquency, 1950 (transl. into Japanese)
Delinquents in the Making, 1952 (transl. into Italian and French)

by Eleanor Touroff Glueck

The Community Use of Schools, 1927
Extended Use of School Buildings, 1927
Evaluative Research in Social Work, 1936

by Sheldon Glueck

Mental Disorder and the Criminal Law, 1925
Probation and Criminal Justice (Editor), 1933
Crime and Justice, 1936; republished, 1945
Cases on Criminal Law (with Livingston Hall), 1940
War Criminals: Their Prosecution and Punishment, 1944 (transl. into Spanish)
The Nuremberg Trial and Aggressive War, 1946 (transl. into Japanese)
Criminal Law and Enforcement (with Livingston Hall), 1951
Crime and Correction: Selected Papers, 1952
The Welfare State and the National Welfare (Editor), 1952

PHYSIQUE and DELINQUENCY

By Sheldon *and* Eleanor Glueck

HARPER & BROTHERS PUBLISHERS NEW YORK

Grateful acknowledgment is made to The Commonwealth Fund and Harvard University Press for permission to reprint material from UNRAVELING JUVENILE DELINQUENCY by Sheldon and Eleanor Glueck. Copyright 1950 by The Commonwealth Fund.

Library of Congress Catalog card number: 56-6432

DEDICATION

To the late EARNEST A. HOOTON, teacher and friend, who long ago directed our attention to the possible role of body build in human behavior.

Table of Contents

Preface

The present volume is the first in a series of monographs growing out of a comprehensive research into persistent juvenile delinquency, encompassed in *Unraveling Juvenile Delinquency* (published in 1950). In the Preface to that volume, we pointed out that the term "unraveling" was deliberately chosen to stress a continuing quest for the causal mechanisms of persistent delinquency. The findings of *Unraveling* were so challenging that we have been impelled to a further and more penetrating analysis of our vast store of basic data, in the conviction that it still holds secret many clues to a better understanding of the causes, treatment, and prevention of antisocial behavior. The time, effort, and expense involved in the initial assembling of the basic materials call for their deeper and more meaningful analysis. As our knowledge of and our "feel" for the data grow, we see new paths along which to venture.

The data presented in *Unraveling* are essentially descriptive. There was no systematic attempt made to interrelate the findings derived from the study of the family and personal background of the delinquent and non-delinquent boys who were the subjects of that research with the data that emerged from the anthropometric, physical, psychological, and psychiatric examinations. Such integration of the findings as we did make was not the result of any statistical intercorrelation of the materials of one area of the research with those of another, but emerged from the descriptive analysis of each aspect of the inquiry. We noted the necessity for further exploration of the data of *Unraveling* in order to modify and to make more specific the rather broad generalizations to which we necessarily had to limit ourselves at that stage.

The present volume deals with a subject—the role of body build in the complex of forces involved in delinquency—which, on the whole, has not had an appeal to American criminologists, who are largely of the sociological persuasion. We ourselves have long been eclectic in our studies of the crime problem; and in determining on a "breakdown" of our data by physique type, we are concerned merely with a deeper penetration into one of many relevant areas suggested by the research project. It is our intent to follow this breakdown with several others having to do with other aspects of juvenile delinquency.

Those who have struggled with investigations in the biosocial field know what a veritable *terra incognita* it is. Conclusions must always be regarded as approximations; and the aim of the scientific explorer is constantly to improve these approximations. What we say in the present volume about the relationship between physique and delinquency is but part of a larger whole. We are well aware of its imperfections; but even a piece of tangible fact is worth more than a totality of guesswork or speculative theorizing.

A volume could be devoted to describing our frustrations in the analysis and presentation of the data, reflected in innumerable discussions, reassessments of procedure, revisions, and rewritings. However, we have emerged from the battle of thoughts and words with a satisfying sense of modest achievement. Certainly we have learned much in the process of breaking down the barriers of misunderstanding between ourselves as criminologists and those far more skilled than we in the related disciplines on which we have had to draw.

One of the greatest struggles was to find a statistical method that would fortify and make more meaningful our inspectional analysis of the data. In this we have had the fruitful advice of Professor Frederick Mosteller of the Harvard Department of Social Relations, who called our attention to a method of "multiple comparisons" recently developed (and as yet unpublished) by Professor John W. Tukey of the Department of Mathematics of Princeton University. (Professor Tukey advises us that he does not know of any analysis, by this method, of "a body of data of comparable size and complexity which will have been analyzed more carefully and conservatively" than ours.) Our chief statistical consultant, Professor Jane Worcester of the Harvard School of Public Health, has guided us not only in the employment of this new method but in the basic statistical issues that arose in the course of the inquiry. Mrs. Rose Kneznek, Executive Secretary of the Bureau of Business Research of the Harvard Graduate School of Business Administration, has devoted much time and thought both to numerous computational problems and to the preparation and checking of the statistical data in all the tables and in the text of the manuscript. Dr. Worcester and Mrs. Kneznek have both read most of the final manuscript and have made constructive editorial suggestions. We are deeply indebted to all these experts, whose unsparing advice has been invaluable during our two years of intensive devotion to this project.

The reader may be surprised to learn that approximately 8000 computations of one sort or another were made at the Bureau of Business Research of the Harvard Business School during the course of the analysis, of which some 5000 are represented in this volume. The ones that were discarded are not wholly lost, as the reader will see in the "Explanation of the Statistical Method" by Jane Worcester, in Appendix A.

Although the statistical management of the data seemed at first to be the most crucial of our problems, we also had to keep in mind the rigid requirements of the anthropologic discipline. To educate ourselves we turned for advice to Professor Earnest A. Hooton, a friend and mentor of many years; Dr. Carl Seltzer, who had originally classified the subjects of *Unraveling* into somatotypes; Professor William W. Howells, who succeeded Professor Hooton as head of the Department of Anthropology at Harvard University; and Professor C. Wesley Dupertuis of the School of Medicine, Western Reserve University. Professor Dupertuis, who is a physical anthropologist, is the only one among them who has read the entire manuscript. He has in fact (and most profitably for us), used a fine-tooth comb on two complete drafts of the manuscript, one finished in the spring of 1954 and since completely rewritten, and the one here presented.

In order to derive some notion of the possible reactions of geneticists to this presentation, we consulted Robert Levine, Assistant Professor of Biology of Harvard University, with whom relevant portions of the first two chapters were discussed.

To ascertain something of the possible receptiveness of psychologists to the constitutional approach, especially those concerned with the study of personality, we submitted several chapters to Professor Gordon W. Allport of the Department of Social Relations of Harvard University.

Needless to add, we are alone responsible for the formulation of the inquiry and the analysis and interpretation of the findings.

For the painstaking day-to-day "grind" in the statistical aspects of this manuscript, we are indebted not only to Mrs. Rose Kneznek but to certain members of her staff in the Harvard Bureau of Business Research—Miss Eleanor G. May, Assistant Executive Secretary of the Bureau; Mrs. Bertha W. Daniels and Mrs. Louise B. Sullivan, who made the tabulations on I.B.M. machines; Mrs. Mabel A. Kelly and Mrs. Joy K. Thoburn, who carried out the vast majority of the computations under the direction of Mrs. Kneznek and Miss May; and Miss Caroline M. Timmerman, who so expertly typed the tables and exhibits.

As regards our own staff, only three have been directly involved—Mrs. Esther A. Ghostlaw, Richard E. Thompson, and Mrs. Sheila Murphrey. The others—Mrs. Mildred P. Cunningham, George F. McGrath, John E. Burke, Mrs. Mary H. Moran, and Mrs. Barbara H. Siegfriedt—have helped us more than they realize by their patient and loyal devotion to their various duties on other aspects of our over-all research program which had to go forward despite our own preoccupation with the preparation of this volume. They have quietly and efficiently carried on their work with a minimum of infringement on our time.

To Mrs. Ghostlaw, who with seemingly limitless cheeriness and rare competence has typed and retyped numerous drafts of each chapter, deciphering the scribblings of both of us in script that would try the patience of handwriting experts, we owe not only the final emergence of an accurate manuscript properly assembled but also an infectious buoyancy which has carried us safely over many "rough times" in the course of this enterprise.

Richard E. Thompson, our research assistant, has served in numerous capacities throughout this project—digesting relevant articles and books, checking footnotes, serving as a liaison between us and the Bureau of Business Research, keeping track of materials, assembling data, acting in other words as librarian of the project and able on short notice to produce out of a welter of data any needed bit that we required.

To Mrs. Murphrey we are grateful for the quiet efficiency with which she has carried on the miscellany of administrative and secretarial duties entailed in a research program such as ours. There are innumerable behind-the-scenes aspects of a project needing wise handling, to which she has brought excellent judgment and finesse.

Our indebtedness as always is great to Dean Erwin N. Griswold of the Harvard Law School for his unflagging interest in and encouragement of our work, and to the foundations (notably the Ford Foundation) which have seen fit to contribute toward its support.

One final word before we invite the reader to plunge *in medias res*. We wish that more refined tests and methods had been available when we assembled the raw materials of *Unraveling Juvenile Delinquency* on which the current inquiry is based. In a research of this kind which involves so many areas, concern is to be expected on the part of experts in each discipline encompassed, regarding the "underpinnings" on which the structure has been reared. Some psychologists, for example, may question the reliability of the

Rorschach Test as a means of deriving the character traits used in this study; some psychiatrists may feel that more effective methods of determining traits of temperament could have been used; some anthropologists may take issue with the idea of somatotyping or the way in which the somatotyping was done; some sociologists may feel that insufficient stress was given to certain sociocultural influences; some statisticians may not like the method of multiple comparisons that has been used in interpreting the findings. Although such criticisms may have some justification, the test of the soundness of a project such as ours rests, in the final analysis, on the clinical "good sense" and the internal consistency of the integrated result.

We have wrought as best we could with the materials at our command; we can only welcome improvement on our handiwork.

SHELDON AND ELEANOR GLUECK

Harvard Law School
June, 1955.

PHYSIQUE and DELINQUENCY

I

General Orientation

From time immemorial—in folklore, philosophic speculation, and literature—there have been attempts to link forms of bodily structure to traits of temperament, character, and conduct. The vigorous antics of Shakespeare's energetic shrew-tamer, Petruchio, the jealousy and envy of the "lean and hungry" Cassius, the indolence and gluttony of the fat knight, Sir John Falstaff, the compensatory villainies of the "deformed, unfinished" Richard III—these are among the more familar illustrations from literature.

In modern times there have been more scientific and systematic attempts to relate body morphology to traits of temperament and personality—among them the pioneering works of Kretschmer[1] and Sheldon.[2]

Is there anything to this alleged biologic affinity of body type to various temperamental and mental traits and, in turn, to conduct? Especially, is there any evidence that somatopsychic structure plays a significant role in delinquency? Since we have some valuable original data which might throw light on this issue, we devote the present volume to it, by intercorrelating traits of personality and character and sociocultural factors of home and family life with physique types, in a representative sample of persistent delinquents contrasted with a matched sample of true non-delinquents.

To focus attention on one aspect of the causal complex in delin-

*Footnotes will be found at the end of each chapter.

quency does not of course imply non-awareness of the others or a notion that they are unimportant. There is indeed a growing conviction that the complex phenomenon of delinquency is not likely to be accounted for by any simplistic concept of unitary "cause" or "theory."[3] Acts of delinquency are varied, having in common only the fact that they are evidence of maladjustment of the individual to one or another of the diverse prohibitions of legal norms and codes. Therefore causal sequences leading to violations of the law must probably also vary. As research proceeds, certain sequences may be found to carry more etiologic weight than others; but it is still true that it is a diversity of traits and factors which, working together in differing degrees and circumstances, bring about the end result of antisocial behavior.

The variety of etiologic influences involved in delinquency makes it possible to place under the microscope for intensive study each of numerous participating factors. Perhaps the analysis of physique as related to temperamental and mental traits and environmental influences will yield some valuable insights.

It should be said at the outset that the present work is not animated by any notion of respectful reawakening of the somnolent Lombrosian theory that "*the* criminal" is a distinct hereditary species of "atavistic" or of degenerative nature. Nor is it begun with any preconception that bodily structure is the most weighty etiologic factor, or matrix of influence, in criminogenesis. It is merely found to be a promising focus of attention—among others we plan to explore in subsequent monographs—in pursuit of more intensive analyses of the intricacies of delinquency than was possible in our prior researches, including even the most comprehensive work, *Unraveling Juvenile Delinquency*.[4]

UNRAVELING JUVENILE DELINQUENCY

In the present volume, then, we continue the task of *Unraveling Juvenile Delinquency* begun in the work of that title in which were presented the first fruits of a farflung inquiry into the causes of juvenile delinquency, through a comparison of 500 persistent delinquents and 500 proven non-delinquents. Detailed account of the sampling process is rendered in *Unraveling Juvenile Delinquency*. Here it need only be pointed out that we studied *persistent* and therefore true delinquents, rather than boys who once or twice during their lives had stolen a toy, sneaked into a motion picture theater, or played hooky—something that many children indulge in by way of experimental deviation from legally dictated norms of conduct. We were interested in the unquestionably "pathologic" in terms of delinquency to compare with the unquestionably healthy. The 500 delinquents were therefore drawn from the two industrial schools of Massachusetts. Much time, effort, and ingenuity were spent to find, in the Boston public schools, 500 true non-delinquents, to match with the 500 delinquents in terms of age, general intelligence (I.Q.), ethnico-racial derivation,[5] and residence in economically and socioculturally underprivileged areas of Greater Boston. General conclusions must be qualified to take account of these aspects of the two samples compared. However, experience with a prediction table based on five factors of family life that were found most markedly to differentiate delinquents from non-delinquents,[6] as well as other, indirect, evidence derived from a prior study,[7] would seem to indicate that the samples in question are more typical of the general situation than might offhand be supposed.

Basic data for comparison of the delinquents and the control group were derived from intensive exploration into the family background of these two groups of boys, their physique, their health, certain aspects of their intelligence, their temperament, and their personality and character structure.

The general control of the ethnico-racial factor greatly enhances the reliability of the morphologic findings, in that the differences found to exist in the body structure of delinquents and non-delinquents,[8] and between the boys of the various physique types, can be considered roughly (though not completely) independent of the influence of ethnic origin on the measurements involved.[9] Apart from this, the intensive verification of the raw materials that entered into the original research[10] gives promise of enhanced reliability of the correlation tables in the analysis encompassed in the present work, advantaged as it is by the employment of a carefully selected control group. It should be pointed out also that no other investigation involving somatotypes or body types exists which includes on so extensive a scale the findings of Rorschach tests, or of psychiatric investigation and sociological inquiry.[11]

Finally, attention should be called to an important methodologic principle governing the original investigation and the gathering of the raw materials for *Unraveling Juvenile Delinquency*. From the start, we insisted that each segment of the inquiry—somatic, intellectual, characterial (Rorschach Test), temperamental-emotional (psychiatric), and sociocultural—be explored independently of every other. No investigator in any of these areas was given access to the findings of the other segments of the research. To be sure, this had some drawbacks; but our experience has demonstrated that the advantages in terms of the ultimate reliability of the data have far outweighed any handicaps. There was no "reading in" or "tainting" of the raw materials of any one area through information obtained from any other line of the investigation. Reasoning in a circle was strictly eschewed. The psychiatrist had no access to the Rorschach Test findings on the boy he was interviewing; the anthropologists were not shown the Rorschach or psychiatric data. The Rorschach experts interpreted the test protocols obtained by other psychologists without prior knowledge of whether the test-responses were from delinquents or non-delinquents. We ourselves put the pieces of the puzzle together.

The reliability of the facts thus obtained from independent and neutralized sources, by various methods and different personnel, revealed an essential harmony reflected, for example, in the consistency of the psychiatric and Rorschach diagnoses when the cases investigated day by day over several years were finally compared;[12] and further reflected in the finding that the three diagnostic-prognostic (predictive) tables we prepared from the most differentiative social, Rorschach, and psychiatric data turned out to have equally high power in distinguishing delinquents from non-delinquents.[13]

Evidences of the internal consistency and reliability of the basic data, from which the tentative conclusions in *Unraveling* were drawn, fortify our conviction of the merit of undertaking the present inquiry.

Over 400 traits and factors were included in *Unraveling* in the mass comparisons of delinquents and the control group of non-delinquents. These comparisons yielded some fundamental insights into the forces at play in the etiologic dynamics of persistent juvenile delinquency. The summation of the major resemblances and dissimilarities between the delinquents and the non-delinquents indicated that the separate findings, independently gathered, integrate into a dynamic pattern which is neither exclusively biologic nor exclusively sociocultural, but which derives from an interplay of certain somatic, temperamental, intellectual, and sociocultural forces:

The delinquents as a group [were found to be] distinguishable from the non-delinquents: (1) *physically,* in being essentially mesomorphic in constitution (solid, closely knit, muscular); (2) *temperamentally,* in being restlessly energetic, impulsive, extroverted, aggressive, destructive (often sadistic) . . . ; (3) *in attitude,* by being hostile, defiant, resentful, suspicious, stubborn, socially assertive, adventurous, unconventional, non-submissive to authority; (4) *psychologically,* in tending to direct and concrete, rather than symbolic, intellectual expression, and in being less methodical in their approach to problems; (5) *socioculturally,* in having been reared to a far greater extent than the control group in homes of little understanding, affection, stability, or moral fibre by parents usually unfit to be effective guides and protectors or . . . desirable sources for emulation and the construction of a consistent, well-balanced, and socially normal superego during the early stages of character development.

While in individual cases the stresses contributed by any one of the above pressure-areas of dissocial-behavior tendency may adequately account for persistence in delinquency, in general the high probability of delinquency is dependent upon the interplay of the conditions and forces from all these areas.

In the exciting, stimulating, but little-controlled and culturally inconsistent environment of the underprivileged area, such boys readily give
expression to their untamed impulses and their self-centered desires by
means of various forms of delinquent behavior. Their tendencies toward
uninhibited energy-expression are deeply anchored in soma and psyche
and in the malformations of character during the first few years of life.[14]

The first assay of the materials that formed the basis of *Unraveling
Juvenile Delinquency* called, naturally, for comparing the delinquents and non-delinquents *en masse*. The next logical step is a
more definitive analysis on the basis of significant "breakdowns" of
the mass data. Indeed, we anticipated this necessity in *Unraveling*
when we said:

Some of the more important questions that will concern us in further,
more detailed explorations of our materials are:
What causal syndromes can be inductively arrived at and defined
by means of correlation of the various factors within each level of the inquiry? What syndromes will emerge from a comparison of delinquents
and non-delinquents on the basis of a breakdown into ethnico-racial
groupings? Into somatotypes? . . .
Further, what somatopsychic types will emerge from detailed cross-
correlations between somatotypes and various characterial and personality
traits? A more exact appreciation of the significance of constitutional
typology in the causation of persistent delinquency than has yet been
established awaits the result of such correlations.[15]

General Purposes of the Inquiry

What, then, happens when the synthetic entities, delinquents and
non-delinquents, are broken down into the four comprehensive
physique types (mesomorphic, ectomorphic, endomorphic, and balanced) within which individual somatotypes can be classified, and
when selected traits and factors originally described in *Unraveling
Juvenile Delinquency* are re-assessed in terms of this fourfold cleav-
age? This is a question of great importance, not only for obtaining
deeper insights into the etiology of delinquency but as a practical
basis for preventive and therapeutic programs. The knowledge that
a delinquent is a mesomorph or endomorph or ectomorph or of

balanced physique yields little explanation of his antisocial behavior. While it is generally known, for example, that a mesomorph is a person of muscular, closely-knit, athletic build, the *special significance for delinquency* of such physical characteristics becomes apparent only through consideration of the intermediary traits of temperament, personality, and character that distinguish the mesomorph from other body types.

CLASSIFICATION OF SOMATOTYPES

From an anthropologic point of view, delinquents and non-delinquents are synthetic groups, made up of a combination of individuals belonging to different somatotypes. The reader who wishes to learn the technical details of classification of human beings into morphologic types is referred to William H. Sheldon's work, *The Varieties of Human Physique*,[16] or his more recent *Atlas of Men*.[17] Here it suffices to state briefly that Sheldon's somatotyping method, which is a significant improvement on the classic but cruder work of Kretschmer, consists of classifying the fundamental tendencies or thrusts of body structure of persons into somatotypes according to the respective degree of participation of each of the major constitutional components—endomorphy, mesomorphy, and ectomorphy. The following definitions of these presumably fundamental building-blocks of body structure are from Sheldon's *The Varieties of Human Physique*:

Endomorphy means relative predominance of soft roundness throughout the various regions of the body. When endomorphy is dominant the digestive viscera are massive and tend relatively to dominate the bodily economy. The digestive viscera are derived principally from the *endodermal* embryonic layer.

Mesomorphy means relative predominance of muscle, bone, and connective tissue. The mesomorphic physique is normally heavy, hard, and rectangular in outline. Bone and muscle are prominent and the skin is made thick by a heavy underlying connective tissue. The entire bodily economy is dominated, relatively, by tissues derived from the *mesodermal* embryonic layer.

Ectomorphy means relative predominance of linearity and fragility. In proportion to his mass, the ectomorph has the greatest surface area and hence relatively the greatest sensory exposure to the outside world. Relative to his mass he also has the largest brain and central nervous system. In a sense, therefore, his bodily economy is relatively dominated by tissues derived from the *ectodermal* embryonic layer.[18]

On the basis of certain key bodily measurements and indices, and of skilled observation, an individual can be identified by three numerals, indicating his position on a seven-point scale in terms of the strength of each of the above-described three constitutional components.[19] Thus, a person rated as 171 is an *extreme mesomorph,* that is, very strong in bone and muscle structure and very weak in both the soft-roundness of the endomorphic component of body build and the linear-fragile ectomorphic component; a 444 is a person who is essentially poised at the midpoint of participation of the three fundamental somatic components; and so on.

By Sheldon's method, many individual somatotypes have been found to exist; in his latest book he identifies no fewer than eighty-eight of them, and he guesses that further exploration would turn up even more.[20] The method of somatotyping followed by our consulting anthropologist, Dr. Carl C. Seltzer, is not, strictly, that of Sheldon; but it has yielded highly reliable results.[21] For the purposes of intercorrelational analysis, individual somatotypes have to be subsumed under more general physique-pattern categories. On the basis of careful anthropologic measurements and of disciplined scrutiny and comparison of the standardized photographs of our delinquents and non-delinquents, Dr. Seltzer classified the individual somatotypes according to component dominance, as shown in the following table from *Unraveling*:[22]

It will be observed not only that mesomorphy predominates in the bodily structure of a majority of the delinquents (60.1%) but that despite the initial matching of the delinquents and the non-delinquent controls by ethnico-racial derivation, twice the proportion of mesomorphs are found among the delinquents as among the non-

INCIDENCE OF SOMATOTYPE COMPONENT DOMINANCE

Endomorphic Component Dominance	496 Delinquents		482 Non-Delinquents	
	No.	%	No.	%
Extreme Endomorphs	6	1.2	24	5.0
Endomorphs	14	2.8	23	4.8
Mesomorphic Endomorphs	16	3.2	7	1.5
Ectomorphic Endomorphs	23	4.6	18	3.7
Subtotal	59	11.8	72	15.0
Mesomorphic Component Dominance				
Extreme Mesomorphs	115	23.2	34	7.1
Mesomorphs	84	16.9	59	12.2
Endomorphic Mesomorphs	66	13.3	15	3.1
Ectomorphic Mesomorphs	33	6.7	40	8.3
Subtotal	298	60.1	148	30.7
Ectomorphic Component Dominance				
Extreme Ectomorphs	9	1.8	70	14.5
Ectomorphs	25	5.0	71	14.7
Endomorphic Ectomorphs	21	4.2	15	3.1
Mesomorphic Ectomorphs	17	3.4	35	7.3
Subtotal	72	14.4	191	39.6
No Component Dominance				
Balanced Types	67	13.5	71	14.7

delinquents. It is to be noted also that there are only a third as many delinquents as there are non-delinquents of ectomorphic physique (14.4%:39.6%).

These findings constitute a major reason for the present inquiry.

CLASSIFICATION OF "PHYSIQUE TYPES"

For the purposes of the present research, the four comprehensive classes of component dominance—endomorphic, mesomorphic, ecto-morphic, and balanced (no component dominance)—have been related to certain basic traits and sociocultural factors culled from

Unraveling. We shall refer to the classes of component dominance as "physique types," "body types," or "morphologic types," to distinguish them from individual "somatotypes." The use of these comprehensive physique patterns rather than of individual somatotypes results in some blunting of the relationship to them of traits and factors; but owing to the smallness of numbers that would result from a breakdown by somatotypes rather than by physique types, this was the only feasible method of procedure. Even the division of each of the three component dominance groups of the above table into its four subclasses, yielding twelve subtypes instead of three general classes (not counting the balanced which has no subtypes), would have too greatly fractionized our materials. Moreover, statistical analysis of the differences between the two purer subtypes within each major class (e.g., extreme mesomorphs and mesomorphs combined) as opposed to the total class which includes *all* the types (i.e., extreme mesomorphs, mesomorphs, endomorphic mesomorphs, and ectomorphic mesomorphs) shows that employment of the more comprehensive typology does not, except in three traits out of sixty-seven included in this study, bring about any result significantly different from that which emerges from the more general classification.[23]

As the analysis of our findings proceeds, the reader will see that much information of value is derived by a correlation of traits and factors with the four comprehensive body-type patterns. Significant clues emerging from such a broadly based comparison of trait-incidence among the physique types and among delinquents as opposed to non-delinquents can later be pursued by other workers using more refined somatotype groupings but involving larger samples of cases.

ORIGIN OF SOMATOTYPES

In the kind of analysis here undertaken, a distinction needs to be made between the origin of the *somatotypes,* on which the four, more general, "physique types" to be used in this study are based, and the origin of certain physical, psychiatric, and psychologic *traits* which are to be correlated with the physique types.

As to the somatotypes, the basic assumption is that their constituents are rooted essentially in constitution. The question arises whether "constitution" means heredity in a genetic sense. Even the most dedicated constitutional anthropologists, such as William H. Sheldon, from whose basic work we quote, confess some doubt as to the extent and nature of the genic content and hereditary mechanisms involved in the origin and differentiation of somatotypes:

We know almost nothing yet concerning the influence of heredity upon somatotypes. Stature and bodily build may be a direct result of heredity carried in the genes or an indirect result of such heredity largely through its influence upon the physiology and chemistry of the body. Or perhaps food or early environmental factors may play a part in the final determination of the somatotype. It seems fairly certain that particular endocrine variations are constant accompaniments of at least the more extreme variations in somatotype, but this fact does not answer the question of the influence of heredity, for the remote cause of the endocrine dominances and that of the dominances of bodily components may be identical and may lie far back among the genes.[24]

Although disclaiming knowledge as to the exact hereditary mechanisms involved, Sheldon and his colleagues define "constitution" in terms which, while not ignoring early environmental influences, anchor the somatotypes ultimately and largely in heredity:

. . . . Constitution refers to those aspects of the individual which are relatively more fixed and unchanging—morphology, physiology, endocrine function, etc.—and may be contrasted with those aspects which are relatively more labile and susceptible to modification by environmental pressures, i.e., habits, social attitudes, education, etc. . . . Although by constitution we refer to the relatively stable aspects of a person's endowment, we do not mean to insist, and indeed do not believe, that the human constitution is an altogether fixed and unalterable hereditary entity. We mean by constitution the basic, underlying pattern of the living individual, as it is at the time when the individual is studied. *That constitution is closely determined by heredity is highly probable, but we do not know that it is entirely so determined.* [Author's italics.][25]

The status of the question has more recently been summarized in the opinion that "the relation of body build to heredity is fairly well established as quite direct, but is influenced by the extent to which the environment allows development of innate potentials."[26]

Thus, while not attributing physique types, at the present undeveloped stage of scientific inquiry, exclusively to genetic origins, it seems reasonable to assume that the components of body morphology are nearer to the hereditary border of the biosocial spectrum than to the sociocultural. It is in this sense that we have employed the breakdown of our cases into four major physique types as a basic principle of analysis.

Origin of Traits

What, now, of the origins of traits?[27] The concept of somatotype, and the fourfold "body-type" classification according to constitutional component-dominance which we derived therefrom, are of value in the formulation of views regarding the probable orientation of certain of the physical, psychologic, and psychiatric traits in this research toward the genetic side of the heredity-environment scale. We assume that the respective degrees of participation of hereditary and environmental influences in the laying down of a trait can be ordered along a bipolar biosocial continuum. At one extreme are traits which are either rooted directly in a complex of specific genes or are more indirectly hereditary (as through the mediating operation of the glandular system); at the other extreme are traits in which there is only a low degree of hereditary determination and which are in large measure socioculturally conditioned. In the present state of knowledge it is impossible to determine exact degrees of participation of the innate and the acquired in the structuring of different traits. Yet a reasonable induction is possible from our data. Where significant variation in the incidence of a trait occurs among the body types of the *non-delinquents* (uncomplicated, that is, by its association with delinquency), it should be reasonable to infer that the trait is oriented toward the constitutional border of the biosocial spectrum. For it does not seem probable that body structures of such contrasting embryonic influences and physical characteristics as the muscular, athletic mesomorph and the thin, fragile ectomorph would possess in equal incidence such traits as sensitivity, for example. And, indeed, an examination of the relevant table (pp. 123-24) shows that the mesomorphs as a group (whether non-delinquent or delinquent) are, as might be expected, least sensitive, while the ectomorphs are most sensitive. From findings of this kind, plus the fact that inter-correlation of our sociocultural factors with physique types largely discloses *no significant variation in incidence among non-delinquents,* it seems reasonable to conclude that those traits in our series which vary significantly in incidence among the physique types of the non-delinquents somehow owe their derivation more to constitutional than to sociolcultural influences. We say "somehow," because our research materials do not permit us to say whether such traits are directly genetic, or are rather the indirect result of the differential responses to the conditioning influences exerted by the environment on physiques of such varying constitutional composition as the meso-morphic, ectomorphic, and endomorphic. A trait can be either directly and specifically attributable to certain genes, or indirectly laid down in the personality structure by the general inherited in-clinations of the various physique types to respond selectively to environmental influences.[28] In this indirect line of heredity we are, to be sure, dealing in large measure with sociocultural influences; but such traits are conditioned originally and fundamentally by the inherited anatomic and physiologic-endocrinologic structure of the particular physique type, which inclines it to respond to sociocultural stimuli in a certain way.[29]

Even in the most carefully designed research into the highly com-plex nature-nurture problem it would be difficult to disentangle the genetic roots from the interacting environmental influences. Even before a child is born, both genetic and non-genetic influences are operative; not only the unfolding of the potentialities of the genes but also the operation of various intra-uterine environmental influences. But apart from this permeative difficulty, it is impossible, from the kind of data on which the present research is based, to arrive at anything but a very indirect and imperfect inference regarding the operation of hereditary influences in the affinity of various traits to one or another of the structurally differentiated physique types. For want of the kind of genetic records of several generations which are indispensable to a more definitive study of heredity, we must be content with the rough substitute of determining the significantly differentiative incidence within the body types of the traits of our non-delinquents (who constitute the norm).

We are proceeding on the assumption, then, that when significant variation is present in trait-incidence among body types of non-delinquents, there is reasonable ground to infer that the trait is essentially related to body type, that is, oriented in constitution, although removed from the genes by one or more steps. It should be pointed out, however, that one cannot be certain that *absence* of variation means that the trait is largely attributable to sociocultural conditioning; because there may well be traits which are essentially hereditary (eye color, for example) though they do not vary with body type.[30] Thus, in the analysis of the traits, we can speak with some assurance of their relationship to body structure only about those in which significant variation is found in their incidence among the physique types of the non-delinquents. When such variation is not found, we cannot be certain that the trait is (a) essentially hereditary or (b) largely attributable to sociocultural conditioning.

MEANING OF "CONSTITUTIONAL ORIENTATION"

By "constitutional orientation" of a trait, then, we mean that it is significantly tied in with physique type, although we are unable to say whether it is *directly* (genetically) constitutional or *indirectly* so (i.e., because of the varied structure of the body types and their differential response to stimuli). Since, on the one hand, the science of genetics has not yet demonstrated conclusively which traits of temperament, personality, and character are determined in the genes, and since, on the other, reasoning in respect to constitutional influence must perforce deal not with specific, sharply defined entities but with broad body *types* which result from varying degrees of participation of the primary constitutional elements, we can at best speak only of a reasonable probability that in the production of certain traits there is more involvement of innately determined constitution than of environmental conditioning.[31] There is of course no attempt to specify any nature-nurture ratio in individual traits.

It should be emphasized that while we assume that fundamental variations in body structure probably reflect basic differences in the physiologic-endocrinologic apparatus which mediates between body build and psychologic traits, we of course realize that as far as conduct is concerned, even genetically anchored traits are not fixed in their ultimate development but are more in the nature of *potentials*.[32] Both environment and heredity are always involved in the process of laying down the complex traits analyzed in this research. We believe, however, that at least as a basis for fruitful hypotheses concerning the relationship of biologically grounded traits to delinquency, it is possible to distinguish from among traits associated with delinquency those which probably have an essentially constitutional orientation as defined above.

Succeeding chapters will show the value of the concept of body type as an "organizing principle"[33] by means of which can be inductively assembled, through intercorrelations, those physical and neurologic characteristics, intellectual qualities, personality and character traits, and responses to environmental stimuli which have a special affinity for, or influence upon the delinquency of, one or another of the four physique types.

NOTES

1. E. Kretschmer, *Physique and Character,* trans. by W. J. H. Sprott (New York: Harcourt, Brace, 1926). For a study of delinquency involving a Kretschmerian typology, see W. A. Willemse, *Constitution-Types*

in Delinquency (New York: Harcourt, Brace; London: Kegan Paul, Trench, Trubner, 1932).

2. W. H. Sheldon, with the collaboration of S. S. Stevens and W. B. Tucker, *The Varieties of Human Physique* (New York: Harper & Brothers, 1940). For a study applying Sheldon's somatotype system to delinquency, see W. H. Sheldon with the collaboration of E. M. Hartl and E. McDermott, *Varieties of Delinquent Youth* (New York: Harper & Brothers, 1949). For a brief history of the precursors of Kretschmer and Sheldon, see Sheldon, *The Varieties of Human Physique,* pp. 10-28, and M. Verdun, *Le Caractère et ses Corrélations, Tome I, Caractère— Milieu–Constitution* (Paris: J. B. Baillière et Fils, 1950), pp. 15-19.

3. A major reason for the slow progress in understanding the etiology of deviant behavior is the *a priori* overemphasis on and isolation of either the biopsychiatric approach or the sociocultural one, with little effort to recognize that behavior is the product of the mutual interplay of organism and environment. Dr. Bernard Glueck's observation of many years ago—"a factor is not a cause unless and until it becomes a motive"—is still a counsel of wisdom.

4. Sheldon and Eleanor Glueck, *Unraveling Juvenile Delinquency* (New York: The Commonwealth Fund, 1950). A popular version of this work, without tables, has been published by Harper & Brothers, New York, 1952, under the title, *Delinquents in the Making: Paths to Prevention. Unraveling Juvenile Delinquency* will hereinafter sometimes be referred to as *Unraveling.*

5. The following table is constructed from the data of Table IV-6, *Unraveling Juvenile Delinquency.*

6. See S. Axelrad and S. J. Glick, "Application of the Glueck Social Prediction Table to 100 Jewish Delinquent Boys," *The Jewish Social Quarterly,* Vol. XXX, No. 2 (1953), pp. 127-136; R. E. Thompson, "A Validation of the Glueck Social Prediction Scale for Proneness to Delinquency," *The Journal of Criminal Law, Criminology and Police Science,* Vol. 43, No. 4 (November-December, 1952), pp. 451-470; report prepared by Dr. Eveoleen Rexford, Director of the Douglas A. Thom Clinic for Children, Boston, (June 1954, unpublished as yet); "Predicting Juvenile Delinquency," Research Bulletin No. 124 (April 1955), published by the Department of Institutions and Agencies, Trenton, N. J. As this goes to press, we are in a position to include two more references to successful validations of the Glueck Social Prediction Table, reported on at the Third International Congress of Criminology, in London, September 1955. The first, by Mrs. I. Lloyd Brandon, involves a psychiatric and social study of adult sex offenders at Sing Sing Prison, New York;

Ethnic Origin

Ethnic Origin	Delinquents										Non-Delinquents									
	Meso-morph		Endo-morph		Ecto-morph		Bal-anced		Total		Meso-morph		Endo-morph		Ecto-morph		Bal-anced		Total	
	No.	%	No.	%	No.	%	No.	%	No.	%	No.	%	No.	%	No.	%	No.	%	No.	%
Old American	24	8.0	8	13.6	3	4.2	3	4.5	38	7.7	8	5.4	9	12.5	9	4.7	9	12.1	35	7.2
Italian	94	31.5	7	11.9	11	15.5	11	16.7	123	24.8	55	36.9	12	16.7	40	20.9	14	19.4	121	25.0
Irish	50	16.7	15	25.3	11	15.5	16	24.2	92	18.6	24	16.1	10	13.9	39	20.4	18	25.0	91	18.8
Slavic	18	6.0	2	3.4	6	8.5	6	9.1	32	6.5	10	6.7	3	4.2	11	5.8	8	11.1	32	6.6
Jewish	5	1.7	2	3.4	2	2.8	0	0.0	9	1.8	0	0.0	7	9.7	3	1.6	0	0.0	10	2.1
French, etc.	18	6.0	2	3.4	5	7.0	5	7.6	30	6.1	7	4.7	1	1.4	15	7.9	2	2.8	25	5.2
English, etc.	61	20.4	19	32.2	27	38.1	17	25.9	124	25.1	30	20.1	20	27.8	58	30.4	15	20.8	123	25.4
Chinese	1	0.3	0	0.0	0	0.0	0	0.0	1	0.2	0	0.0	0	0.0	0	0.0	0	0.0	0	0.0
Portugese, Spanish	7	2.3	2	3.4	0	0.0	3	4.5	12	2.4	6	4.0	0	0.0	5	2.6	1	1.4	12	2.5
Near East	13	4.3	0	0.0	3	4.2	2	3.0	18	3.6	5	3.4	5	6.9	6	3.1	3	4.2	19	3.9
Swedish, etc.	8	2.8	2	3.4	3	4.2	3	4.5	16	3.2	4	2.7	5	6.9	5	2.6	2	2.8	16	3.3
Total	299	100.0	59	100.0	71	100.0	66	100.0	495	100.0	149	100.0	72	100.0	191	100.0	72	100.0	484	100.0

the second, reported on by Dr. Augusta Bonnard, involves a follow-up investigation of maladjusted children treated at the East London Child Guidance Clinic of the London County Council. Details will be available when these two reports are published. These experiments involve such a variety of investigators, of subjects to whom the Table was applied, and of locales as to be hardly attributable to the "long arm of coincidence." The Youth Board of New York City is presently engaged in applying the Social Prediction Table to boys of the ages of 5½ to 6½ entering the first grade of two public schools in the Bronx. In one of these the boys predicted to be delinquent are given clinical treatment (including visits by social workers to the home); in the other, not. It is planned to follow up the two sets of cases to check on the effectiveness of the prediction instrument and on the success of early clinical intervention in checking the transformation of potential delinquents into actual ones.

7. "The effectiveness of this kind of service [clinical study, diagnosis and the making of recommendations to a juvenile court] in preventing recidivism was tested in a study conducted by Sheldon and Eleanor Glueck. In this study the subsequent court records of 1,000 boys who had been referred by the Juvenile Court to the Judge Baker Guidance Center were examined 5 years after study at the clinic. It was found that 88 percent of the boys had continued their misconduct. Seventy percent had been convicted of serious offenses and a third had been arrested four or more times. It was concluded that child guidance service of the variety provided to the Boston Juvenile Court was ineffectual in reducing recidivism.

"The possibility that even this poor record was better than that of children who had not been examined at the clinic was then tested by the Judge Baker research staff. This was done by ascertaining the court records of 1,000 other boys who came before the court in the same years and who were not examined at the clinic. When this study showed very similar percentages of recidivism, the directors of the clinic wrote off the study-and-recommendations method of delinquency prevention as useless, calling the experiment 'the close of another chapter in criminology.' (Healy, William; Bronner, Augusta F.; and Shimberg, Myra E.: The close of another chapter in criminology, *Mental Hygiene* 19:208-222, 1935)." H. L. Witmer and E. Tufts, *The Effectiveness of Delinquency Prevention Programs,* Children's Bureau Publication No. 350 (Washington, D. C.: U. S. Dept. of Health, Education, and Welfare, Social Security Administration, 1954), pp. 36-37.

8. See *Unraveling,* Chapter XV, "Bodily Constitution."

9. To match 500 delinquents with 500 non-delinquents by the four

variables of age, general intelligence, ethnic derivation, and residence in underprivileged urban areas was no easy task; and we certainly claim no perfection in the matching. However, if the reader will consult pages 33-39 and Appendix B. of *Unraveling,* we believe he will see evidence of meticulous care in this difficult task. In a future analysis of aspects of the raw materials that entered into *Unraveling,* we plan (among others) a breakdown of the data by ethnico-racial derivation and by intelligence levels.

10. See *Unraveling,* Part Two, "The Technique."

11. See other studies involving somatotype and traits of temperament, character, or personality, such as: W. A. Willemse, *op. cit.;* W. H. Sheldon, *The Varieties of Temperament* (New York: Harper & Brothers, 1942); C. C. Seltzer, F. L. Wells, and E. B. McTernan, "A Relationship Between Sheldonian Somatotype and Psychotype," *Journal of Personality,* Vol. 16, No. 4 (June 1948), pp. 431-436; Sheldon, *Varieties of Delinquent Youth;* C. C. Seltzer, "Constitutional Aspects of Juvenile Delinquency," Cold Spring Harbor Symposia on Quantitative Biology, Vol. XV (1951), pp. 361-372; C. W. Heath in collaboration with L. Brouha, L. W. Gregory, C. C. Seltzer, F. L. Wells, and W. L. Woods, *What People Are: A Study of Normal Young Men* (Cambridge: Harvard University Press, 1945); N. S. Kline and A. N. Oppenheim, "Constitutional Factors in the Prognosis of Schizophrenia (Further Observations)," *American Journal of Psychiatry,* Vol. 108, No. 12 (June 1952), pp. 909-911; B. Di Tullio, *Principi Di Criminologia Clinica* (Rome: Instituto Di Medicina Sociale, 1954). The above are among the more relevant contributions; no attempt has been made to list all the literature that might possibly be relevant. This was done in a comprehensive analysis by R. M. Snodgrass. See his "Crime and the Constitution Human: A Survey," Journal of Criminal Law, Criminology, and Police Science, Vol. 42 (1951-52), pp. 18-52.

12. *Unraveling,* pp. 242-243, note 8, reproduced as Appendix F of the present volume.

13. *Ibid.,* Chap. XX.

14. *Ibid.,* pp. 281-282.

15. *Ibid.,* p. 285.

16. New York: Harper & Brothers, 1950.

17. W. H. Sheldon, with the collaboration of C. W. Dupertuis and E. McDermott, *Atlas of Men* (New York: Harper & Brothers, 1954).

18. *Ibid.,* pp. 5-6.

19. "These components can be scaled against *continuous* scales, and it is only for purposes of convenience that we divide these scales by means

of 7 points at equal-appearing intervals. Given sufficient refinement of method, these scales could be subdivided indefinitely. Conversely, the coarseness of the units used can be made greater at will." *Ibid.*, p. 64.

20. *Ibid*, p. 17.

21. In Appendix B of this volume, a statement by Dr. Seltzer is reproduced from *Unraveling*, describing the precautions taken in assessing the body structure of boys in this study, for the purpose of arriving at a reliable classification of physique types.

22. Adapted from Table C-68 in Appendix C of *Unraveling*, p. 343.

23. The computations are on file in our laboratory at Harvard Law School. The three traits, the incidence of which is somewhat beclouded by the use of the more inclusive classification of body type, are Susceptibility to Contagion, which is found to occur in 32.4% of non-delinquent boys of ectomorphic component dominance (including all the types), as compared with 10.1% of extreme ectomorphs alone (the difference between them being at the .001 level of significance); Strength of Grip, which is high in 72.1% of extreme delinquent mesomorphs as contrasted with 63.3% in all the mesomorphic delinquents (the difference being significant at the .001 level); and Conscientiousness, which significantly differentiates extreme endomorphic delinquents from all endomorphic delinquents (at the .02 level of significance).

24. *The Varieties of Human Physique,* pp. 227-228. Sheldon adds, in a footnote, that "Davenport has produced apparently valid evidence that at least three specific genetic factors, and probably a fourth, determine body build."

25. *Ibid.*, pp. 1-2, note 1. In his latest work, Sheldon emphasizes the genetic core of the somatotype although assigning importance also to the role of nutrition: "The phenotype (literally, the form now appearing) is of course an expression of the state of nutrition, and it is also an expression of an underlying genetic influence which is carried in all of the bodily cells and may be referred to as the genotype of the individual. The genotype is at work throughout the life of a living organism, transmitting its own individual stamp to the new material used for replacement, as it did originally in the first emergence of the organism into its characteristic structure. The life of an organism is an expression of a reciprocal relationship going on continuously from conception to death, between the genotype and the flow of nourishing substance yielded to the organism by the environment." *Atlas of Men,* p. 19.

26. L. Alexander, *Treatment of Mental Disorder* (Philadelphia: Saunders Co., 1953), p. 20. Compare the following: "This close alliance between constitution and heredity has placed constitution on the side of

heredity in the heredity-environment dichotomy. It will be only by achieving a holistic viewpoint towards constitution that the dissolution of this dichotomy will be accomplished and hereditary and environmental factors can both be assigned their proper relative roles as constitutional determinants in any given case. . . . The inherited determinants of constitution are best thought of as potentials, rather than as quantitatively fixed, genetically determined entities." D. H. Russell, W. T. Vaughan, Jr., and G. King, "A Contribution From Child Psychiatry Towards a Broader Concept of Constitution," *Diseases of the Nervous System,* Vol. X, No. 9 (Sept. 1949), pp. 2-3.

27. G. Allport has shown how confused are the concept and name "trait" in the writings of psychologists, psychiatrists, and others; and he has done yeoman service in trying to bring some tangible order out of the chaos. Both in *Unraveling* and in the present work we have not attempted to be strictly technical in the use of the term; we have employed "trait" in a general sense, to include even some data derived from medical examination and from intelligence tests. But it would appear that most of the temperamental and emotional traits of personality and character derived from the psychiatric and Rorschach examinations employed in our research fulfill the more basic identifying criteria presented by Allport; namely, greater generalization of a trait than is true of an ordinary habit, and the dynamic or "determinative" nature of a trait in the following sense: "It is not the stimulus that is the crucial determinant in behavior that expresses personality; it is the trait itself that is decisive. Once formed, a trait seems to have the capacity of directing responses to stimuli into characteristic channels. This emphasis upon the dynamic nature of traits, ascribing to them a capacity for guiding the specific response, is variously recognized by many writers." G. W. Allport, "The Personality Trait," in M. H. Marx, ed., *Psychological Theory* (New York: The Macmillan Co., 1952), pp. 503-507. See, also, G. W. Allport, *Personality* (New York: Henry Holt & Co., 1937, 1948), Chap. XI, "The Theory of Traits." See, also, R. B. Cattell, *Description and Measurement of Personality* (Yonkers, N. Y.: 1946), pp. 59-91.

28. "Is it the type of metabolism or biochemical relationships associated with given body builds that provides the physiologic substratum for defective functioning? Or is the relation due rather to the sort of reactions to life experiences that are most suitable to these people by virtue of their constitutional equipment? Or is it the constitutional equipment itself that predisposes the person to certain sensitivities to environmental influences and to certain types of experiences? As a concrete example, is

it the possible superior physiologic functioning of the mesomorph compared to the ectomorph that provides him with greater psychosomatic resistiveness to developing schizophrenia or once having developed it to recover from it? Or could it be his greater capacity to fight—the type of reaction he finds most rewarding with his particular equipment? Or is is that people of athletic build are more favored in our society, are more accepted and admired, find greater opportunity for satisfaction and security? The same question, *mutatis mutandis,* may be applied to the other extremes of body type—for instance, the greater nervous sensitivity of the ectomorph to outer stimulation that has been pointed out by Sheldon, Draper and others." L. Alexander, *op. cit.,* p. 22.

29. It would not seem probable that with reference to most of the traits included in this research—complex and only fairly definable as they are—there is a direct and specific line of hereditary linkage between any identifiable gene or set of genes and some particular trait, except perhaps in respect to such traits, for example, as physiologic sensitivity. "Specialized traits, such as musical or mathematical ability, lend themselves most easily to studies in heredity. . . . The study of the role of heredity in the development of individual differences in generalized traits presents difficult problems. Evidently such traits are affected by many genes whose descent cannot be traced in any simple or Mendelian way. It is difficult to study the inheritance of generalized qualities through the science of genetics." F. Osborn, *Preface to Eugenics,* rev. ed. (New York: Harper & Brothers, 1951), p. 83.

"No simple connection exists between most observable characters of the developed human being and a single gene; and . . . *a single gene,* by being part of the network of developmental reactions, *will often influence more than a single character."* C. Stern, *Principles of Human Genetics* (San Francisco: W. H. Freeman and Co., 1949), p. 36.

30. See F. Osborn, *op. cit.,* pp. 13-14. Considering the nature and complexity of the traits analyzed in our work, such a possibility would seem to be remote; but if it does exist, our data and method do not enable us to isolate such uniformly hereditary traits.

31. Compare the titles "Some Dominant Hereditary Defects in Which Environment Plays Practically No Part" and "Recessive Defects Little Affected by the Environment," in Osborn, *op. cit.,* pp. 10 and 13.

32. "Biological inheritance provides the stuff from which personality is fashioned and, as manifested in the physique at a given time-point, determines trends and sets limits within which variation is constrained. There are substantial reasons for believing that different genetic struc-

tures carry with them varying potentialities for learning, for reaction time, for energy level, for frustration tolerance. Different people appear to have different biological rhythms: of growth, of menstrual cycle, of activity, of depression and exaltation. . . . Personality is also shaped through such traits of physique as stature, pigmentation, strength, conformity of features to the culturally fashionable type, etc. Such characteristics influence a man's needs and expectations." C. Kluckhohn and H. A. Murray, *Personality in Nature, Society and Culture* (New York: Alfred Knopf, 1948), p. 39.

"The personality is a configuration or *gestalt* made up of a great number of elements which have been organized and mutually adjusted to form a more or less coherent, functional whole. At the foundation of this configuration lie the innate, inherited qualities of the individual; such things as his capacity for receiving and responding to stimuli, for muscular coordination, for habit formation and for those complex processes of association which are subsumed under the term intelligence. All these qualities are, presumably, functions of the individual's organic structure and, as such, are influenced by heredity and biological mutation. Since we know that the organic structure is never identical for any two persons the qualities in question might be expected to present a corresponding range of individual variation. Experimentally this can be shown to be the case, but unfortunately for those who believe in a genetic solution for all psychological and social ills, experiments also show the presence of a complicating factor of extreme importance. The qualities in question are not determined exclusively by heredity but are modified through their exercise. It seems that any one of them can be improved by training. There is good reason to believe that there are physiologically determined limits to what training can do for the individual. Thus no amount of it can transform a moron into an Einstein. However, the limits seem to be wide enough to permit of the same degree of innate ability showing markedly different results in interaction with environments of different sorts. Although psychologists are busily at work on the problem, they are still unable to distinguish between innate and acquired ability and until they can do this no conclusions as to the inheritance of psychological qualities can be really valid." R. Linton, "Some Functional, Social, and Biological Aspects of Offenses and Offenders," *Federal Probation*, Vol. V, No. 2, p. 19.

33. Compare the following statement from another set of data intercorrelated with somatotypes: "It is well to emphasize that we do not feel that somatotype is the final determining factor in the type or prognosis

of schizophrenia. The ultimate answers probably lie in the biochemical and biophysical fields. Direct approach to the problem through biochemistry and biophysics has, however, only resulted in a welter of data that are consistent only in the fact that they are extremely variable. We have already obtained considerable information from other patients of the larger study, which leads us to believe that many physiological responses —and ultimately the biochemical and biophysical relations upon which they rest—vary in direct relationship with somatotype. . . . The introduction of somatotyping as an 'organizing principle' may quite possibly make order out of what is now chaos because of individual differences." N. S. Kline and A. M. Tenny, "Constitutional Factors in the Prognosis of Schizophrenia," *American Journal of Psychiatry,* Vol. 107, No. 6 (December 1950), pp. 434-441. See also N. S. Kline, N. Wertheimer, C. G. Dyer, A. Schenker, B. Rubin, and R. Sniffen, "Patterns of Biochemical Organization Related to Morphology," *American Journal of Psychiatry,* Vol. 109, No. 8 (Feb. 1953), pp. 603-611.

Aims, Design, Method

Aims of the Inquiry

At the close of the preceding chapter we spoke in general terms of the objectives of the present research. The inquiry proceeds on the hypothesis that, if body structure is relevant to delinquency, then (a) at least some *traits* should be found to vary significantly in their association with delinquency of the body types, reflecting a greater influence on the delinquency of some types than on others, and (b) the effect on delinquency of some *sociocultural factors* should be found to vary among the physique types.

Let us now set forth more specifically the major questions that flow from these assumptions, with which we shall be concerned in the analyses of traits and social factors to follow:

(1) Among the traits that had been found in *Unraveling Juvenile Delinquency* significantly to distinguish delinquents from non-delinquents in the mass, which ones have a varied influence on the delinquency of the body types?

(2) Of the traits that had *not* been found in *Unraveling* to distinguish delinquents from controls, which ones are now found to discriminate between the two within one or another body type?

(3) Which traits are found to vary significantly among the physique types of the non-delinquents (among which the incidence of a trait is not complicated by the fact of delinquency), making reasonable an inference that such traits are of essentially constitutional orientation? And what clusters of traits are found to distin-

guish one physique type from another irrespective of delinquency?

(4) Among the sociocultural factors (largely concerning home and family environment) that had been found in *Unraveling* to be associated with delinquency, which ones are now found to have a *varying* criminogenic influence on the four physique types?

We would hope (a) that even imperfect answers to the above questions may lead to more specific knowledge about the role of physique in delinquency than was derived in *Unraveling Juvenile Delinquency* from the finding of a significant difference in body structure between delinquents and non-delinquents in the mass, and (b) that important clues to a further definition of the task of managing juvenile delinquency both in its preventive and its therapeutic aspects may thereby be derived. If body structure, through the intermediary of traits adhering to it and through a selective response to environmental pressures, contributes in different ways to the delinquent behavior of boys of the four physique types, such knowledge is obviously of value.

How we proceed to obtain answers to the questions we have set will be indicated later; but first a word about the traits and sociocultural factors included in the inquiry.

Traits and Sociocultural Factors

A major problem in circumscribing the present research was to eliminate from among the more than 400 traits and sociocultural factors in *Unraveling Juvenile Delinquency* those which either are not essential or are unsuitable to the attainment of our present objectives. The data in *Unraveling* are largely of two kinds—primary, because they pertain to the entire group of boys (delinquents and non-delinquents alike), and subsidiary, because they refer only to a portion of the delinquents or non-delinquents. For example, *broken homes* is a "primary" factor, divided into two categories, *broken homes* and *homes not broken*. A "subsidiary" factor is one which subdivides and further describes the status of the boys from broken homes, such as *age at which the first break in the home occurred,* or *nature of first break in the home.*

The subsidiary factors have not been included in the present inquiry. Some primary factors have also been eliminated, either because of a resultant smallness of numbers after the totals were broken down into body types or because of their inadequacy for our present purposes. Certain data, for example, too remote in time from direct influence on the boys, such as the economic circumstances and education of their grandparents, were eliminated, as well as those which could not possibly be deemed "causative" of delinquency because in the great majority of instances they arose after the onset of delinquency. Such a factor, for example, is *membership in gangs.* In all, 109 personality traits and sociocultural factors were finally included in the analysis of the four physique groups.

In the aspect of the inquiry dealing with the influence of *traits* on the delinquency of each of the body types, 67 traits are involved. These encompass certain physical and neurologic conditions; some constituents of intelligence; traits of character and personality structure and dynamics obtained through the Rorschach ("ink blot") Test; and traits derived from psychiatric examination of the boys, reflecting emotional dynamics and conflicts, appetitive-aesthetic tendencies, personality orientation, and a psychiatric diagnosis. The line of inquiry analyzing the influence of aspects of the *environment* on the delinquency of boys of the four body types encompasses 42 sociocultural factors relating largely to the activities and quality of home and family life.

Listed below are the 67 traits and 42 sociocultural factors involved. The numbers on the left correspond to the table numbers in this volume; the numbers in parentheses on the right refer to the original tables in *Unraveling Juvenile Delinquency.*

TRAITS

Developmental Health History
  1. Health in Infancy (xiv-1)
  2. Susceptibility to Contagion (xiv-3)
  3. Restlessness in Early Childhood (xiv-2)
  4. Enuresis (xiv-2)

Neurologic Findings
    5. Irregular Reflexes (xiv-6)
    6. Cyanosis (xiv-13)
    7. Dermographia (xiv-13)
    8. Tremors (xiv-13)

Other Physical Findings
    9. Genital Development (xiv-9)
    10. Strength of Hand Grip (xiv-4)

Some Aspects of Intelligence
    11. Verbal Intelligence (D-11)
    12. Performance Intelligence (D-12)
    13. Originality (xvii-1)
    14. Banality (xvii-3)
    15. Powers of Observation (xvii-4)
    16. Intuition (xvii-7)
    17. Tendency to Phantasy (xvii-8)
    18. Common Sense (xvii-6)
    19. Method of Approach to Problems (xvii-10)
    20. Potential Capacity for Objective Interests (xvii-11)

Basic Attitudes to Authority and Society
    21. Social Assertiveness (xviii-2)
    22. Defiance (xviii-3)
    23. Submissiveness (xviii-4)
    24. Ambivalence to Authority xviii-5)

Feelings of Resentment, Anxiety, Inferiority, and Frustration
    25. Feeling of Insecurity (xviii-7)
    26. Feeling of Not Being Wanted or Loved (xviii-8)
    27. Feeling of Not Being Taken Care Of (xviii-9)
    28. Feeling of Not Being Taken Seriously (xviii-10)
    29. Feeling of of Helplessness (xviii-12)
    30. Feeling of Not Being Appreciated (xviii-11)
    31. Fear of Failure and Defeat (xviii-13)
    32. Feeling of Resentment (xviii-14)

Feelings of Kindliness and Hostility
    33. Surface Contact With Others (xviii-17)
    34. Hostility (xviii-22)

35. Suspiciousness (xviii-23)
36. Destructiveness (xviii-24)
37. Feeling of Isolation (xviii-25)
38. Defensive Attitude (xviii-26)

Dependence and Independence
39. Dependence on Others (xviii-27)
40. Feeling of Being Able to Manage Own Life (xviii-32)

Goals of Strivings
41. Narcissistic Trends (xviii-33)
42. Receptive Trends (xviii-35)
43. Masochistic Trends (xviii-34)
44. Destructive-Sadistic Trends (xviii-36)

Some General Qualities of Personality
45. Emotional Lability (xviii-37)
46. Self-Control (xviii-38)
47. Vivacity (xviii-39)
48. Compulsory Trends (xviii-40)
49. Extroversive Trends (xviii-41)
50. Introversive Trends (xviii-42)

Deep-Rooted Emotional Dynamics
51. Sensitivity (xix-1)
52. Suggestibility (xix-1)
53. Inadequacy (xix-1)
54. Stubbornness (xix-1)
55. Adventurousness (xix-1)
56. Motor Responses to Stimuli (xix-1)
57. Emotional Instability (xix-1)

Appetitive-Aesthetic Tendencies
58. Aestheticism (xix-2)
59. Sensuousness (xix-2)
60. Acquisitiveness (xix-2)

Personality Orientation
61. Conventionality (xix-3)
62. Self-Criticism (xix-3)
63. Conscientiousness (xix-3)
64. Practicality (xix-3)

Some Aspects of Mental Pathology
 65. Emotional Conflicts (xix-4)
 66. Neuroticism (xviii-43)
 67. Psychopathy (xviii-43)

SOCIOCULTURAL FACTORS

Nativity of Parents
 68. Nativity of Parents (ix-2)

Pathology of Parents
 69. Delinquency of Father (ix-10)
 70. Alcoholism of Father (ix-10)
 71. Emotional Disturbance in Father (ix-10)
 72. Physical Ailment in Father (ix-10)
 73. Delinquency of Mother (ix-10)
 74. Alcoholism of Mother (ix-10)
 75. Emotional Disturbance in Mother (ix-10)
 76. Physical Ailment in Mother (ix-10)

Economic Conditions
 77. Financial Dependence of Family (ix-14)
 78. Management of Family Income (x-1)
 79. Gainful Employment of Mother (x-9)

Physical Aspects of Home
 80. Crowding of Home (viii-7)
 81. Cleanliness and Orderliness of Home (viii-8)
 82. Household Routine (x-2)
 83. Cultural Renfiement in Home (x-3)

Instability of Home and Neighborhood
 84. Broken Home (xi-8)
 85. Rearing by Parent Substitute (xi-12)
 86. Frequency of Moving (xiii-2)

Atmosphere of Family Life
 87. Dominance of Mother in Family Affairs (x-8)
 88. Self-Respect of Parents (x-4)
 89. Ambition of Parents (x-5)
 90. Conduct Standards of Family (x-6)

Evidence of Family Disunity
  91. Compatibility of Parents (x-7)
  92. Family Group Recreations (x-11)
  93. Parents' Interest in Children's Friends (x-12)
  94. Recreational Facilities in Home (x-13)
  95. Family Cohesiveness (x-14)

Affection of Family for Boy
  96. Rank of Boy Among Siblings (xi-5)
  97. Attachment of Father to Boy (xi-13)
  98. Attachment of Mother to Boy (xi-14)
  99. Attachment of Siblings to Boy (xi-18)

Feeling of Boy for Parents
  100. Attachment of Boy to Father (xi-15)
  101. Acceptability of Father to Boy for Emulation (xi-16)
  102. Attachment of Boy to Mother (xi-17)

Supervision and Discipline of Boy
  103. Supervision by Mother (x-10)
  104. Discipline by Father (xi-22)
  105. Physical Punishment by Father (xi-23)
  106. Scolding or Threatening by Father (xi-23)
  107. Discipline by Mother (xi-22)
  108. Physical Punishment by Mother (xi-23)
  109. Scolding or Threatening by Mother (xi-23)

It must be remembered that the particular traits and sociocultural factors included are only samples or indicia of many more that may actually be involved in differentiating the influence of traits and social factors on the delinquency of any one physique type from the others. Therefore any patterns or syndromes that may emerge from the analyses to follow are necessarily incomplete; they can be but suggestive fragments of larger wholes. For example, it will be seen that *cyanosis* (bluish discoloration of the skin resulting from inadequate oxygenization of the blood), although not distinguishing delinquents from non-delinquents as a whole, has some indirect significance in the delinquency of endomorphs (see Table 6, p. 54). Although the influence of this neurologic disturbance on the delinquency of endomorphs is significant, its true nature and meaning can be determined only if cyanosis is viewed as but one element in a pathologic syndrome. However, the suggestiveness of the clue may lead to further fruitful investigation. The same may be said for other bits of our necessarily limited data.

ILLUSTRATION OF TABULAR PRESENTATION

We seek answers to our questions—tentative as some of them must necessarily be—through detailed analysis of the 67 traits and 42 sociocultural factors. The following is an illustration of the tables dealing with traits. We present it at this point only to explain the meaning of the components of the tables.

ILLUSTRATIVE TABLE

		Defensive Attitude					
		Column 1		Column 2		Column 3	
	Physique Type	Delinquents		Non-Delinquents		Difference in Percentages	P
		No.	%	No.	%		
Line 1	*Total*	243	56.0	183	45.0	11.0	.01
Line 2	Mesomorph	150	56.2	59	47.6	8.6	
Line 3	Endomorph	29	56.9	30	50.0	6.9	
Line 4	Ectomorph	35	58.3	73	44.5	13.8	
Line 5	Balanced	29	51.8	21	35.5	16.3	

As will be noted from the illustrative table, each trait—here *defensive attitude*—is considered from two points of view: The horizontal dimension makes possible a comparison of trait-incidence *among delinquents and non-delinquents* of each body type; the vertical makes possible a comparison of trait-incidence among the *body types* of the delinquents, on the one hand, and the non-delinquent control group, on the other. Thus, in Line 1, the number 243 and its accompanying percentage (56.0%) indicate that of all the delinquents who could be classified both as to *defensive attitude* and by *body type*, 243 possess this trait. On the other hand, of the non-delinquents who were classifiable as to this particular trait and physique type, only 183 (45.0%) proved to have the trait.[1] The probability (P<.01) given at the right of Line 1 (computed by Chi-square method)* represents the significance of the difference in the incidence of the trait between the *totals* of delinquents and of non-delinquents, and says, in effect, that in samples of this size a difference as great as or greater than the 11.0% actually found could occur by chance less frequently than once in a hundred times.

It will be noted that the table includes (in Column 3) the differences in percentages between the delinquents and non-delinquents of each body type; and the question may arise in the minds of some readers as to why Chi-square probabilities are not presented to indicate the statistical significance of these differences. The Chi-square computation, although the best method available when we began this inquiry, soon proved not to be entirely suitable, because its use in the comparison of delinquents and non-delinquents by physique types presupposes that we are dealing with four independent samples.[2] Actually, however, these are not independent samples but parts of two wholes (i.e., delinquents, non-delinquents) which had been matched by ethnic derivation,[3] but not by physique type. A method of determining significance was needed which would take into account the interdependence of the component parts of the totals and also indicate the *locale* of variations in the incidence of traits among the delinquents of the four physique types, among the non-delinquents of the four physique types, and among the differences between the delinquents and non-delinquents of each physique type in relation to such differences within the other physique types.

At the suggestion of Frederick Mosteller, Professor of Mathematical Statistics in the Department of Social Relations of Harvard University, and with the concurrence of our statistical consultant, Jane Worcester, Professor of Biostatistics of the Harvard School of Public Health, we adopted a recently developed method of "multiple comparisons" better suited to our purpose. (See statement on statistical method by Jane Worcester in Appendix A.)

---

* Throughout this volume Chi is represented by X.

Turning now to the vertical dimension of the illustrative table, this shows the incidence of the trait within each of the four physique types among the delinquents on the one hand, and among the non-delinquents on the other. Here, too, the Chi-square method was originally used to determine the significance of any observed variation in the incidence of a trait. Although its applicability for this purpose is justified, it does not pinpoint the exact locale of variations in the incidence of a trait among pairs of physique types. Therefore, the method of multiple comparisons, which deals with the significance of variation between pairs of physique types, was used for this purpose as well.

The use of computations of significance is familiar to many readers; but for the benefit of those who are not acquainted with the need of this discipline to check the reliability of conclusions found on mere inspection of figures, an illustration may be given from the table: One of the aims of the present research is to determine whether the influence of certain traits is greater on the delinquency of one body type than on that of the others. Referring now to the illustrative table, simple inspection of the percentage differences between the delinquents and non-delinquents of each body type does show variation. One might conclude, offhand, that the difference in the incidence of *defensive attitude* between the mesomorphic delinquents and non-delinquents (8.6%), on the one hand, and the delinquents and non-delinquents of balanced physique type (16.3%), on the other, is clearly greater in the latter than the former. However, appearances may be deceiving; and in fact, computation by the method of multiple comparisons shows that the variation between the differences in question occurs at such a low level of reliability that the probabilities are considerable that it is due to chance.

This raises the question of the level of statistical significance. The line at which this is drawn is partly a matter of convention and partly suggested by the nature of the materials. While conscious of the desirability of conservatism in interpretation, we have not always adhered to the .01-.05 Chi-square level used in *Unraveling*. This departure was made because computations by Dr. Worcester on our materials, comparing actual with expected outcomes, showed the .01-.10 level of significance derived by the method of multiple comparisons to be sufficiently reliable for the purposes of the current inquiry. (See Appendix A.) However, we have sometimes rejected an interpretation based on a .10 level of significance, because the internal logic of the table did not seem to us to warrant its use.

Occasionally, statistical computation tells one story while clinical and criminologic interpretation tells another. We have not always permitted the procrustean bed of mathematical statistics to cut down a suggestive finding when there seemed reasonable justification to include it. We regard mathematical statistics as adjuncts both to inspectional analysis and to our long familiarity with the data. Readers who prefer to pin their faith on the proposition that under no circumstances is a statistical difference significant unless there is only one chance in a hundred (or a thousand) that a difference as great or greater could occur by accident or random sampling, will be throwing into the discard some findings that are both clinically relevant and highly suggestive of fruitful hypotheses.

In this connection, our view is that not all the findings or clues turned up in the swampy area of biosocial research need be regarded as definitive in terms of whether they will surely recur in other samples; there are some which are valuable as hypotheses to be further tested both in research and in clinical practice.

PATTERNS OF TRAIT ANALYSIS

The findings resulting from the analysis of the illustrative table in both its horizontal and vertical dimensions represent only one of several patterns emerging from the data. The horizontal dimension, it will be recalled, makes possible a consideration of the association of a trait with the delinquency of the physique types; and the vertical an inference as to whether a trait has an essentially constitutional orientation.

As regards a determination of the *association of the traits with delinquency,* four categories emerge:

Group 1: Traits which, in *Unraveling,* were *not* found to be associated with delinquency (that is, did not distinguish delinquents as a whole from non-delinquents as a whole) and are now also *not* found to differentiate the delinquents from the non-delinquents in any of the *body types.*

Group 2: Traits which were *not* originally found to distinguish delinquents as a whole from non-delinquents as a whole but are now found to differentiate the delinquents from the non-delinquents in *one or more of the body types.*

Group 3: Traits which were found in *Unraveling* to differentiate delinquents from non-delinquents as a whole and do *not* now show a significantly greater differentiation between the delinquents and non-delinquents of one body type than of any other.

Group 4: Traits which were found in *Unraveling* to distinguish delinquents from non-delinquents in the mass and are now found to differentiate the delinquents from the non-delinquents of some (not all) physiques more than from others.

As regards determination of whether a trait associated with delinquency may be inferred to have a constitutional orientation, four categories emerge:

Type A: Traits which vary significantly in incidence among the four body types of the *non-delinquents,* but are not found to vary among the body types of the delinquents.

Type B: Traits which vary significantly among the body types of both the *non-delinquents and the delinquents.*

Type C: Traits which do not vary significantly among the body types of the non-delinquents but do vary among those of the *delinquents.*

Type D: Traits which do not vary significantly among the body types of either the non-delinquents or the delinquents.

By such categorization, arrived at inductively, it becomes possible to classify the traits within patterns involving both their association with the delinquency of the body types and the probably constitutional orientation of the traits. For example, the table used as an illustration (see p. 32) will be found on analysis to fall into Group 3, Type D (above), i.e., a *defensive attitude* significantly differentiates delinquents from non-delinquents in the mass; and in the breakdown into physique types the difference between the delinquents and non-delinquents of each body type is not significantly greater or less than in the other body types, which means that the trait is not found to have a greater impact on the delinquency of one body type than on any other. In addition, this trait has not been found to vary in incidence among the physique types of the non-delinquents or the delinquents. Thus on the available evidence, an inference that the trait is constitutionally oriented cannot be made.

The reader can readily make the various combinations from both strands of the analysis. What these combinations or patterns mean in terms of the influence of the traits on delinquency of the four physique types and their probable constitutional orientation is reserved for the chapters that follow, in which each trait is analyzed in all its aspects.

Our focus in the analyses of the traits that are to follow in the four succeeding chapters is on a consideration of *every* aspect of a table. In order to make this possible, it is necessary to determine from each table:

(a) The significance of the *difference* in the incidence of a trait in the *total group* of delinquents as compared with the total group of non-delinquents (as measured by Chi-square), in order to have a standard against which to measure the differences between the delinquents and non-delinquents of each physique type.

(b) The significance of the *difference* between the delinquents and non-delinquents of *each body type* as contrasted with the difference between the delinquents and non-delinquents of every other body type, in order to determine (by the method of multiple comparisons) whether a trait has a greater or lesser influence on the delinquency of one body type than of another.

(c) The significance of any variation in the incidence of a trait among the body types of the *delinquents,* to assist in determining the role of body structure in the complex of delinquency-inducing traits and factors.

(d) The significance of any variation in the incidence of a trait among the body types of the *non-delinquents,* to determine whether an inference is reasonably supportable that the trait is of constitutional orientation.

As regards determination of (a) above, namely the significance of the difference in the incidence of a trait in the total group of delinquents as compared with the total group of non-delinquents, this will be arrived at by scanning Line 1 (see Illustrative Table, p. 32) of each table, in which appear the percentages of delinquents and of non-delinquents possessing a given trait. If the *difference* in incidence between the delinquents as a group and the non-delinquents as a group occurs at the .01–.05 level (as determined by Chi-square) we conclude that there exists a significant association of the trait with delinquency.

Having determined whether a trait is or is not associated with delinquency in the *mass* of cases, we turn next to step (b) of the analysis of the table, the object of which is to determine whether a trait which was found to be associated with delinquency in the mass continues to be associated about equally with the delinquency of all four body types or has a significantly greater or a lesser association with the delinquency of one body type than the others; or, if not originally found to be significantly associated with delinquency in the mass, whether, in the breakdown into physique types, it is now found to be related to the delinquency of some particular physique type.

To accomplish these purposes, we must examine not merely Lines 2, 3, 4, and 5 of a table, but also Column 3; and we must further examine the computations of probability that will henceforth be presented beneath Column 3, which indicate (by the method of multiple comparisons) whether any differences actually obtained are of sufficient reliability (i.e., fall within the .01–.10 range of probability adopted in this research as the level of significance). Where the probability level is less trustworthy than the limits drawn, it is not set down, although occasionally a probability of .15 will be adverted to in the text as indicating a trend worthy of further exploration in other samples.

In taking step (c), which deals with determining whether there is significant variation in the incidence of a trait among the body types of the *delinquents,* we examine Column 1 in each table, and the index of probability appearing beneath Column 1 which will indicate (by the method of multiple comparisons) whether observed differences between the incidence of a trait in the various body types are or are not essentially due to chance. The computation not only makes it possible to determine whether a variance found in the incidence of a trait among the delinquents is statistically reliable, but it also establishes the significant differences in the incidence of a trait between pairs of body types.

Step (d) of the analysis, determination of divergence in the incidence of a trait among the body types of the *non-delinquents,* is accomplished in the same fashion as is step (c).

The reader will soon become acquainted with all the ramifications of the strands of the analysis, consideration of which will be clearer if it is realized that each table must be viewed as a unit, expressive of the interrelationship of its parts. In the majority of tables, the analysis is not difficult. There are some, however, in which the outcome in terms of the differential influence of a trait on the delinquency of the body types is not clear. A word of caution is necessary in contemplating such tables. It must be borne in mind that while causal association is determined by a *difference* in incidence of a trait between delinquents and non-delinquents, such a difference depends on its incidence not merely among delinquents but also among non-delinquents. Thus, when it is found that a difference in trait-incidence exists between the delinquents and non-delinquents of any particular body type, this may be due either to (a) a significantly greater (or lesser) incidence of that trait in that body type than in the others among the *delinquents,* or (b) a significantly greater (or lesser) incidence of that trait in that body type than in the others among the *non-delinquents.* It is therefore necessary to analyze the origins of a difference between delinquents and controls within a body type to determine whether this is brought about largely by the first or second of these influences. The two results not only have different origins but different meanings, which should become clear as we proceed with the analysis and when we summarize in Chapter VII the various patterns into which the traits are found to fall.

"Association" and "Causation"

Before closing this chapter, a few words are in order regarding the concepts of *association* and *causation.*

Those who have worked in any field of human behavior realize how extremely difficult it is to clarify causal implications.

When a significant relationship between two facts emerges, there is statistical "association," but not necessarily "causation" in the sense of an *influence of one trait or factor upon the other.* If, for example, some research disclosed a high association between fluctuations in the length of women's skirts in Paris over a certain period and fluctuations in the political parties which had control of the United States Congress during the same period, one would be hard put to it to explain the *etiologic* interrelationship of the two phenomena. At best, it would be remote, indirect, and tied in with a great many other subtle influences. An association found statistically, even by the most sensitive mathematical formulae, must have some basis in experience or reason. The associations in our tables (i.e., the significant differences in trait-incidence between delinquents and non-delinquents and those between the various body types) do have such a basis.

It is also essential for the concept of "causation," as opposed to the broader and more indefinite "association," that the phenomena involved be related in temporal sequence. One must avoid the familiar cart-before-the-horse fallacy. Both in *Unraveling* and in the present study we have laid aside traits and factors which did not meet this sequence-in-time test. Thus, as has been pointed out, we have eliminated from consideration the factor *membership in gangs* as an influence in originating delinquency because we found that, in the vast majority of instances among our delinquents, gang membership occurred *after* the onset of delinquency and it could not therefore have been causal in the above sense. The onset of persistent delinquency occurred before the age of eight among 48% of our delinquents, and in the eighth to the tenth year in an additional 39%, making a total of almost nine-tenths of the entire group who showed delinquent tendencies before the time when the gang, "largely on adolescent phenomenon,"[4] played a part in the life of some of our boys.[5]

Where temporal sequence does occur consistently in a definite order from the presence of a certain factor or group of factors to the presence of a tendency to delinquency, we can rationally assume that these successive events not only follow each other but follow *from* each other. In other words, we can legitimately assume, for practical purposes, the existence of a system of cause-and-effect in the generally accepted sense; that is to say, we have, in such a situation, not merely association but *etiologic association*. Moreover, we can test it by experiments designed to modify or eliminate the conditions that have been found to precede delinquency in one sample of cases in order to check on whether or not the subsequent result in a new sample turns out to be delinquency or non-delinquency.

Where the interacting elements are of such nature as to indicate clearly that the horse comes before the cart, relatively clean-cut causal sequence is then traceable. This is true, for example, in the relationship of a somatotype to a personality trait, on the obvious assumption that body type precedes sociocultural conditioning. But even in such sequences reciprocal influences may sometimes be at work. Certainly, in the case of parent-child, child-sibling, and child-companion relationships, we are dealing with a complex process of *interstimulation* and *interresponse* in which it is sometimes difficult to establish the temporal sequence of events.

The concept of temporal sequence does not exclude the fact that two or more interrelated traits or factors may in turn be the product of a third or fourth influence which is often not clearly apparent on the surface. There are degrees of directness or indirectness in the causal association of traits and factors with delinquency or physique type. Such a trait, for example, as *sensitivity* (Table 51) is not directly implicated in the criminogenic complex, as is shown by the fact that it fails to distinguish delinquents from non-delinquents either as a whole or within any body type. Yet in the case of both delinquents and non-delinquents there is a much greater incidence of the trait among ectomorphs than among mesomorphs; and it may well be that this trait is indirectly related to delinquency in being associated with other traits that do distinguish delinquents from non-delinquents or in effecting a special reaction to certain environmental stimuli on the part of ectomorphs. The interrelationship of causal forces is so complex that ordinarily one can be certain of little more than that an association between two variables is probably not due to chance.

It must also be borne in mind that etiologic influence is typically multiple and complex, consisting of numerous traits and factors of which each is but a part of the causal nexus. It is very doubtful whether, standing alone, any single trait or factor analyzed in this study would be sufficient to account for delinquency. Moreover, while "cause" requires a totality of influences indispensable to the result, it cannot be exactly determined how much weight each of the traits contributes to any theoretical total causal influence.[6]

Another important point (already mentioned in Chapter I) is that a *variety* of combinations of specific factors or causal patterns can account for a uniform result in terms of antisocial behavior. Just as death, although always the same terminal event, is nonetheless the result of a variety of preceding sequences of influence, so the end product of persistent delinquency, or of some trait of personality or character, may have in its etiologic background a variety of different sequences leading to the same ultimate result.

Finally, it must be kept in mind that we are not attempting the clinical task of analyzing causal sequences in individual cases, but are rather approaching the problem via *mass* comparisons of delinquents and non-delinquents. In dealing with problems of human behavior in society we must be content with accepting "cause-and-effect" to signify, not a hundred per cent relationship, but rather a high *probability* of relationship. Even in the physical sciences, generalizations are not stated in terms of absolute inevitability in each and every instance, but only of high probability in the mass. The statistical method of comparing delinquents as a group with non-delinquents as a group is not designed to bring out any point-to-point causal tie-in that will always hold good for each and every case. It is rather intended to disclose whether or not the general run of cases possessing a certain cluster of traits is much more likely to be delinquent than a group not so loaded down or impelled. In other words, we are concerned with discovering the general relationships of certain traits and precipitating factors to a course of antisocial conduct among each of the four body types.

When, therefore, in the following pages we sometimes resort to such expressions as "etiologic" or "causal" or "criminogenic" or "having the greatest impact on delinquency," in place of "associated with delinquency," we do so in the foregoing context.

PLAN OF PRESENTATION

Analysis of materials of such great complexity is hazardous. We ask the reader to follow patiently with us each step in the exposition. This is not a work into which one can dip here and there; there is no cream to be skimmed off the whole milk. The varied impact of a particular trait on the delinquency of boys of the four physique types is meaningful only as it adds or subtracts a piece to the growing mosaic of delinquency-causation that we are patiently attempting to design from a large array of traits and factors which have been gathered and verified with care. We interpret the data guardedly, and we emphasize that the findings are to be considered more in the nature of hypotheses worthy of more intensive and extensive exploration on other samples of cases than as definitive and final conclusions.

Chapters III to VI are devoted to an analysis of the influence of the 67 traits on the delinquency of boys of the four physique types. In Chapter VII the traits are summarized. Chapters VIII and IX are devoted to the influence on the delinquency of boys of the four physique types of the 42 sociocultural factors, dealing largely with home and family life.

In Chapter X the traits and sociocultural factors not found to play a selective role in the delinquency of the four physique types are summarized. In Chapters XI to XIV all the findings are integrated by physique type in terms of the selective influence on the delinquency of boys of each body type of the traits and sociocultural factors that have been found to be associated with delinquency. Chapter XV is devoted to a consideration of the implications of the findings for the more effective management of juvenile delinquency. In Chapter XVI we present some suggestive etiologic hypotheses which are worthy of testing on large samples of cases.

NOTES

1. The numbers of cases involved in the total group of delinquents and non-delinquents in each table are not exactly the same totals (and percentages) presented in the tables in *Unraveling* because they now encompass only those boys for whom the particular trait and the physique groupings were available. However, they remain very close to the totals in *Unraveling*.

2. See distribution of physique types, Chapter I, p. 9.

3. See distribution of ethnic origins by physique types, Chapter I, p. 17, note 5.

4. Of some 1200 cases of gang membership studied in Chicago, only 1.5% of the boys were six to twelve years old, while 63% were classified

as adolescents. F. M. Thrasher, *The Gang* (Chicago: University of Chicago Press, 1932), 2nd Rev. Ed., p. 36. "The lure of the gang is undoubtedly due in part to the fact that the gang boy is in the adolescent stage which is definitely correlated with gang phenomena. Although this period has no exact limits for any individual, it includes broadly for the boy the years from twelve to twenty-six." *Ibid.,* p. 80.

5. Somewhat over half the delinquent boys (56%) compared to only 0.6% of the non-delinquents ultimately became gang members.

6. We have made an approach to this in our various prediction tables based on *weighted* "scores." See, for example, the tables in *Unraveling,* pp. 260-280. While no opportunity has yet arisen for testing the validity of the prediction table based on Rorschach Test findings and that derived from psychiatric traits, the Social Prediction Table in that study has been validated. See Chapter I, p. 16, note 6.

III

Physical and Neurologic Traits

We are now ready to begin the analysis of the 67 traits encompassed in this research. We ask the reader's patience in what may, to some, prove a tedious journey. Again we must repeat that there are no short-cuts to the attainment of the objectives of the study. The task is a complicated one and is subject to many pitfalls. If the imagination of the reader is stirred, as ours has been, in threading our way through the network of findings, the reward should be great in deepening his knowledge of why children become delinquent and what more effective preventive measures can be applied than have as yet been possible.

DEVELOPMENTAL HEALTH HISTORY

First let us examine a few evidences of the physical condition of the boys in infancy and early childhood. This information was derived largely from their mothers, often supplemented from social agency and hospital reports. Although in *Unraveling Juvenile Delinquency* we had gathered considerably more information than we present here, most of it had to be excluded from the present study of the special impact of various physical conditions on the delinquency of boys of different physique types, because of the smallness of numbers involved once the breakdown into body types was made.

HEALTH IN INFANCY

Examination of Table 1[1] dealing with *health in infancy* shows a relatively low incidence of poor health among both delinquents and non-delinquents, despite the fact that they were all reared in underprivileged urban centers.

(a) However, the factor of *poor health in infancy* was found to be significantly (but only slightly) associated with delinquency in general. (b) In the breakdown of the total group into physique types a significant difference was not found to exist in the influence of

Table 1 (XIV-1). POOR HEALTH IN INFANCY

Percentages of the Respective Physique Type Totals

Physique Types	Delinquents		Non-Delinquents		Difference in Percentages between Delinquents and Non-Delinquents	Probability (Based on X^2 Test)
	No.	%	No.	%		
TOTAL	73	14.7	45	9.3	5.4	.01
Mesomorph	41	13.7	12	8.1	5.6	
Endomorph	8	13.5	9	12.5	1.0	
Ectomorph	14	19.7	16	8.3	11.4	
Balanced	10	15.1	8	11.1	4.0	

Significance of Differences between Physique Types

Mesomorph–Endomorph	-	-	-
Mesomorph–Ectomorph	-	-	-
Mesomorph–Balanced	-	-	-
Endomorph–Ectomorph	-	-	-
Endomorph–Balanced	-	-	-
Ectomorph–Balanced	-	-	-

this trait on the delinquency of the four body types, despite what appears on inspection to be a greater impact on the delinquency of the ectomorphs. (c) Nor is a significant variation in the incidence of this trait established among the physique types of the delinquents. (d) *Poor health in infancy* is not found to vary significantly among the physique types of the non-delinquents, and therefore an inference of its essentially constitutional orientation is not justified on the evidence at hand.

In view of these findings, *poor health in infancy* cannot be deemed to exert a differential criminogenic impact among physique types. It is significantly, although only slightly, related to delinquency both in the mass and probably in the four physique types on whose delinquency it does not have a dissimilar criminogenic impact.

SUSCEPTIBILITY TO CONTAGION

Information regarding resistance to contagious diseases (as judged by the frequency and severity of such illnesses as measles, whooping

Table 2 (XIV-3). SUSCEPTIBILITY TO CONTAGION

Percentages of the Respective Physique Type Totals

Physique Types	Delinquents		Non-Delinquents		Difference in Percentages between Delinquents and Non-Delinquents	Probability (Based on X^2 Test)
	No.	%	No.	%		
TOTAL	131	27.0	96	20.0	7.0	.02
Mesomorph	87	30.0	22	15.0	15.0	
Endomorph	8	13.6	6	8.3	5.3	
Ectomorph	15	21.4	61	32.4	−11.0	
Balanced	21	31.8	7	9.7	22.1	

Significance of Differences between Physique Types

Mesomorph-Endomorph	.05	-	-
Mesomorph-Ectomorph	-	.02	.02
Mesomorph-Balanced	-	-	-
Endomorph-Ectomorph	-	.01	-
Endomorph-Balanced	.10	-	-
Ectomorph-Balanced	-	.02	.02

cough, chicken pox, mumps, scarlet fever, and other typical childhood contagions) was derived not only from questioning of the mother but from reports of doctors and social workers who had treated the boys or had had close association with their families. If a boy had not had contagious diseases his immunity was rated as *good*. If he had only a few such illnesses unaccompanied by much fever, had not been considered "sick," did not cry much or complain of discomfort or pain, he was judged to have *fair* immunity.

(a) Table 2 indicates that *susceptibility to contagion* is implicated in delinquency, as shown by a significant (albeit slight) difference in incidence of this trait among the delinquents and non-delinquents. (b) This condition appears to play a negative role in the case of ectomorphs, *absence* of susceptibility to contagion being more associated with delinquency in that physique type. (c) It varies in incidence among the delinquents, being significantly less characteristic of delinquent endomorphs than of delinquent mesomorphs and delinquent boys of balanced type. (d) *Susceptibility to contagion* also varies in incidence among the body types of the non-delinquents, making it reasonable to infer that it represents a constitutional tendency. It is distinctly more characteristic of ectomorphs than of all other physique types. (But see footnote 23 of Chap. 1.)

This probably constitutionally oriented trait, although usually occurring more frequently among ectomorphs than among boys of other body types, is far less of a positive influence in the delinquency of the ectomorphs than it is in that of mesomorphs and boys of balanced physique.

EXTREME RESTLESSNESS IN EARLY CHILDHOOD

Extreme restlessness in childhood refers to the inability to "sit still," always wanting to be "on the go," according to parents, teachers, and family physicians.

(a) Table 3 shows that *extreme restlessness in early childhood* is substantially more characteristic of delinquents as a group than of non-delinquents. (b) Analysis of differences by body types reveals a varied impact of this trait on their delinquency, its criminogenic influence being significantly heavier on ectomorphs than on mesomorphs. (c) A variation in the incidence of this trait is found among

the body types of the delinquents, however, ectomorphic delinquents being as a group more restless in early childhood than
mesomorphs or endomorphs, and delinquents of balanced type more
restless than mesomorphs. (d) Inasmuch as this characteristic is not
found to vary significantly among the body types of the non-delin-

Table 3 (XIV-2). EXTREME RESTLESSNESS IN EARLY CHILDHOOD

Percentages of the Respective Physique Type Totals

Physique Types	Delinquents		Non-Delinquents		Difference in Percentages between Delinquents and Non-Delinquents	Probability (Based on x^2 Test)
	No.	%	No.	%		
TOTAL	295	59.6	147	30.4	29.2	.01
Mesomorph	156	52.2	40	26.8	25.4	
Endomorph	35	59.3	23	31.9	27.4	
Ectomorph	59	83.1	65	34.0	49.1	
Balanced	45	68.2	19	26.4	41.8	

Significance of Differences between Physique Types

Mesomorph-Endomorph	-	-	-
Mesomorph-Ectomorph	.01	-	.05
Mesomorph-Balanced	.10	-	-
Endomorph-Ectomorph	.05	-	-
Endomorph-Balanced	-	-	-
Ectomorph-Balanced	-	-	-

quents, an inference that it is constitutionally oriented cannot, on
the evidence at hand, be made.

A variation in the association of this characteristic with the delinquency of the physique types cannot be attributed to any significant differences in the incidence of this trait among the body types
of the non-delinquents, but when *extreme restlessness* in early childhood occurs among ectomorphs it is more of a danger signal of
potential delinquency than when it occurs in other body types.

ENURESIS

(a) In respect to *enuresis* (bedwetting persisting beyond the years of its normal expectancy), Table 4 reveals that delinquents as a group are more enuretic than non-delinquents. (b) In the breakdown of the totals into body types, it is found that while *enuresis* is associated with the delinquency of all the physiques, no reliable dif-

Table 4 (XIV-2). ENURESIS IN EARLY CHILDHOOD

Percentages of the Respective Physique Type Totals

Physique Types	Delinquents		Non-Delinquents		Difference in Percentages between Delinquents and Non-Delinquents	Probability (Based on X^2 Test)
	No.	%	No.	%		
TOTAL	141	28.5	67	13.8	14.7	.01
Mesomorph	69	23.1	15	10.1	13.0	
Endomorph	17	28.8	13	18.1	10.7	
Ectomorph	31	43.7	30	15.7	28.0	
Balanced	24	36.4	9	12.5	23.9	

Significance of Differences between Physique Types

Mesomorph-Endomorph	-	-	-
Mesomorph-Ectomorph	.05	-	-
Mesomorph-Balanced	-	-	-
Endomorph-Ectomorph	-	-	-
Endomorph-Balanced	-	-	-
Ectomorph-Balanced	-	-	-

ferences among the body types occur in its relation to their delinquency at the level of significance adopted for this inquiry. (c) There is, however, a variation in the incidence of *enuresis* among the delinquents, a higher proportion of ectomorphic than mesomorphic delinquents being bedwetters. (d) Since a significant variation in the incidence of *enuresis* among the body types of the non-delinquents is not established, an inference of an essentially constitutional orientation of this tendency cannot be made. Whether heredity plays a dominant role in *enuresis* or whether faulty toilet training and habituation are dominant cannot be determined from the evidence at hand.[2]

The fact that *enuresis* is found to vary in incidence among the delinquents would certainly indicate that, regardless of its origins, its occurrence among ectomorphs is more of a danger signal of delinquency than when it occurs, for example, in mesomorphs.

Neurologic Findings

In making neurological tests, our examining physician was concerned with irregular reflexes, cyanosis, dermographia, and tremors.

IRREGULAR REFLEXES

The reflexes for which examination was made were the pupillary, abdominal, cremasteric (testicular), and patellar (knee-jerk). The physician recorded marked deviation from the accepted norm of deep or superficial reflexes, the presence of which might or might not, in itself, be of diagnostic significance.

(a) Table 5 does not reveal a significant association between *irregular reflexes* and delinquency, the incidence of this factor among delinquents and non-delinquents being very similar. (b) In the breakdown of the total groups of delinquents and non-delinquents into physique types, a significant difference is not found in the criminogenic impact of *irregular reflexes* on the four body types. There is, therefore, no reliable evidence of an association of this trait with delinquency either in the mass or among the body types. (c) Nor is a significant divergence found to exist in the incidence of *irregular reflexes* among the delinquents of the four physique types. (d) Since a significant variation in the incidence of *irregular reflexes* is not found among the body types of the non-delinquents, there is no ground in our data for the inference that this trait has an essentially constitutional orientation.

To sum up, since the incidence of *irregular reflexes* is not found to be proportionally different among delinquents and non-delinquents, either in general or in any body type, and since it does not vary among the physique types of the delinquents or the non-delinquents, an inference cannot be made that *irregular reflexes* are associated with delinquency or that they are constitutionally oriented.

Table 5 (XIV-6). IRREGULAR REFLEXES

Percentages of the Respective Physique Type Totals

Physique Types	Delinquents		Non-Delinquents		Difference in Percentages between Delinquents and Non-Delinquents	Probability (Based on X^2 Test)
	No.	%	No.	%		
TOTAL	169	34.2	185	38.3	-4.1	.20
Mesomorph	107	35.9	58	38.9	-3.0	
Endomorph	14	23.7	26	36.1	-12.4	
Ectomorph	27	38.0	74	38.9	-0.9	
Balanced	21	31.8	27	37.5	-5.7	

Significance of Differences between Physique Types

Mesomorph-Endomorph	-	-	-
Mesomorph-Ectomorph	-	-	-
Mesomorph-Balanced	-	-	-
Endomorph-Ectomorph	-	-	-
Endomorph-Balanced	-	-	-
Ectomorph-Balanced	-	-	-

CYANOSIS

Cyanosis, which is a neurologic trait, is a blue discoloration of the skin resulting from inadequate oxygenization of the blood.

(a) A significant association was not found in *Unraveling* between *cyanosis* and delinquency, the incidence of this condition being similar among delinquents and non-delinquents (Table 6). (b) However, a comparison of the differences in incidence of *cyanosis* between the delinquents and non-delinquents of the physique types now reveals that there is variation in its delinquency-related impact among the body types. It now appears that *cyanosis* has more of a bearing on the delinquency of endomorphs than of mesomorphs. What the nature of this association is we are unable to say. Obvi-

Table 6 (XIV-13). CYANOSIS

(Categories: Marked and Slight)

Percentages of the Respective Physique Type Totals

Physique Types	Delinquents		Non-Delinquents		Difference in Percentages between Delinquents and Non-Delinquents	Probability (Based on X^2 Test)
	No.	%	No.	%		
TOTAL	205	41.5	208	43.1	-1.6	.70
Mesomorph	109	36.6	59	39.6	-3.0	
Endomorph	31	52.6	22	30.5	22.1	
Ectomorph	36	50.7	94	49.5	1.2	
Balanced	29	43.9	33	45.9	-2.0	

Significance of Differences between Physique Types

Mesomorph-Endomorph	-	-	.10
Mesomorph-Ectomorph	-	-	-
Mesomorph-Balanced	-	-	-
Endomorph-Ectomorph	-	.05	-
Endomorph-Balanced	-	-	-
Ectomorph-Balanced	-	-	-

ously it can be only an indirect one arising from a complex of conditions involving inadequate oxygenization of the blood. (c) A variation is not found in the incidence of *cyanosis* among the body types of the delinquents at the established level of significance; although inspection would seem to indicate a lesser incidence of *cyanosis* among the mesomorphic than of endomorphic and ectomorphic delinquents, this cannot be viewed as definitive in the light of a probability of .15. (d) But *cyanosis* is found to vary significantly in incidence among the body types of the non-delinquents, which permits of an inference that it is probably of constitutional orientation. Endomorphic non-delinquents are significantly less cyanotic as a group than are ectomorphs.

The relevance of the greater association of *cyanosis* with the delinquency of endomorphs than of mesomorphs is certainly worthy of further exploration. It is a clinical sign of importance, the nature of which is, however, not definable from the data we have at hand.

DERMOGRAPHIA

Another finding that has emerged from the neurological examination of our boys has to do with the presence of *dermographia,* a con-

Table 7 (XIV-13). DERMOGRAPHIA

(Categories: Marked and Slight)

Percentages of the Respective Physique Type Totals

Physique Types	Delinquents		Non-Delinquents		Difference in Percentages between Delinquents and Non-Delinquents	Probability (Based on x^2 Test)
	No.	%	No.	%		
TOTAL	223	45.2	280	58.0	-12.8	.01
Mesomorph	113	38.0	88	59.1	-21.1	
Endomorph	33	55.9	43	59.8	-3.9	
Ectomorph	44	62.0	114	60.0	2.0	
Balanced	33	50.0	35	48.6	1.4	

Significance of Differences between Physique Types

Mesomorph-Endomorph	.10	-	-
Mesomorph-Ectomorph	.02	-	.05
Mesomorph-Balanced	-	-	-
Endomorph-Ectomorph	-	-	-
Endomorph-Balanced	-	-	-
Ectomorph-Balanced	-	-	-

dition indicated by reddish tracings on the skin made by light stroking with the nail. This would seem to reflect some physiologic sensitivity.

(a) *Dermographia* is seen in Table 7 to be less characteristic of delinquents as a group than of non-delinquents; hence it is negatively associated with delinquency. (b) It is further evident that the association of *dermographia* with delinquency varies among the body types. The *absence* of the clinical sign of *dermographia* is more significant in relation to the potential delinquency of mesomorphs than to that of ectomorphs. (c) A variation in the incidence of this trait is found among the body types of the delinquents, differentiating mesomorphs from ectomorphs and also from endomorphs and perhaps, though not definitively, from boys of balanced physique. The mesomorphic delinquents as a group have among their number a lesser proportion of boys of sensitive skin. (d) Since this characteristic is not found to vary significantly among the body types of the non-delinquents, an inference that it is constitutionally oriented cannot, on existing evidence, be made.

Whether *dermographia* is or is not of constitutional orientation, it is evident that the absence of dermographia is more significant in relation to the potential delinquency of mesomorphs than to that of ectomorphs.

TREMORS

Turning now to the neurologically induced tendency to involuntary trembling, it was found that about a fifth of both the delinquents and the non-delinquents had this characteristic.

(a) It is seen in Table 8 that a significant association between the neurologic sign of *tremors* and delinquency was not established in *Unraveling*. (b) In breaking the totals down into physique types, there emerge no significant differences between the delinquents and non-delinquents in any of them. (c) Nor is a significant variation found in the incidence of this condition among the physique types of the delinquents. (d) It may reasonably be inferred, however, that the neurologic symptom of *tremors* is essentially constitutional in tendency, since a significant variation is found in its incidence among the physique types of the non-delinquents, the ectomorphs being more markedly characterized by *tremors* than the mesomorphs and endomorphs.

To summarize, the presence of *tremors* is not found to be associated with delinquency in general or with the delinquency of any

Table 8 (XIV-13). TREMORS

(Categories: Marked and Slight)

Percentages of the Respective Physique Type Totals

Physique Types	Delinquents		Non-Delinquents		Difference in Percentages between Delinquents and Non-Delinquents	Probability (Based on X^2 Test)
	No.	%	No.	%		
TOTAL	92	18.8	102	21.1	-2.3	.50
Mesomorph	50	16.9	23	15.4	1.5	
Endomorph	7	11.9	7	9.7	2.2	
Ectomorph	18	25.3	58	30.6	-5.3	
Balanced	17	25.8	14	19.4	6.4	

Significance of Differences between Physique Types

Mesomorph-Endomorph	-	-	-
Mesomorph-Ectomorph	-	.05	-
Mesomorph-Balanced	-	-	-
Endomorph-Ectomorph	-	.02	-
Endomorph-Balanced	-	-	-
Ectomorph-Balanced	-	-	-

of the four physique types. This condition is probably of constitutional orientation.

OTHER PHYSICAL FINDINGS

There are two other physical findings which may be revealing. These pertain to genital development and strength of hand grip.

GENITAL UNDERDEVELOPMENT

(a) An association between *genital underdevelopment* and delinquency was not established in *Unraveling* (Table 9). (b) No significant contrast emerges in the relationship of this characteristic to the delinquency of each physique type. Therefore, it cannot be said

Table 9 (XIV-9).   GENITAL UNDER-DEVELOPMENT

(Categories: Marked and Slight)

Percentages of the Respective Physique Type Totals

Physique Types	Delinquents		Non-Delinquents		Difference in Percentages between Delinquents and Non-Delinquents	Probability (Based on X^2 Test)
	No.	%	No.	%		
TOTAL	56	11.5	65	13.5	-2.0	.50
Mesomorph	20	6.7	7	4.7	2.0	
Endomorph	11	18.6	20	27.7	-9.1	
Ectomorph	18	25.3	31	16.5	8.8	
Balanced	7	10.6	7	9.7	0.9	

Significance of Differences between Physique Types

Mesomorph-Endomorph	-	.02	-
Mesomorph-Ectomorph	.05	.02	-
Mesomorph-Balanced	-	-	-
Endomorph-Ectomorph	-	-	-
Endomorph-Balanced	-	.05	-
Ectomorph-Balanced	-	-	-

that any significant association has been established between *genital underdevelopment* and delinquency, in any body type. (c) There is, however, significant variation in the incidence of this trait among the physique types of the delinquents. This is evident in the contrast between mesomorphs and ectomorphs, the mesomorphs, as a group, being more developed than the ectomorphs. (d) *Genital underdevelopment* may be said to be essentially constitutional in orientation, since it is found to vary significantly in incidence among the physique types of the non-delinquents, a higher proportion of endomorphs being genitally underdeveloped than of mesomorphs or boys of balanced type. Mesomorphs as a group are not only clearly less underdeveloped than endomorphs but also than ectomorphs.

Since *genital underdevelopment* is not found to be significantly associated with delinquency in general or with that of any of the four body types, it cannot be inferred that this probably constitutional trait is criminogenic.

STRENGTH OF HAND GRIP

Strength of hand grip was measured by a standard hand dyna-

Table 10 (XIV-4). STRENGTH OF HAND GRIP

(Dynamometric Strength - 75 Kilograms and over)

Percentages of the Respective Physique Type Totals

Physique Types	Delinquents		Non-Delinquents		Difference in Percentages between Delinquents and Non-Delinquents	Probability (Based on x^2 Test)
	No.	%	No.	%		
TOTAL	251	51.4	210	43.9	7.5	.02
Mesomorph	186	63.3	109	73.6	-10.3	
Endomorph	25	43.1	27	38.1	5.0	
Ectomorph	12	17.1	45	23.9	-6.8	
Balanced	28	42.4	29	30.3	12.1	

Significance of Differences between Physique Types

Mesomorph-Endomorph	.05	.01	-
Mesomorph-Ectomorph	.01	.01	-
Mesomorph-Balanced	.05	.01	.05
Endomorph-Ectomorph	.05	-	-
Endomorph-Balanced	-	-	-
Ectomorph-Balanced	.05	-	-

mometer, the results as given in Table 10 representing an average of the grip of both hands.

(a) The difference between the delinquents and non-delinquents in this regard, though slight, is significant, and reflects somewhat greater peripheral strength among the delinquents as a group. (b) Variation is further revealed in the impact of *strength of hand grip* on the delinquency of the four physique types; its influence is greater when occurring in boys of balanced physique, at least in contrast to mesomorphs. (c) The trait varies significantly in incidence among the body types of the delinquents, the most important finding being that mesomorphic delinquents have as a group a stronger hand grip than the boys of the other physique types. (But see note 23, Chap. 1.) (d) This trait is found to vary significantly in incidence among the body types of the non-delinquents, which makes it possible to infer that it is constitutionally oriented. It significantly differentiates the mesomorphs from each of the other body types, mesomorphs as a group having greater peripheral strength.

The relationship to delinquency of the probably constitutionally oriented trait, *strength of hand grip,* is especially high when it occurs in boys of balanced physique as contrasted with mesomorphs. Since, irrespective of whether they are delinquents or not, a significantly greater proportion of mesomorphs than of other boys have a strong hand grip, whatever role this trait may play in delinquency, it is related to the fact that mesomorphs as a group have greater peripheral strength than boys of other body types. But in the case of boys of balanced physique who, normally, are not as strong in hand grip, the atypical occurrence of such strength in them must be regarded as one of the constellation of influences that are especially related to their delinquency.

The foregoing traits are but a sampling of the entire series to be analyzed in this study. However, even at this early stage, there is a hint that many of the characteristics which distinguish delinquents from non-delinquents operate in varying degree in connection with the delinquency of the four physique types and that the traits exerting a special influence within any body type tend to cluster into a meaningful syndrome. This will not become sufficiently clear or convincing until other traits, analyzed in the succeeding chapters, fall into their appropriate patterns.

NOTES

1. The reader is reminded that the table number appearing in parentheses at the right of the title serves as a reference to tables in *Unraveling* which deal with the same factor in a mass comparison of the 500 delinquents and 500 non-delinquents who formed the subject of that volume.

2. Michaels binds together persistent enuresis, juvenile delinquency and psychopathic personality. J. J. Michaels, *Disorders of Character* (Springfield, Ill.: C. C. Thomas, 1955).

IV

Aspects of Intelligence;
Character Structure

Continuing the analysis, we turn in this chapter to those traits which reflect some aspects of intelligence and of the basic character structure of the boys. With the exception of Verbal and Performance Intelligence determined by the Wechsler-Bellevue Test, the traits presented in this chapter were derived by the Rorschach Test (see Appendix F).

SOME ASPECTS OF INTELLIGENCE

First we deal with verbal and performance ability, bearing in mind that the 500 delinquents and 500 non-delinquents described in *Unraveling Juvenile Delinquency* had been initially matched, case by case, by their over-all intelligence quotient as determined by the Wechsler-Bellevue Test. For this reason, any specific resemblances and differences emerging in their verbal and performance ability ar all the more significant.

Next our focus will be on a determination of the extent to which the following aspects of intelligence play a differential role in the antisocial behavior of boys of various physique types: Originality, Banality, Power of Observation, Intuition, Tendency to Phantasy, Common Sense, Method of Approach to Problems, and Potential Capacity for Objective Interests.

62

LOW VERBAL INTELLIGENCE

Verbal intelligence consists essentially of the capacity to do intellectual tasks requiring the use of abstract reasoning and memory, in which the approach to meaning tends to be through a structure of intermediate symbols rather than through concrete physical things. Thus the Wechsler-Bellevue verbal battery is made up of the

Table 11 (App. D-11). LOW VERBAL INTELLIGENCE

(Wechsler Verbal I.Q. below 80)

Percentages of the Respective Physique Type Totals

Physique Types	Delinquents		Non-Delinquents		Difference in Percentages between Delinquents and Non-Delinquents	Probability (Based on X^2 Test)
	No.	%	No.	%		
TOTAL	136	27.5	78	16.2	11.3	.01
Mesomorph	94	31.5	19	12.8	18.7	
Endomorph	10	17.0	8	11.1	5.9	
Ectomorph	13	18.2	35	18.3	-0.1	
Balanced	19	28.8	16	22.2	6.6	

Significance of Differences between Physique Types

Mesomorph-Endomorph	.05	-	-
Mesomorph-Ectomorph	.10	-	.05
Mesomorph-Balanced	-	-	-
Endomorph-Ectomorph	-	-	-
Endomorph-Balanced	-	-	-
Ectomorph-Balanced	-	-	-

following six subtests: Vocabulary, Information, Similarities, Comprehension, Arithmetic Reasoning, and Memory Span.[1]

(a) Despite the over-all matching of delinquents with non-delinquents in general intelligence (derived from averaging verbal and performance scores of the Wechsler-Bellevue Test), it was found in *Unraveling* that more delinquents than non-delinquents have a *low verbal intelligence* (Table 11). (b) Breakdown into physique types now reveals a variation in the relationship of *low verbal intelligence* to delinquency in mesomorphs as contrasted with ectomorphs, *low verbal intelligence* in the former being more likely to be associated with delinquency than when it occurs in ectomorphs. (c) Significant variation is found in the incidence of inferior verbal intellect among the body types of the delinquents, the mesomorphs as a group being endowed with less verbal ability than the endomorphs and ectomorphs. (d) Since a significant differentiation in incidence of this trait is not established among the body types of the non-delinquents, an inference cannot be made on the evidence of this table alone that low verbal intelligence verges toward the constitutional pole of the biosocial spectrum. This may, however, be a trait which has a hereditary basis despite the fact that it is not found to vary significantly among the physique types.

To sum up, on the evidence in Table 11 it cannot be concluded that *verbal intelligence* is of constitutional orientation, although other evidence may establish it to be hereditary. *Low verbal intelligence* is associated with delinquency, however, and is found to be more potent in inducing mesomorphs to delinquency than ectomorphs (and perhaps endomorphs).

HIGH PERFORMANCE INTELLIGENCE

Performance ability relates to the "hand-minded" aspects of intelligence, in which the approach to meaning tends to be by way of direct physical relationships, with a minimum dependence on intermediary symbols and abstractions. The five substests of the Wechsler-Bellevue performance battery consist of Digit Symbol, Picture Completion, Picture Arrangement, Block Design, and Object Assembly.[2] It was found in *Unraveling* that delinquents do not accumulate a large repertoire of symbols, their generalizations being closely geared to concrete realities.

(a) *High performance intelligence* was not found in *Unraveling* to be related to delinquency, similar proportions of delinquents and non-delinquents having good performance ability (Table 12). (b) A breakdown into physique types reveals, however, that *high performance ability* is positively related to the delinquency of endomorphs and the boys of balanced physique as contrasted with mesomorphs, among whom it is found, contrariwise, that *low performance intelligence* contributes to their delinquency. (c)

Table 12 (App. D-12). HIGH PERFORMANCE INTELLIGENCE

(Wechsler Performance I.Q. 101 and over)

Percentages of the Respective Physique Type Totals

Physique Types	Delinquents		Non-Delinquents		Difference in Percentages between Delinquents and Non-Delinquents	Probability (Based on X^2 Test)
	No.	%	No.	%		
TOTAL	195	39.3	203	42.0	-2.7	.50
Mesomorph	96	32.1	67	45.0	-12.9	
Endomorph	25	42.5	22	30.5	12.0	
Ectomorph	30	42.2	83	43.4	1.2	
Balanced	44	66.6	31	44.0	22.6	

Significance of Differences between Physique Types

Mesomorph- Endomorph	-	-	.10
Mesomorph- Ectomorph	-	-	-
Mesomorph- Balanced	.01	-	.02
Endomorph- Ectomorph	-	-	-
Endomorph- Balanced	.05	-	-
Ectomorph- Balanced	.05	-	-

Performance intelligence is seen to vary among the physique types of the delinquents, those of balanced physique having, as a group, better performance ability than the delinquents of the other body types. (d) On the evidence of the table a constitutional orientation cannot be ascribed to *performance intelligence,* since it is not found to vary significantly in incidence among the body types of the non-delinquents. This may, however, be a trait which is hereditary though it does not vary with body type.

Summarizing, it is evident that *good performance ability,* when occurring in boys of balanced physique, is more likely (in conjunction with other factors, of course) to embroil them in delinquency than when it occurs in mesomorphs. Contrastingly, in the latter it is rather the *absence* of high *performance ability* that is associated with delinquency. It would seem that the presence of *high performance ability* in the balanced type, which is poised equally between the three bodily components, adds to the armamentarium of capacities that tip the scales in the direction of delinquency, while in the case of mesomorphs their *lack* of ability for skillful use of their hands appears to contribute to their need to seek outlets for their energies in socially unacceptable ways. The difference between these two reactions requires further exploration.

ORIGINALITY

Originality (as derived from the Rorschach Test) results from an unconventional way of perception, experience, or thought, and is, in its positive aspect, a genuine and often productive expression of the personality; while, in its negative aspect, it may lead to estrangement from the community, to a lack of common sense, to "queerness," and the like.

(a) A significant association was not found in *Unraveling* between *originality* and delinquency, the incidence of this factor among delinquents and non-delinquents being very similar (Table 13). (b) In the breakdown of the total groups of delinquents and of non-delinquents into physique types, a significant difference is also not disclosed in the delinquency-inducing impact of *originality* on the four body types. There is, therefore, no evidence of a significant association of *originality* with the delinquency of any particular physique. (c) Nor is a significant variation found in the incidence of *originality* among the four physique types of the delinquents. (d) Since significant variation in the incidence of this trait does not exist among the body types of the non-delinquents, it cannot be inferred, on the evidence at hand, that *originality* is essentially of constitutional orientation.

In brief, since *originality* is not found to differentiate delinquents from non-delinquents, either as a group or in any body type, and

Table 13 (XVII-1). ORIGINALITY

(Categories: Marked and Slight)

Percentages of the Respective Physique Type Totals

Physique Types	Delinquents		Non-Delinquents		Difference in Percentages between Delinquents and Non-Delinquents	Probability (Based on X^2 Test)
	No.	%	No.	%		
TOTAL	134	27.7	124	25.9	1.8	.70
Mesomorph	87	29.9	35	23.7	6.2	
Endomorph	13	22.4	15	21.4	1.0	
Ectomorph	20	28.2	55	28.9	-0.7	
Balanced	14	21.9	19	26.8	-4.9	

Significance of Differences between Physique Types

Mesomorph–Endomorph	-	-	-
Mesomorph–Ectomorph	-	-	-
Mesomorph–Balanced	-	-	-
Endomorph–Ectomorph	-	-	-
Endomorph–Balanced	-	-	-
Ectomorph–Balanced	-	-	-

since it is not found to vary in incidence among the physique types of the non-delinquents, it cannot be inferred that this trait is either criminogenic or constitutionally oriented.

BANALITY

Banality is defined as the complete or comparative inability to think in other than the most commonplace terms and concepts; this is often to be found as a consequence of conventionality.

(a) A significant association was not established between *banality* and delinquency, the incidence of this characteristic among delinquents and non-delinquents being very similar (Table 14). (b) In the breakdown of the total group of delinquents and of non-delinquents into physique types, a significant difference is also not established in the association of *banality* with the delinquency of

Table 14 (XVII-3). BANALITY

(Categories: Marked and Slight)

Percentages of the Respective Physique Type Totals

Physique Types	Delinquents		Non-Delinquents		Difference in Percentages between Delinquents and Non-Delinquents	Probability (Based on X^2 Test)
	No.	%	No.	%		
TOTAL	123	26.1	142	30.9	-4.8	.20
Mesomorph	75	26.6	54	37.5	-10.9	
Endomorph	16	27.6	17	25.8	1.8	
Ectomorph	15	22.0	54	29.8	-7.8	
Balanced	17	27.0	17	25.0	2.0	

Significance of Differences between Physique Types

Mesomorph-Endomorph	-	-	-
Mesomorph-Ectomorph	-	-	-
Mesomorph-Balanced	-	-	-
Endomorph-Ectomorph	-	-	-
Endomorph-Balanced	-	-	-
Ectomorph-Balanced	-	-	-

the four body types. There is, therefore, no sound evidence of a relationship of *banality* to the delinquency of any body type. (c) Nor is a significant divergence found in the incidence of this trait among the physique types of those boys who do become delinquents. (d) Since significant variation of *banality* does not exist among the four physique types of the non-delinquents, it cannot be inferred that this trait is essentially of constitutional orientation.

To sum up, since *banality* does not differentiate delinquents from non-delinquents, either as a group or in any body type, and since this trait does not vary in incidence among the physique types of the non-delinquents, it cannot be inferred that *banality* is either criminogenic or constitutionally oriented.

MARKED POWER OF OBSERVATION

Marked power of observation includes both the ability to observe accurately and the ability to maintain such accuracy of observation

Table 15 (XVII-4). MARKED POWER OF OBSERVATION

Percentages of the Respective Physique Type Totals

Physique Types	Delinquents		Non-Delinquents		Difference in Percentages between Delinquents and Non-Delinquents	Probability (Based on x^2 Test)
	No.	%	No.	%		
TOTAL	308	63.9	334	70.3	−6.4	.05
Mesomorph	177	61.2	100	68.1	−6.9	
Endomorph	40	67.8	45	65.3	2.5	
Ectomorph	49	70.0	137	72.9	−2.9	
Balanced	42	65.6	52	73.2	−7.6	

Significance of Differences between Physique Types

Mesomorph-Endomorph	-	-	-
Mesomorph-Ectomorph	-	-	-
Mesomorph-Balanced	-	-	-
Endomorph-Ectomorph	-	-	-
Endomorph-Balanced	-	-	-
Ectomorph-Balanced	-	-	-

at a fairly constant level. A prerequisite of this is a fairly accurate visual memory and a certain amount of attentive concentration.

(a) *Lack* of a *marked power of observation* is slightly and significantly (at the .05 level) associated with delinquency (Table 15).

(b) In the breakdown of the total group into physique types, there does not emerge a significant variation in the association of this trait with delinquency. (c) Nor is the incidence of a *marked power of observation* found to vary significantly among delinquents of the four body types. (d) Since the incidence of this trait does not reliably differ among the physique types of the non-delinquents, an inference of its essentially constitutional orientation is not justified.

In the light of the foregoing analysis, a *marked power of observation* cannot be deemed to exert a differential criminogenic impact on the physique types. It is questionably, and, at the most only slightly, related to delinquency in the mass, but its criminogenic role in the four body types, on which it does not have a varied impact, is not clearly established.

INTUITION

Intuition is the ability to penetrate quickly some or all of the factors in a given situation, experience, or task, not by conscious deductive or inductive reasoning, but by sensing the quality of the factors involved or at least one aspect of their quality. *Intuition* does not necessarily lead to constructive results. For instance, if it is combined with a lack of mental control or with flightiness it may lead to an entirely distorted mental picture of a situation or to a quite inadequate solution of a problem.

(a) As has been true of all the qualitative aspects of intelligence thus far described, so too as regards *intuition*; there is no essential difference between our delinquents as a group and the non-delinquents in the presence of this trait (Table 16). (b) In the breakdown of the totals of delinquents and non-delinquents by physique types, a significant difference fails to emerge in the impact of *intuition* on the delinquency of the four body types, despite what appears on inspection to be a negative association with the delinquency of boys of balanced type. There is, therefore, no evidence of a significant relationship of *intuition* to the delinquency of any body type. (c) Nor is a reliable variation found in the incidence of this trait among the delinquents of the four physique types. (d) Since no significant diversity in the incidence of *intuition* is found among the non-delinquents of the four physique types, it cannot be inferred that this trait is essentially of constitutional orientation.

In brief, since *intuition* does not differentiate delinquents from non-delinquents either as a group or in any body type, and since the

Table 16 (XVII-7). INTUITION

(Categories: Marked and Slight)

Percentages of the Respective Physique Type Totals

Physique Types	Delinquents		Non-Delinquents		Difference in Percentages between Delinquents and Non-Delinquents	Probability (Based on X^2 Test)
	No.	%	No.	%		
TOTAL	79	16.3	75	15.7	0.6	.90
Mesomorph	51	17.6	19	12.8	4.8	
Endomorph	7	11.9	8	11.5	0.4	
Ectomorph	14	20.3	33	17.5	2.8	
Balanced	7	10.8	15	21.5	-10.7	

Significance of Differences between Physique Types

Mesomorph–Endomorph	-	-	-
Mesomorph–Ectomorph	-	-	-
Mesomorph–Balanced	-	-	-
Endomorph–Ectomorph	-	-	-
Endomorph–Balanced	-	-	-
Ectomorph–Balanced	-	-	-

trait is not found to vary in incidence among the physique types of the non-delinquents, it cannot be inferred that *intuition* is either criminogenic or constitutionally oriented.

TENDENCY TO PHANTASY

The *tendency to phantasy* refers to the invention of something which is not taken from reality, or to a combination of elements taken from reality in a way which does not conform to that reality. Phantasy may be productive or receptive. Actually, there are many intermediate states and combinations of these two extremes. In either case, phantasy may lead to a merely arbitrary neglect of certain elements in reality or to a consistent elaboration of well perceived elements into a product of phantasy.

Table 17 (XVII-8). TENDENCY TO PHANTASY

(Categories: Marked and Slight)

Percentages of the Respective Physique Type Totals

Physique Types	Delinquents		Non-Delinquents		Difference in Percentages between Delinquents and Non-Delinquents	Probability (Based on X^2 Test)
	No.	%	No.	%		
TOTAL	188	39.1	153	32.5	6.6	.05
Mesomorph	111	38.4	36	24.4	14.0	
Endomorph	18	30.5	20	28.6	1.9	
Ectomorph	31	43.7	68	36.8	6.9	
Balanced	28	45.2	29	42.0	3.2	

Significance of Differences between Physique Types

Mesomorph-Endomorph	-	-	-
Mesomorph-Ectomorph	-	.10	-
Mesomorph-Balanced	-	.10	-
Endomorph-Ectomorph	-	-	-
Endomorph-Balanced	-	-	-
Ectomorph-Balanced	-	-	-

(a) The *tendency to phantasy* is shown to be only slightly but significantly associated with delinquency (Table 17). (b) A significant difference in the association of this tendency with the delinquency of the four body types does not emerge, despite what appears from inspection of the table to be a greater impact on the delinquency of boys of mesomorphic physique. (c) This is supported by the fact that variation is not established in the incidence of this trait among the body types of the delinquents. (d) Since the *tendency to phantasy* varies in incidence among the physique types of the non-delinquents, being less characteristic of mesomorphs than of ecto-morphs or boys of balanced physique, an inference of its essentially constitutional orientation is permissible.

On the basis of the above findings, it would be well to explore further the *tendency to phantasy* which, though not found to have a greater criminogenic impact on any one body type than on any other, may well be more involved in the delinquency of mesomorphs than of boys of the other physique types just because it is found to be less characteristic of non-delinquent mesomorphs than of ecto-morphs and boys of balanced physique, but not found in this sample to vary among the delinquents of the four body types.

LACK OF COMMON SENSE

Common sense is the faculty of thinking and acting in the ways of the community. It may be present even if some acts of the individual run counter to accepted mores. There may, for instance, be a conflict between *common sense* and a phantasy-induced thirst for adventure.

(a) *Lack* of *common sense* is slightly but significantly associated with delinquency (Table 18). (b) The breakdown of the total group into physique types fails to reveal a statistically significant variation in the criminogenic influence of this trait on the body types despite what appears from inspection to be a greater impact on boys of ectomorphic physique. (c) Nor is the incidence of this trait found to vary significantly among delinquents of the four body types. (d) The incidence of *common sense* does not differ significantly among the physique types of the non-delinquents, and on this evidence an inference of its essentially constitutional orientation is therefore not justified.

In view of the foregoing, the *lack of common sense* cannot be deemed to exert a differential criminogenic impact on the physique types. It is slightly but significantly related to delinquency both in

Table 18 (XVII-6). COMMON SENSE

(Categories: Marked and Slight)

Percentages of the Respective Physique Type Totals

Physique Types	Delinquents		Non-Delinquents		Difference in Percentages between Delinquents and Non-Delinquents	Probability (Based on X^2 Test)
	No.	%	No.	%		
TOTAL	357	75.2	376	80.7	−5.5	.05
Mesomorph	224	77.5	122	84.7	−7.2	
Endomorph	39	68.4	52	74.3	−5.9	
Ectomorph	42	64.6	144	78.7	−14.1	
Balanced	52	81.2	58	84.1	−2.9	

Significance of Differences between Physique Types

Mesomorph-Endomorph	−	−	−
Mesomorph-Ectomorph	−	−	−
Mesomorph-Balanced	−	−	−
Endomorph-Ectomorph	−	−	−
Endomorph-Balanced	−	−	−
Ectomorph-Balanced	−	−	−

the mass and probably in the four body types. On the available evidence, this trait cannot be said to be constitutional in tendency.

UNMETHODICAL APPROACH TO PROBLEMS

An *unmethodical approach to problems* pertains to the way in which an intellectual problem or some task is typically attacked and how the individual tries to master it.

(a) An *unmethodical approach to problems* was found, in *Unraveling,* to be significantly associated with delinquency (Table 19). (b) In the breakdown of the totals into physique types, a significant variation does not emerge in the influence of this trait on delinquency among the body types. (c) Diversity is nevertheless revealed among the physique types of the delinquents, a lesser proportion of meso-morphs than of delinquents of balanced type being *unmethodical in their approach to problems.* (d) Since no variance is found in the incidence of this characteristic among the body types of the non-delinquents, there is no basis for an inference that this trait is oriented in constitution.

The evidence in the table precludes a definitive conclusion that *unmethodical approach to problems* is either constitutional in

Table 19 (XVII-10). UNMETHODICAL APPROACH TO PROBLEMS

Percentages of the Respective Physique Type Totals

Physique Types	Delinquents		Non-Delinquents		Difference in Percentages between Delinquents and Non-Delinquents	Probability (Based on X^2 Test)
	No.	%	No.	%		
TOTAL	380	78.8	297	65.0	13.8	.01
Mesomorph	219	74.8	93	65.0	9.8	
Endomorph	48	84.2	39	60.0	24.2	
Ectomorph	57	82.7	116	64.8	17.9	
Balanced	56	88.9	49	70.0	18.9	

Significance of Differences between Physique Types

Mesomorph-Endomorph	-	-	-
Mesomorph-Ectomorph	-	-	-
Mesomorph-Balanced	.05	-	-
Endomorph-Ectomorph	-	-	-
Endomorph-Balanced	-	-	-
Ectomorph-Balanced	-	-	-

emphasis or has a greater bearing on the delinquency of any one physique type than of any other, despite what appears from inspection to be a lesser association of this characteristic with the delinquency of mesomorphs. A check on another sample of cases is indicated, however, because of the significant difference in the incidence of the trait between the mesomorphic delinquents and those of balanced physique.

POTENTIAL CAPACITY FOR OBJECTIVE INTERESTS

(a) A *potential capacity for genuine objectivity* was found in *Unraveling* to be less characteristic of delinquents than of non-delinquents (Table 20). It would appear, therefore, that the delinquents had more of a tendency to be non-objective, that is, to be interested

Table 20 (XVII-11). POTENTIAL CAPACITY FOR OBJECTIVE INTERESTS

(Categories: Marked and Slight)

Percentages of the Respective Physique Type Totals

Physique Types	Delinquents		Non-Delinquents		Difference in Percentages between Delinquents and Non-Delinquents	Probability (Based on X^2 Test)
	No.	%	No.	%		
TOTAL	164	44.5	163	54.3	-9.8	.02
Mesomorph	108	46.6	49	48.5	-1.9	
Endomorph	13	32.5	23	54.7	-22.2	
Ectomorph	25	49.0	65	56.6	-7.6	
Balanced	18	40.0	26	61.9	-21.9	

Significance of Differences between Physique Types

Mesomorph–Endomorph	-	-	-
Mesomorph–Ectomorph	-	-	-
Mesomorph–Balanced	-	-	-
Endomorph–Ectomorph	-	-	-
Endomorph–Balanced	-	-	-
Ectomorph–Balanced	-	-	-

in something merely or predominantly for the sake of gaining prestige, earning money, having success, procuring the attention, affection, or protection of others. (b) This table affords a good illustration of the pitfalls of interpretation made merely on inspection of percentages. Despite what appears to be a much greater criminogenic impact of the trait in question on endomorphs and boys of balanced physique, a statistically significant variation is not established. (c) Nor does the proportion of *potential capacity for objective interests* vary significantly among delinquents of the four body types. (d)

The incidence of this trait does not differ significantly among the physique types of the non-delinquents, and therefore the evidence in the table does not support an inference of its essentially constitutional orientation.

In view of the foregoing, *potential capacity for objective interests* cannot be deemed to exert a differential criminogenic impact on the physique types. It is, however, significantly related to delinquency both in the mass and in the four physique types.

Basic Attitudes to Authority and Society

We turn now to various traits in the character structure of our boys as determined by the Rorschach Test. First we consider basic attitudes to authority and society, which are attitudes important for the genesis and establishment of the individual's psychological situation in the social group. The attitude toward authority is of special significance since, in our culture, most individuals experience society as authority, at first through the medium of the family (the parents), later through school, church, and other agencies of society. These attitudes concern basic ways by which the individual attempts to establish his place, his security, and his share in society and in life. The possession of at least a minimal standard of traditional attitudes toward parents, teachers, society, law, and other sources and symbols of authority is indispensable to a child's adjustment to the prohibitions, taboos, and demands imposed by the social order and the various groups within which he must develop an emotionally wholesome and behaviorally law-abiding *modus vivendi*.

Our first concern is with the selective impact on the delinquency of boys of the four physique types of the traits of social assertiveness, defiance, submissiveness, and ambivalence to authority.

SOCIAL ASSERTIVENESS

Unlike self-assertion, which usually implies a genuine, spontaneous self, *social assertiveness* refers to the rather superficial quality of asserting one's will and ambitions.

(a) *Social assertiveness* was found in *Unraveling* to be significantly associated with delinquency (Table 21). (b) Although the break-down into physique types does not reveal a significant variation in the association of the trait with the delinquency of the body types, there is some possibility of a greater impact of *social assertiveness* on the delinquency of mesomorphs than of ectomorphs. (c) Variation in the incidence of this trait among delinquents is reflected in the

Table 21 (XVIII-2). SOCIAL ASSERTIVENESS

(Categories: Marked and Slight)

Percentages of the Respective Physique Type Totals

Physique Types	Delinquents		Non-Delinquents		Difference in Percentages between Delinquents and Non-Delinquents	Probability (Based on χ^2 Test)
	No.	%	No.	%		
TOTAL	178	45.3	81	20.2	25.1	.01
Mesomorph	121	51.3	27	21.1	30.2	
Endomorph	19	40.5	5	8.0	32.5	
Ectomorph	20	33.9	35	22.0	11.9	
Balanced	18	35.3	14	26.9	8.4	

Significance of Differences between Physique Types

Mesomorph-Endomorph	–	.05	–
Mesomorph-Ectomorph	.10	–	–
Mesomorph-Balanced	–	–	–
Endomorph-Ectomorph	–	.05	–
Endomorph-Balanced	–	.05	–
Ectomorph-Balanced	–	–	–

finding that mesomorphic delinquents are, as a group, more socially assertive than ectomorphic delinquents. (d) It may be inferred that this trait is probably of constitutional orientation because it varies significantly in incidence among the body types of the non-de-linquents, there being a lower incidence of *social assertiveness* among endomorphs than among boys of the other physiques.

Although the evidence is insufficient to conclude that the constitutionally oriented trait of *social assertiveness* is more largely involved in the delinquency of mesomorphs (at least in contrast to ectomorphs), the likelihood of this is worth exploring in another and larger sample of cases.

DEFIANCE

Unlike social assertion, which is a rather superficial quality, *defiance* is aggressive self-assertion born out of deeper insecurity or weakness and, therefore, often indiscriminate in its aims and

Table 22 (XVIII-3). DEFIANCE

(Categories: Marked and Slight)

Percentages of the Respective Physique Type Totals

Physique Types	Delinquents		Non-Delinquents		Difference in Percentages between Delinquents and Non-Delinquents	Probability (Based on X^2 Test)
	No.	%	No.	%		
TOTAL	223	50.4	52	11.5	38.9	.01
Mesomorph	125	47.2	17	12.3	34.9	
Endomorph	29	50.9	5	7.5	43.4	
Ectomorph	31	50.8	21	11.6	39.2	
Balanced	38	63.3	9	13.6	49.7	

Significance of Differences between Physique Types

Mesomorph–Endomorph	-	-	-
Mesomorph–Ectomorph	-	-	-
Mesomorph–Balanced	.10	-	-
Endomorph–Ectomorph	-	-	-
Endomorph–Balanced	-	-	-
Ectomorph–Balanced	-	-	-

means, and usually directed against somebody or something rather than toward a positive goal.

(a) *Defiance* is significantly associated with delinquency, young offenders as a group being far more defiant than non-delinquents

(Table 22). (b) In the breakdown of the total group of delinquents and of non-delinquents into physique types, a significant difference is not found in the association of this trait with the delinquency of the four body types. (c) A possibly reliable variation is found in the incidence of *defiance* among the physique types of the delinquents, reflected in the suggestion (at the .10 level of confidence) that delinquents of balanced physique are, as a group, more defiant than mesomorphic delinquents. However, other evidence in this table does not warrant a stress on this finding. (d) *Defiance* is not found to vary significantly among the physique types of the non-delinquents, and therefore an inference of its essentially constitutional orientation is not here justified.

The trait of *defiance,* which is clearly associated with delinquency, cannot be said to lean toward the constitutional end of the biosocial spectrum, and is not conclusively found to have a differential criminogenic impact on the four physique types.

MARKED SUBMISSIVENESS

In contrast to defiance, which is aggressive self-assertion, *marked submissiveness* is the abandonment of self-assertion in an attempt to gain security by submitting to others, especially to those who are believed stronger (originally, one or both of the parents and later, also, the more anonymous power of institutions, public opinion, conventional usage, and the like).

(a) As might be anticipated, the delinquents as a whole were found in *Unraveling* to be far less submissive to authority than the non-delinquents (Table 23). (b) Nothing can be added on this score to what was established in that work, since a significant variation is not found in the delinquency-inducing impact of this trait among the body types, even though inspection alone would seem to indicate that *lack* of *marked submissiveness* among the endomorphs is more likely to result in delinquency than in other body types. (c) The incidence of this trait is, however, not found to differ significantly among the delinquents of the four physique types. (d)

Since a significant variation is found in the incidence of *marked submissiveness* among the non-delinquents, a higher proportion of endomorphs than of mesomorphs and ectomorphs possessing the trait, it can be assumed that this characteristic is probably oriented in constitution.

Although the influence of *lack* of *marked submissiveness* on the

Table 23 (XVIII-4). MARKED SUBMISSIVENESS

Percentages of the Respective Physique Type Totals

Physique Types	Delinquents		Non-Delinquents		Difference in Percentages between Delinquents and Non-Delinquents	Probability (Based on X^2 Test)
	No.	%	No.	%		
TOTAL	127	26.8	375	80.0	-53.2	.01
Mesomorph	76	27.0	113	77.4	-50.4	
Endomorph	13	22.4	63	90.0	-67.6	
Ectomorph	18	26.5	146	78.4	-51.9	
Balanced	20	30.8	53	79.1	-48.3	

Significance of Differences between Physique Types

Mesomorph-Endomorph	-	.10	-
Mesomorph-Ectomorph	-	-	-
Mesomorph-Balanced	-	-	-
Endomorph-Ectomorph	-	.10	-
Endomorph-Balanced	-	-	-
Ectomorph-Balanced	-	-	-

delinquency of the four physique types does not vary at the level of significance required in this research, the difference between the impact of the trait on the mesomorphs and the endomorphs (at the .15 level) encourages exploration of another sample of cases to determine whether the *absence* of *marked submissiveness* when it occurs in endomorphs (who are found as a group to be normally more submissive to authority than boys of other body types) plays more of a role in their delinquency than it does among the other body types.

AMBIVALENCE TO AUTHORITY

Ambivalence to authority is the result of contradictory or conflicting feelings, such as a coexistence of defiant and submissive

Table 24 (XVIII-5). AMBIVALENCE TO AUTHORITY

(Categories: Marked and Slight)

Percentages of the Respective Physique Type Totals

Physique Types	Delinquents		Non-Delinquents		Difference in Percentages between Delinquents and Non-Delinquents	Probability (Based on X^2 Test)
	No.	%	No.	%		
TOTAL	157	40.6	69	19.6	21.0	.01
Mesomorph	75	32.9	20	19.1	13.8	
Endomorph	27	52.9	7	11.9	41.0	
Ectomorph	24	45.3	29	20.8	24.5	
Balanced	31	57.4	13	26.6	30.8	

Significance of Differences between Physique Types

Mesomorph-Endomorph	.05	—	.05
Mesomorph-Ectomorph	-	-	-
Mesomorph-Balanced	.05	-	-
Endomorph-Ectomorph	-	-	-
Endomorph-Balanced	-	-	-
Ectomorph-Balanced	-	-	-

strivings, of assertive and dependent attitudes. Some of our delinquents were neither clearly defiant nor clearly submissive to authority; they were ambivalent. But reasonable consistency in response to authoritative demands is necessary for continued adjustment to the obligations and prohibitions imposed by conventional society.

(a) *Ambivalence to authority* was found in *Unraveling* to be more characteristic of delinquents as a group than of non-delinquents

(Table 24). (b) Analysis of differences by body type shows a variation in the association of this trait with delinquency. *Ambivalence to authority* has a heavier impact on the delinquency of endomorphs (in contrast to mesomorphs, at least). In other words, *ambivalence to authority,* when occurring in endomorphs is more likely to contribute to their delinquency than when it occurs in mesomorphs. (c) Variation is found in the incidence of this trait among the body types of the delinquents, there being significantly *less ambivalence to authority* among mesomorphic offenders as a group than among endomorphic and the balanced type. (d) Since this characteristic is not found to vary significantly among the body types of the non-delinquents, an inference that it is constitutionally oriented cannot be made.

Although it cannot be said that *ambivalence to authority* is a constitutionally focused trait, it nevertheless plays a differential role in the delinquency of the physique types, as evidenced by its lesser impact on the delinquency of mesomorphs than of endomorphs.

FEELINGS OF RESENTMENT, ANXIETY, INFERIORITY, AND FRUSTRATION

The tensions and anxieties which assail many youngsters in underprivileged urban areas may operate with special selective force in propelling boys of one or another physique type toward maladjustment and delinquency. Reflective of these disturbances is the group of traits with which we now deal—feelings of insecurity or anxiety, of not being wanted or loved, of not being taken care of; feelings of not being taken seriously, of helplessness and powerlessness, of not being recognized or appreciated; fear of failure and defeat; and finally a feeling of resentment, all determined from the Rorschach Test.

MARKED FEELING OF INSECURITY

While insecurity and anxiety are emotional involvements not only in pathological cases but also in many normal persons, *enhanced insecurity and/or anxiety* designates a state in which these feelings exert a decidedly stronger influence within the personality dynamics —either quantitatively or qualitatively—than is usual in the average person. Such feelings may, however, remain largely unconscious.

(a) In comparing our delinquents and non-delinquents in the mass, it was found in *Unraveling* that the delinquents suffered *less* than the non-delinquents from *marked feelings of insecurity*

Table 25 (XVIII-7). ENHANCED FEELINGS OF INSECURITY

(Categories: Marked and Slight)

Percentages of the Respective Physique Type Totals

Physique Types	Delinquents		Non-Delinquents		Difference in Percentages between Delinquents and Non-Delinquents	Probability (Based on X^2 Test)
	No.	%	No.	%		
TOTAL	84	18.5	124	28.8	-10.3	.01
Mesomorph	51	18.8	33	26.6	-7.8	
Endomorph	7	12.7	22	33.3	-20.6	
Ectomorph	16	25.0	56	31.5	-6.5	
Balanced	10	16.1	13	21.0	-4.9	

Significance of Differences between Physique Types

Mesomorph–Endomorph	-	-	-
Mesomorph–Ectomorph	-	-	-
Mesomorph–Balanced	-	-	-
Endomorph–Ectomorph	-	-	-
Endomorph–Balanced	-	-	-
Ectomorph–Balanced	-	-	-

and/or anxiety (Table 25). (b) In the breakdown of the total group into physique types a significant difference is not found in the association of this trait with the delinquency in the four body types, despite what appears on inspection to be a more potent effect of *lack* of a *marked feeling of insecurity* and anxiety when occurring in endomorphs, than when it occurs in other boys. (c) Nor is the incidence of a *marked feeling of insecurity* found to vary significantly among the four body types of the delinquents. (d) The percentage of this deep-seated feeling does not differ significantly among the physique types of the non-delinquents, and there is therefore no basis for an inference of its essentially constitutional orientation.

In view of the foregoing, *marked feelings of insecurity* cannot be deemed to exert a differential criminogenic impact on the physique types. Lack of such feelings is, however, significantly related to delinquency both in the mass and in the four body types.

MARKED FEELING OF NOT BEING WANTED OR LOVED

Not being wanted or loved is the feeling that one is not accepted, not included, or even rejected by others. It is a sense of a lack of positive human relationship to a particular group or person, especially to parents and other members of the family, in early childhood. This feeling is very often repressed and becomes unconscious. It may lead to an exaggerated need for affection, recognition, or success.

(a) There is no evidence of a significant association between the *marked feeling of not being wanted or loved* and delinquency, the incidence of this trait among delinquents and non-delinquents being very high in both, and quite similar (Table 26). (b) In the analysis of differences, through the breakdown of the total group of delinquents and of non-delinquents into physique types, a significant variation is not found in the impact of this deep-seated feeling on the delinquency of the four body types. There is, therefore, no reliable evidence of an association of this trait with the delinquency of any physique type. (c) Nor does a significant variation exist in the incidence of the *marked feeling of not being wanted or loved* among the physique types of the delinquents. (d) Since no clear variation in the incidence of this trait is revealed among the physique types of the non-delinquents, it cannot be inferred that it is essentially of constitutional orientation.

To sum up, since the *marked feeling of not being wanted or loved* does not differentiate delinquents from non-delinquents, either as a group or in any body type, and since this deep-seated trait is not found to vary in incidence among the physique types of the non-

Table 26 (XVIII-8). MARKED FEELING OF NOT BEING WANTED OR LOVED

Percentages of the Respective Physique Type Totals

Physique Types	Delinquents		Non-Delinquents		Difference in Percentages between Delinquents and Non-Delinquents	Probability (Based on χ^2 Test)
	No.	%	No.	%		
TOTAL	343	84.1	337	88.0	-3.9	.20
Mesomorph	198	80.8	97	88.2	-7.4	
Endomorph	42	89.4	47	83.9	5.5	
Ectomorph	53	89.8	138	89.6	0.2	
Balanced	50	87.7	55	87.3	0.4	

Significance of Differences between Physique Types

Mesomorph–Endomorph	-	-	-
Mesomorph–Ectomorph	-	-	-
Mesomorph–Balanced	-	-	-
Endomorph–Ectomorph	-	-	-
Endomorph–Balanced	-	-	-
Ectomorph–Balanced	-	-	-

delinquents, it cannot be inferred that it is either criminogenic or constitutionally oriented.

FEELING OF NOT BEING TAKEN CARE OF

The sense of *not being taken care of* is the feeling that there is no active interest on the part of others (especially of parents), or help from them, in situations in which one deems himself entitled to such interest and help. Once this feeling is established it may outlast the particular situation which produced it.

(a) It is in connection with a trait such as the *feeling of not being taken care of* that the value of a breakdown of the total group of delinquents, and of non-delinquents, into body types is well illustrated. In *Unraveling* an association was not found between the trait and delinquency, since it did not significantly distinguish delinquents from non-delinquents (Table 27). (b) But a breakdown into physique types now reveals that the *feeling of not being taken care of* bears a significant association to the delinquency of *mesomorphs*;

Table 27 (XVIII-9). FEELING OF NOT BEING TAKEN CARE OF

(Categories: Marked and Slight)

Percentages of the Respective Physique Type Totals

Physique Types	Delinquents		Non-Delinquents		Difference in Percentages between Delinquents and Non-Delinquents	Probability (Based on x^2 Test)
	No.	%	No.	%		
TOTAL	96	29.2	75	24.7	4.5	.30
Mesomorph	74	36.5	18	18.8	17.7	
Endomorph	7	17.9	11	31.4	-13.5	
Ectomorph	9	20.9	32	25.2	-4.3	
Balanced	6	13.6	14	30.4	-16.8	

Significance of Differences between Physique Types

Mesomorph-Endomorph	.05	–	.05
Mesomorph-Ectomorph	–	–	.10
Mesomorph-Balanced	.02	–	.05
Endomorph-Ectomorph	–	–	–
Endomorph-Balanced	–	–	–
Ectomorph-Balanced	–	–	–

it is rather its *absence* that is somehow criminogenically involved among boys of the other three physique types. (c) As might be expected from the above finding, the trait is found to vary among the body types of the delinquents, a higher proportion of the mesomorphs than of the endomorphs or balanced (and possibly, though not definitively, than of the ectomorphs) having the *feel-*

ing of not being taken care of. (d) This characteristic does not vary sufficiently among the body types of the non-delinquents to permit of an inference that it inclines toward the constitutional end of the biosocial spectrum.

To sum up, although the *feeling of not being taken care of* was not found in *Unraveling* to differentiate delinquents from non-delinquents in the mass, it is now evident that its presence has criminogenic implications for mesomorphs. A reasonable hypothesis would seem to be that since the *feeling of not being taken care of* would not appear to be normal to the sturdy, muscular mesomorphs, when it does exist it adds a special impulsion to other criminogenic influences.

FEELING OF NOT BEING TAKEN SERIOUSLY

Not being taken seriously is the feeling that one's own person, interests, ideas, and wishes are not acknowledged and not treated as deserving of respect and consideration for their own sake. This is frequently produced in childhood (often inadvertently) by making a child feel that whatever he does is "child's play," especially if his wishes and interests do not coincide with those of his parents.

(a) A *marked feeling of not being taken seriously* is shown to be negatively associated with delinquency (Table 28). (b) In the breakdown of the total group into physique types, a significant difference is not found in the impact of this trait on the delinquency of the four body types despite what appears from inspection to be more of a negative association with the delinquency of endomorphs and ectomorphs. (c) Nor is the incidence of a *marked feeling of not being taken seriously* found to vary significantly among delinquents of the four body types. (d) Further, this trait does not vary significantly among the physique types of the non-delinquents. An inference of its essentially constitutional orientation is not therefore justified by our evidence, although mere inspection would appear to show that a greater proportion of endomorphs have this feeling than do boys of the other body types.

The *absence* of a *marked feeling of not being taken seriously* cannot be deemed to exert a differential impact on the delinquency of the physique types. It is only slightly related to delinquency both

Table 28 (XVIII-10). MARKED FEELING OF NOT BEING TAKEN SERIOUSLY

Percentages of the Respective Physique Type Totals

Physique Types	Delinquents		Non-Delinquents		Difference in Percentages between Delinquents and Non-Delinquents	Probability (Based on X^2 Test)
	No.	%	No.	%		
TOTAL	165	44.1	185	52.3	-8.2	.05
Mesomorph	100	43.7	50	47.2	-3.5	
Endomorph	22	45.8	38	64.4	-18.6	
Ectomorph	18	36.0	72	51.8	-15.8	
Balanced	25	53.1	25	50.0	3.1	

Significance of Differences between Physique Types

Mesomorph-Endomorph	-	-	-
Mesomorph-Ectomorph	-	-	-
Mesomorph-Balanced	-	-	-
Endomorph-Ectomorph	-	-	-
Endomorph-Balanced	-	-	-
Ectomorph-Balanced	-	-	-

in the mass and probably in the four physique types. It cannot be inferred that the trait is of constitutional orientation.

FEELING OF HELPLESSNESS

The trait previously analyzed, the feeling of not being taken seriously, often leads to a sense of *helplessness and powerlessness—* a particularly frequent, important, and very often unconscious kind of insecurity in which the individual feels himself incompetent, especially as regards changing or influencing anything, and most particularly the course of his own life.

(a) *Absence* of the *feeling of helplessness and powerlessness* is seen to be significantly associated with delinquency (Table 29). (b) The breakdown into physique types fails to uncover a significant difference in the criminogenic impact of this trait among the four body types. What appears to be a difference, at least between meso-morphs and endomorphs, is found to be significant only at a level

Table 29 (XVIII-12). FEELING OF HELPLESSNESS

(Categories: Marked and Slight)

Percentages of the Respective Physique Type Totals

Physique Types	Delinquents		Non-Delinquents		Difference in Percentages between Delinquents and Non-Delinquents	Probability (Based on X^2 Test)
	No.	%	No.	%		
TOTAL	181	42.1	214	55.2	-13.1	.01
Mesomorph	120	46.4	59	53.7	-7.3	
Endomorph	16	33.3	38	65.5	-32.2	
Ectomorph	27	40.9	89	54.6	-13.7	
Balanced	18	32.2	28	49.1	-16.9	

Significance of Differences between Physique Types

Mesomorph-Endomorph	-	-	-
Mesomorph-Ectomorph	-	-	-
Mesomorph-Balanced	-	-	-
Endomorph-Ectomorph	-	-	-
Endomorph-Balanced	-	-	-
Ectomorph-Balanced	-	-	-

which we cannot accept (.15). (c) Nor is the incidence of the *feeling of helplessness and powerlessness* found to vary significantly among the four body types of the delinquents. (d) Since this trait does not differ significantly in incidence among the non-delinquents of the four physique types, an inference of essentially constitutional orientation is not justified on the evidence before us.

In brief, the *feeling of helplessness and powerlessness* cannot be deemed to exert a differential criminogenic impact on the physique types. Significantly related to delinquency both in the mass and in the four physique types, it does not, however, exert a varied influence on their delinquency.

FEELING OF NOT BEING APPRECIATED

The *feeling of not being recognized or appreciated* refers especially

Table 30 (XVIII-11). FEELING OF NOT BEING APPRECIATED

(Categories: Marked and Slight)

Percentages of the Respective Physique Type Totals

Physique Types	Delinquents		Non-Delinquents		Difference in Percentages between Delinquents and Non-Delinquents	Probability (Based on X^2 Test)
	No.	%	No.	%		
TOTAL	145	35.9	84	24.8	11.1	.01
Mesomorph	98	40.0	21	19.3	20.7	
Endomorph	14	28.6	12	25.0	3.6	
Ectomorph	18	32.7	36	27.1	5.6	
Balanced	15	27.8	15	30.6	-2.8	

Significance of Differences between Physique Types

Mesomorph–Endomorph	-	-	-
Mesomorph–Ectomorph	-	-	-
Mesomorph–Balanced	-	-	-
Endomorph–Ectomorph	-	-	-
Endomorph–Balanced	-	-	-
Ectomorph–Balanced	-	-	-

to the impression that one's qualities, gifts, intentions, and achievements are not sufficiently thought of or valued. It often occurs in association with conscious as well as unconscious grandiose ideas and opinions about one's self.

(a) The delinquents as a group were found to have this feeling to a significantly greater extent than the non-delinquents (Table 30).

(b) In the breakdown of the total group into physique types a significant difference is not established in the relationship of this trait to the delinquency of the four body types. What appears on inspection to be a greater impact on mesomorphs may be so, but the variance between mesomorphs and the balanced type is at the .15 level of confidence. (c) Nor is the incidence of the *feeling of not being recognized or appreciated* found to vary significantly between the four body types among the delinquents. (d) Since this trait does not vary significantly among the physique types of the non-delinquents, an inference of its essentially constitutional orientation is, on the evidence at hand, not justified.

In brief, the *feeling of not being recognized or appreciated* cannot safely be deemed to exert a differential impact on the delinquency of the physique types, despite what appears from inspection to be a greater emphasis of this trait in contributing to the delinquency of mesomorphs. Analysis of another sample of cases might prove definitive.

FEAR OF FAILURE AND DEFEAT

The *fear of failure and defeat* is a frequent consequence of anxiety, especially in persons with an over-competitive attitude. This fear may permeate every sphere of life, not only work or play but relations with others. It may lead either to greater effort or to inhibitions, aloofness, and a recoiling from competition.

(a) *Fear of failure and defeat* was found in *Unraveling* to be negatively associated with delinquency, as shown by the considerably *lower* incidence of this trait among the total of delinquents than that of the control group (Table 31). (b) Examination of the differences between delinquents and non-delinquents among the body types indicates variation in degree of association of this trait with delinquency. A difference in the extent of etiologic impact of *fear of failure and defeat* is established between the endomorphs and the balanced group, it having significantly less influence on the delinquency of endomorphs than of boys of balanced physique. (c)

However, no significant variation is found to exist in the incidence of this trait among the body types of the delinquents. (d) The trait varies in percentage among the physique types of the non-delinquents, making it reasonable to infer that it has a constitutional orien-

Table 31 (XVIII-13). FEAR OF FAILURE AND DEFEAT

(Categories: Marked and Slight)

Percentages of the Respective Physique Type Totals

Physique Types	Delinquents		Non-Delinquents		Difference in Percentages between Delinquents and Non-Delinquents	Probability (Based on X² Test)
	No.	%	No.	%		
TOTAL	186	44.3	266	63.6	-19.3	.01
Mesomorph	114	44.7	86	67.7	-23.0	
Endomorph	24	45.3	47	75.8	-30.5	
Ectomorph	23	41.9	106	62.7	-20.8	
Balanced	25	43.8	27	45.0	-1.2	

Significance of Differences between Physique Types

Mesomorph–Endomorph	-	-	-
Mesomorph–Ectomorph	-	-	-
Mesomorph–Balanced	-	.05	-
Endomorph–Ectomorph	-	-	-
Endomorph–Balanced	-	.02	.10
Ectomorph–Balanced	-	.10	-

tation. *Fear of failure and defeat* is *less* characteristic of boys of balanced physique than of the other body types.

This probably constitutionally oriented trait is not found to be significantly associated with the delinquency of boys of balanced physique, in contrast with endomorphs.

FEELING OF RESENTMENT

Resentment is the feeling of frustration, envy, or dissatisfaction, with particular emphasis on the negative wish that others be denied satisfactions or enjoyments that one has himself lacked, rather than the positive hope or attempt to better one's own situation.

(a) The *feeling of resentment* was found in *Unraveling* to be markedly associated with delinquency (Table 32). (b) In the break-down of the total group into physique types, a significant difference is not established in the criminogenic impact of this trait on the

Table 32 (XVIII-14).   FEELING OF RESENTMENT

(Categories: Marked and Slight)

Percentages of the Respective Physique Type Totals

Physique Types	Delinquents		Non-Delinquents		Difference in Percentages between Delinquents and Non-Delinquents	Probability (Based on X^2 Test)
	No.	%	No.	%		
TOTAL	299	74.2	160	51.6	22.6	.01
Mesomorph	190	76.0	44	50.5	25.5	
Endomorph	36	72.0	23	52.3	19.7	
Ectomorph	32	65.3	72	52.5	12.8	
Balanced	41	75.9	21	50.0	25.9	

Significance of Differences between Physique Types

Mesomorph–Endomorph	-	-	-
Mesomorph–Ectomorph	-	-	-
Mesomorph–Balanced	-	-	-
Endomorph–Ectomorph	-	-	-
Endomorph–Balanced	-	-	-
Ectomorph–Balanced	-	-	-

four body types. (c) Nor is the incidence of the *feeling of resentment* found to diverge significantly among the four body types of the de-linquents. (d) Since this trait does not vary significantly among the physique types of the non-delinquents, an inference of its essentially constitutional orientation is not justified on the evidence.

To summarize, the *feeling of resentment,* constitutional emphasis of which is not supported by the findings, cannot be deemed to exert a differential criminogenic impact on the physique types. It is significantly related to delinquency both in the mass and in the four physique types.

The traits of intelligence and character structure analyzed in this chapter have added a few strokes to our developing portrait of the selective characteristics contributing to the delinquency of boys of the four body types. The picture should increase in clarity and perspective as we proceed further.

NOTES

1. For details regarding the nature of the abilities which these sub-tests are designed to measure, and tabulations of findings, see *Unraveling,* pp. 199-202, 351-362.

2. For details regarding these tests and tabulations of findings, see *Unraveling,* pp. 202-204, 351-362.

V

Character Structure (Continued)

In the prior chapter the traits were presented that deal with certain qualitative aspects of intelligence; with basic attitudes to authority and society; and with feelings of resentment, anxiety, inferiority, and frustration. In the present chapter we continue the analysis of the selective impact on the delinquency of boys of the four physique types of other traits of character structure derived from the Rorschach Test. These encompass feelings of kindliness and hostility, feelings of dependence, goals of strivings, and some general qualities of personality.

FEELINGS OF KINDLINESS AND HOSTILITY

Ability to express kindliness and to manage or sublimate feelings of hostility are part of the necessary equipment for social adaptation.

In this area we will be concerned with surface contact with others, hostility, suspiciousness, destructiveness, feeling of isolation, and a defensive attitude.

SURFACE CONTACT WITH OTHERS

Good surface contact with others consists of the ability to get along with people regardless of the underlying attitude, which may be, for instance, one of isolation or even hostility. There may especially be a surface attitude of "keep smiling," without any real friendliness or kindness. This need not be merely simulated or acted; the individual may sincerely believe that he is very friendly and sociable and appears to be so, whereas unconsciously he may be intensely hostile.

(a) *Good surface contact with others* was found in *Unraveling* to be negatively associated with delinquency (Table 33). (b) In breaking down the total group of delinquents and non-delinquents into physique types and comparing the differences, it is now found that

Table 33 (XVIII-17). GOOD SURFACE CONTACT WITH OTHERS

Percentages of the Respective Physique Type Totals

Physique Types	Delinquents		Non-Delinquents		Difference in Percentages between Delinquents and Non-Delinquents	Probability (Based on x^2 Test)
	No.	%	No.	%		
TOTAL	438	91.6	451	96.6	-5.0	.01
Mesomorph	263	92.0	142	98.6	-6.6	
Endomorph	57	96.6	62	91.2	5.4	
Ectomorph	57	82.6	179	96.8	-14.2	
Balanced	61	95.3	68	97.1	-1.8	

Significance of Differences between Physique Types

Mesomorph–Endomorph	-	-	.05
Mesomorph–Ectomorph	-	-	-
Mesomorph–Balanced	-	-	-
Endomorph–Ectomorph	.05	-	.05
Endomorph–Balanced	-	-	-
Ectomorph–Balanced	.10	-	-

good surface contact with others is affirmatively associated with the delinquency of endomorphs and negatively with that of mesomorphs and ectomorphs. (c) The trait varies significantly among the body types of the delinquents, ectomorphic delinquents as a group not manifesting good surface contact with others to the extent that endomorphs or delinquents of balanced physique do. (d) The characteristic is not found to vary in incidence among the body types of the non-delinquents and can therefore not be ascribed to the constitutional pole of the biosocial spectrum.

Good surface contact with others is not found to have a constitutional orientation. It plays a selective role in the delinquency of the physique types.

HOSTILITY

Next we are concerned with the impact of consciously or unconsciously hostile impulses against others, without good reason, on the

Table 34 (XVIII-22). HOSTILITY

(Categories: Marked and Slight)

Percentages of the Respective Physique Type Totals

Physique Types	Delinquents		Non-Delinquents		Difference in Percentages between Delinquents and Non-Delinquents	Probability (Based on X^2 Test)
	No.	%	No.	%		
TOTAL	335	79.6	196	56.0	23.6	.01
Mesomorph	203	79.3	51	50.5	28.8	
Endomorph	40	76.9	30	57.7	19.2	
Ectomorph	48	82.8	88	61.6	21.2	
Balanced	44	80.0	27	50.0	30.0	

Significance of Differences between Physique Types

Mesomorph-Endomorph	-	-	-
Mesomorph-Ectomorph	-	-	-
Mesomorph-Balanced	-	-	-
Endomorph-Ectomorph	-	-	-
Endomorph-Balanced	-	-	-
Ectomorph-Balanced	-	-	-

delinquency of boys of the four physique types. This kind of hostility usually accompanies a fear that the person against whom it is directed is in turn hostile.

(a) *Hostility* was found in *Unraveling* to be markedly associated with delinquency (Table 34). (b) In the breakdown of the total group into physique types, a significant difference in the delinquency-inducing impact of this trait on the four body forms does not emerge. (c) Nor does the incidence of *hostility* vary significantly among the four body types of the delinquents. (d) Further, the incidence of *hostility* does not differ significantly among the physique types of the non-delinquents, and therefore an inference of its essentially constitutional orientation is not justified.

In the light of the table *hostility,* although markedly associated with delinquency, cannot be deemed to exert a differential criminogenic impact on the physique types.

SUSPICIOUSNESS

Suspiciousness has to do with indiscriminate or exaggerated suspicion of others, unwarranted by the situation. The person is usually not aware that he is unduly mistrustful; he thinks rather

Table 35 (XVIII-23). MARKED SUSPICIOUSNESS

Percentages of the Respective Physique Type Totals

Physique Types	Delinquents		Non-Delinquents		Difference in Percentages between Delinquents and Non-Delinquents	Probability (Based on X^2 Test)
	No.	%	No.	%		
TOTAL	221	51.4	106	26.8	24.6	.01
Mesomorph	135	51.3	29	24.6	26.7	
Endomorph	23	47.9	20	35.1	12.8	
Ectomorph	34	53.1	47	28.8	24.3	
Balanced	29	52.7	10	17.5	35.2	

Significance of Differences between Physique Types

Mesomorph-Endomorph	-	-	-
Mesomorph-Ectomorph	-	-	-
Mesomorph-Balanced	-	-	-
Endomorph-Ectomorph	-	-	-
Endomorph-Balanced	-	-	-
Ectomorph-Balanced	-	-	-

that he is being merely cautious or realistic or that he is being perse-
cuted.

(a) It is apparent that *marked suspiciousness* is significantly associated with delinquency, a far higher proportion of delinquents
than of non-delinquents possessing this trait (Table 35). (b) In the
breakdown of the total group into physique types, there is no significant difference in the association of this trait with the delinquency
of the four body types, despite what appears on the surface to be a
lesser role of suspiciousness in the delinquency of endomorphs. (c)
Nor does the incidence of this trait vary significantly among the
body types of the delinquents. (d) Further, the incidence of *marked
suspiciousness* does not vary significantly among the physique
types of the non-delinquents, there being therefore no basis in the
table for an inference of an essentially constitutional orientation
of this trait.

In brief, *marked suspiciousness* is significantly related to antisocial
behavior both in the mass and in the four physique types, but it
does not exert a significantly differential influence on the delinquency
of the body types.

DESTRUCTIVENESS

Now we consider the tendency to destroy, to hurt, to be negativistic.
This may be directed against others or against one's self; usually both
trends run parallel, one often being more manifest, the other more
suppressed. (Destructiveness is not to be confused with destructive-
sadistic trends, which pertain to *goals* of drives.)

(a) *Destructiveness* was found in *Unraveling* to be associated
with delinquency, as shown by the considerable and significant
difference in incidence of this trait between the total of delinquents
and that of the control group, the former being more destructive
than the latter (Table 36). (b) It is now shown to be significantly
associated with delinquency in all body types, but to vary in its influence, having a significantly greater criminogenic impact on mesomorphic boys than ectomorphic. (c) No significant variation exists

in the incidence of *destructiveness* among the body types of the delinquents. (d) However, the trait does vary in incidence among the body types of the non-delinquents, being more characteristic of ectomorphs than of mesomorphs or endomorphs, and thus making it reasonable to infer that it has a constitutional orientation.

To sum up and interpret further: since it is obvious that the ex-

Table 36 (XVIII-24). DESTRUCTIVENESS

(Categories: Marked and Slight)

Percentages of the Respective Physique Type Totals

Physique Types	Delinquents		Non-Delinquents		Difference in Percentages between Delinquents and Non-Delinquents	Probability (Based on X^2 Test)
	No.	%	No.	%		
TOTAL	185	48.4	64	15.7	32.7	.01
Mesomorph	123	51.9	14	11.1	40.8	
Endomorph	19	38.7	5	7.8	30.9	
Ectomorph	19	39.6	35	21.8	17.8	
Balanced	24	50.0	10	17.2	32.8	

Significance of Differences between Physique Types

Mesomorph-Endomorph	-	-	-
Mesomorph-Ectomorph	-	.10	.05
Mesomorph-Balanced	-	-	-
Endomorph-Ectomorph	-	.05	-
Endomorph-Balanced	-	-	-
Ectomorph-Balanced	-	-	-

cessive criminogenic contribution of the constitutionally oriented trait of *destructiveness* to the delinquency of mesomorphs as compared with ectomorphs is associated with its relatively low incidence among mesomorphic *non-delinquents*, it may reasonably be assumed that when this trait is involved in the personality-character structure of mesomorphic boys, it exerts an especially damaging influence.

FEELING OF ISOLATION

Isolation is a feeling of being alone (often combined with a sense of helplessness), and of not being sufficiently capable of giving and receiving love and affection. It may well be accompanied by an appearance and a subjective conviction of being very sociable. This is illustrated, for instance, by the person who is constantly "on the

Table 37 (XVIII-25). FEELING OF ISOLATION

(Categories: Marked and Slight)

Percentages of the Respective Physique Type Totals

Physique Types	Delinquents		Non-Delinquents		Difference in Percentages between Delinquents and Non-Delinquents	Probability (Based on X^2 Test)
	No.	%	No.	%		
TOTAL	166	45.5	126	36.9	8.6	.02
Mesomorph	109	46.2	33	32.7	13.5	
Endomorph	13	38.2	20	41.6	-3.4	
Ectomorph	24	46.1	57	40.1	6.0	
Balanced	20	46.5	16	31.4	15.1	

Significance of Differences between Physique Types

Mesomorph-Endomorph	-	-	-
Mesomorph-Ectomorph	-	-	-
Mesomorph-Balanced	-	-	-
Endomorph-Ectomorph	-	-	-
Endomorph-Balanced	-	-	-
Ectomorph-Balanced	-	-	-

go" and always "making friends" merely to escape awareness of extreme emotional isolation.

(a) The *feeling of isolation* was found in *Unraveling* to be slightly but clearly associated with delinquency (Table 37). (b) In the breakdown of the total group into physique types, a significant difference is not found in the impact of this trait on the delinquency of the four body types. (c) Nor does the incidence of the *feeling of isolation* differ significantly among delinquents of the four physiques. (d) Since this trait does not vary significantly among the body types of the non-delinquents, any inference of its essentially constitutional orientation is not justified on the evidence in the table.

Reviewing the findings, the *feeling of isolation*, although significantly related to delinquency both in the mass and in the four physique types, cannot be deemed to have a differential influence on the delinquency of the latter.

DEFENSIVE ATTITUDE

Unwarranted defensiveness is either exaggerated in proportion to the attack or directed against an imaginary attack. The means of

Table 38 (XVIII-26). DEFENSIVE ATTITUDE

(Categories: Marked and Slight)

Percentages of the Respective Physique Type Totals

Physique Types	Delinquents		Non-Delinquents		Difference in Percentages between Delinquents and Non-Delinquents	Probability (Based on X^2 Test)
	No.	%	No.	%		
TOTAL	243	56.0	183	45.0	11.0	.01
Mesomorph	150	56.2	59	47.6	8.6	
Endomorph	29	56.9	30	50.0	6.9	
Ectomorph	35	58.3	73	44.5	13.8	
Balanced	29	51.8	21	35.5	16.3	

Significance of Differences between Physique Types

Mesomorph-Endomorph	-	-	-
Mesomorph-Ectomorph	-	-	-
Mesomorph-Balanced	-	-	-
Endomorph-Ectomorph	-	-	-
Endomorph-Balanced	-	-	-
Ectomorph-Balanced	-	-	-

defense are varied. Sometimes they consist of a "shell-like" attitude of warding off every approach and erecting a wall around oneself; sometimes they take a more aggressive form, as, for instance, in persons who are very sensitive to any criticism and are provoked by it to defiant or obstinate or opinionated behavior.

(a) A *defensive attitude* was found in the parent study to be significantly associated with delinquency (Table 38). (b) It is clear that the breakdown of the total group into physique types fails to disclose a significant variation in the association of this trait with the delinquency of the body types. (c) Nor is the incidence of a *defensive attitude* found to vary significantly among the four body types of those already delinquent. (d) Further, the incidence of a *defensive attitude* does not differ significantly among the physique types of the non-delinquents, and therefore an inference of essentially constitutional orientation is not justified.

To sum up, a *defensive attitude* is significantly related to delinquency both in the mass and in the body types, but it cannot be deemed to exert a differential criminogenic impact on any of the four physique types.

DEPENDENCE AND INDEPENDENCE

As regards dependence, we consider first several attitudes that reflect the degree to which the delinquents and non-delinquents were emotionally dependent on others or were self-reliant, independent, and secure. The traits to be given special emphasis are dependence on others and the feeling of being able to manage one's own life.

DEPENDENCE ON OTHERS

Dependence on others is defined as the tendency to cling to others rather than to stand on one's own feet. It may evidence itself in relations to loved ones, to employers, or to others who in one way or another furnish protection. Often, the need for dependence is directed indiscriminately toward anyone who appears strong and who may be a potential protector.

(a) *Marked dependence on others* was found in *Unraveling* to be negatively associated with delinquency, as shown by the considerable difference in incidence of the trait between the total group of delinquents and that of the non-delinquents, the former being less dependent on others than the latter (Table 39). (b) Analysis of differences by body type reveals some variation among them in the

Table 39 (XVIII-27). MARKED DEPENDENCE ON OTHERS

Percentages of the Respective Physique Type Totals

Physique Types	Delinquents		Non-Delinquents		Difference in Percentages between Delinquents and Non-Delinquents	Probability (Based on X^2 Test)
	No.	%	No.	%		
TOTAL	296	68.8	399	86.4	-17.6	.01
Mesomorph	173	67.9	121	85.8	-17.9	
Endomorph	39	68.4	65	92.8	-24.4	
Ectomorph	37	64.9	161	87.5	-22.6	
Balanced	47	77.0	52	77.6	-0.6	

Significance of Differences between Physique Types

Mesomorph- Endomorph	-	-	-
Mesomorph- Ectomorph	-	-	-
Mesomorph- Balanced	-	-	-
Endomorph- Ectomorph	-	-	-
Endomorph- Balanced	-	.10	.10
Ectomorph- Balanced	-	-	-

impact of the trait on delinquency, there being far less of an influence of an *absence of marked dependence* on boys of balanced physique than on the endomorphs. (c) Significant variation is not found to exist, however, in the incidence of *marked dependence* among the body types of the delinquents. (d) Since the trait varies in incidence among the physique types of the non-delinquents, there being a lesser incidence among boys of balanced physique than among endomorphs, there is some ground to infer that it has a constitutional emphasis.

It can be concluded that this possibly constitutional trait is essentially non-criminogenic among boys of balanced physique in contradistinction to the considerable etiologic involvement of a *lack of marked dependence* on others in the delinquency of endomorphs. This outcome is attributable to the naturally greater incidence of marked dependence on others in the endomorphic group of non-delinquents than among the non-delinquents of balanced physique.

FEELING OF BEING ABLE TO MANAGE OWN LIFE

The *feeling of being able to manage one's own life* is a deep-seated confidence that one will be able, on the whole, to handle the problems and tasks of life without leaning unduly on others.

Table 40 (XVIII-32). FEELING OF BEING ABLE TO MANAGE OWN LIFE

(Categories: Marked and Slight)

Percentages of the Respective Physique Type Totals

Physique Types	Delinquents		Non-Delinquents		Difference in Percentages between Delinquents and Non-Delinquents	Probability (Based on X^2 Test)
	No.	%	No.	%		
TOTAL	237	73.1	202	63.3	9.8	.01
Mesomorph	147	70.7	59	67.0	3.7	
Endomorph	31	81.6	23	51.1	30.5	
Ectomorph	24	64.9	85	62.5	2.4	
Balanced	35	85.4	35	70.0	15.4	

Significance of Differences between Physique Types

Mesomorph–Endomorph	-	-	.10
Mesomorph–Ectomorph	-	-	-
Mesomorph–Balanced	.10	-	-
Endomorph–Ectomorph	-	-	-
Endomorph–Balanced	-	-	-
Ectomorph–Balanced	-	-	-

(a) Examination of the totals shows that this attitude is more characteristic of delinquents as a group than of non-delinquents, it being thus established that it is associated with delinquency (Table 40). (b) Analysis of differences by body type reveals some variation among them in the impact of the trait on delinquency, endomorphs who are not dependent being more likely to become delinquent than non-dependent lads of balanced type. (c) Variation occurs in the incidence of this trait among the body types of the delinquents, reflected largely in a significantly lesser incidence of this feeling among mesomorphic delinquents than among those of the balanced type. (d) This trait is not found to vary significantly among the body types of the non-delinquents.

In summary, on the evidence at hand the *feeling of being able to manage one's life* cannot be said to have a constitutional emphasis. It plays a lesser criminogenic role among mesomorphs than among endomorphs. It is not clear whether this fact is attributable to a deficiency of this trait among endomorphic non-delinquents, or to the probability that when it does exist in the character structure of endomorphs it is especially likely to make them prone to delinquency; or whether both sets of influences are involved.

GOALS OF STRIVINGS

Our next concern is with some typical goal-aimed ways in which the individual tries to satisfy his needs: by intensive love of self (narcissistic trends); by a more or less conscious expectation that others will take care of one (receptive trends); by a tendency to suffer and to be dependent on others (masochistic trends); or by a tendency to hurt or destroy others (destructive-sadistic trends).

NARCISSISTIC TRENDS

Narcissistic trends reflect love of self resulting in increased need for power, superiority, prestige, status, and admiration.

(a) Presence of *narcissistic trends* is shown to be significantly associated with delinquency (Table 41). (b) The breakdown of the total group into physique types fails to disclose a significant difference in the criminogenic impact of this trait on the four body types, despite the appearance of a greater influence in the case of mesomorphs. (c) Nor is the incidence of *narcissistic trends* found to vary significantly among the delinquents of the four body types. (d) The incidence of this trait does not vary significantly among

Table 41 (XVIII-33). NARCISSISTIC TRENDS

(Categories: Marked and Slight)

Percentages of the Respective Physique Type Totals

Physique Types	Delinquents		Non-Delinquents		Difference in Percentages between Delinquents and Non-Delinquents	Probability (Based on X^2 Test)
	No.	%	No.	%		
TOTAL	108	23.3	63	14.3	9.0	.01
Mesomorph	72	25.7	18	12.7	13.0	
Endomorph	13	22.4	9	13.8	8.6	
Ectomorph	14	21.2	26	15.2	6.0	
Balanced	9	15.0	10	16.4	-1.4	

Significance of Differences between Physique Types

Mesomorph–Endomorph	-	-	-
Mesomorph–Ectomorph	-	-	-
Mesomorph–Balanced	-	-	-
Endomorph–Ectomorph	-	-	-
Endomorph–Balanced	-	-	-
Ectomorph–Balanced	-	-	-

the physique types of the non-delinquents, and therefore an inference of its essentially constitutional orientation is not justified.

In brief, the presence of *narcissistic trends,* although significantly related to delinquency both in the mass and in the four physique types, cannot be deemed to exert a differential criminogenic impact on the body types.

RECEPTIVE TRENDS

Expression of *receptive* (*oral*) *trends* as a typical way in which one satisfies his needs, reflects a more or less unconscious expectation that one will be somehow taken care of by others, the individual not feeling obliged to make any effort to assume his responsibilities. This tendency may take a passive form (waiting for someone else to

Table 42 (XVIII-35). RECEPTIVE TRENDS

(Categories: Marked and Slight)

Percentages of the Respective Physique Type Totals

Physique Types	Delinquents		Non-Delinquents		Difference in Percentages between Delinquents and Non-Delinquents	Probability (Based on X^2 Test)
	No.	%	No.	%		
TOTAL	129	29.6	59	13.8	15.8	.01
Mesomorph	91	35.0	21	16.3	18.7	
Endomorph	12	24.5	8	12.6	11.9	
Ectomorph	16	25.0	16	9.4	15.6	
Balanced	10	15.8	14	21.9	-6.1	

Significance of Differences between Physique Types

Mesomorph-Endomorph	-	-	-
Mesomorph-Ectomorph	-	-	-
Mesomorph-Balanced	.05	-	.05
Endomorph-Ectomorph	-	-	-
Endomorph-Balanced	-	-	-
Ectomorph-Balanced	-	-	.10

provide what one desires); or it may take a more active form leading to outwardly expressed greed, or to attempts to secure the desired object without effort (stealing), or without assuming any obligations.

(a) *Receptive* (*oral*) *trends* were found in *Unraveling* to be more characteristic of delinquents as a group than of non-delinquents; hence an etiologic association with delinquency has been established

(Table 42). (b) Further analysis now reveals some variation in the impact of such trends in the character dynamics on the delinquency of the body types. *Receptive (oral) trends* have significantly *less* bearing on the misconduct of boys of balanced physique than on mesomorphs and ectomorphs. This is one of the very few traits which exert a considerable and quite similar influence on such contrasting physiques as the muscular mesomorph and the fragile ectomorph. (c) Variation in the incidence of *receptive (oral) trends* occurs among the body types of the delinquents, those of balanced physique containing a smaller proportion of boys with this trait than do the mesomorphs. (d) Since the incidence of the trait is not found to vary significantly among the body types of the non-delinquents, an inference that it is constitutional in orientation cannot be made.

To recapitulate, there is inadequate evidence for an assumption that *receptive (oral) trends* have a constitutional emphasis. A higher proportion of mesomorphs and ectomorphs who possess this trait than of boys of balanced physique become delinquent. Since the incidence of the trait is not found to vary significantly among the non-delinquents, its lesser criminogenic influence on boys of balanced type in contrast to mesomorphs and ectomorphs cannot be attributed to any deficiency in such trends among the former, but must be assigned to the fact that, for reasons not clear, when *receptive (oral) trends* are present in the character dynamics of boys of balanced physique, such tendencies are not as likely to incline them toward delinquency as when occurring in boys of the other body types.

MASOCHISTIC TRENDS

(a) *Masochistic trends* (i.e., of a tendency to suffer and to be dependent on others) in the character dynamics was found in *Unraveling* to be negatively associated with delinquency (Table 43). (b) Comparison of differences among physique types does not establish a significant variation in the impact of this trait on delinquency, despite what appears from inspection to be a greater involvement of *masochism* in the misconduct of boys of balanced physique. (The statistical evidence for this cannot be accepted as definitive because the difference in the role of the tendency to self-punishment on boys of balanced physique as contrasted with ectomorphs and endomorphs does not attain the required significance level of at least .10). (c) There is variation, however, in the incidence of *masochistic trends* among the four physique types of the delinquents, ectomorphic

Table 43 (XVIII-34). MASOCHISTIC TRENDS

(Categories: Marked and Slight)

Percentages of the Respective Physique Type Totals

Physique Types	Delinquents		Non-Delinquents		Difference in Percentages between Delinquents and Non-Delinquents	Probability (Based on X^2 Test)
	No.	%	No.	%		
TOTAL	67	15.4	141	37.5	−22.1	.01
Mesomorph	48	18.4	44	38.9	−20.5	
Endomorph	7	13.0	28	45.9	−32.9	
Ectomorph	5	8.2	56	38.6	−30.4	
Balanced	7	11.9	13	22.8	−10.9	

Significance of Differences between Physique Types

Mesomorph-Endomorph	−	−	−
Mesomorph-Ectomorph	.10	−	−
Mesomorph-Balanced	−	−	−
Endomorph-Ectomorph	−	−	−
Endomorph-Balanced	−	.05	−
Ectomorph-Balanced	−	−	−

offenders being significantly less self-punishing than mesomorphic delinquents. (d) This tendency is found to vary sufficiently in incidence among the body types of the non-delinquents to permit of an inference of probably constitutional orientation, a significantly lower incidence of the trait existing among boys of balanced physique than among endomorphs.

In brief, the probably constitutionally oriented trait of *masochism*

cannot be said to have more of an influence on the delinquency of
any one physique type than on that of any other, although there
may possibly be a lesser participation of the trait in contributing to
the delinquency of boys of balanced physique. Only further studies
can reveal its role.

DESTRUCTIVE-SADISTIC TRENDS

Destructive-sadistic trends have to do with the tendency to destroy, to hurt, to be negativistic.

Table 44 (XVIII-36). DESTRUCTIVE-SADISTIC TRENDS

(Categories: Marked and Slight)

Percentages of the Respective Physique Type Totals

Physique Types	Delinquents		Non-Delinquents		Difference in Percentages between Delinquents and Non-Delinquents	Probability (Based on X^2 Test)
	No.	%	No.	%		
TOTAL	187	48.7	66	16.2	32.5	.01
Mesomorph	124	51.9	15	11.9	40.0	
Endomorph	19	38.8	5	7.8	31.0	
Ectomorph	20	41.7	36	22.4	19.3	
Balanced	24	50.0	10	17.2	32.8	

Significance of Differences between Physique Types

Mesomorph-Endomorph	-	-	-
Mesomorph-Ectomorph	-	.10	.10
Mesomorph-Balanced	-	-	-
Endomorph-Ectomorph	-	.05	-
Endomorph-Balanced	-	-	-
Ectomorph-Balanced	-	-	-

(a) *Destructive-sadistic trends* were found in *Unraveling* to be
associated with delinquency, as shown by the considerable and significant difference in incidence of this trait between the total of
delinquents and that of non-delinquents (Table 44). (b) This

mechanism in the underlying character structure continues to be significantly associated with delinquency in all the physique types, but varies in its criminogenic impact. *Destructive-sadistic trends* have less of an association with the delinquency of ectomorphs than of mesomorphs. In other words, destructive-sadistic ectomorphs are less likely to become delinquents than are destructive-sadistic meso-morphs. (c) Significant variation does not occur in the incidence of this trait among the body types of delinquents. (d) The trait varies in incidence among the body types of the non-delinquents, however, making reasonable the inference that it has a constitutional emphasis. Like destructiveness, *destructive-sadistic trends* are more character-istic of ectomorphs than of endomorphs and mesomorphs.

To summarize, the probably constitutionally oriented goal-seeking trait of *destructive-sadistic trends* (like destructiveness), although not excessively frequent among mesomorphs generally, has a heavier delinquency-provoking impact on them than on ectomorphs. Since it is clear that ectomorphs are generally *more* destructive-sadistic than mesomorphs or endomorphs (irrespective of the complicating involvement of delinquency), the lesser criminogenic influence of the trait on ectomorphs is not assignable to this fact. It must rather be considered that such trends, when they exist in an ectomorphic habitus, are less likely to seek overt "acting out" expression in anti-social behavior than when they occur in mesomorphs.

Some General Qualities (Dynamics) of Personality

We now turn to the selective influence on the delinquency of boys of the four physique types of the following dynamics of per-sonality: emotional lability, self-control, vivacity, compulsory trends, extroversive trends, and introversive trends. These qualities, in con-trast to specific attitudes and to the content, direction, and goals of psychic or instinctual tendencies, concern the manner in which drives, emotions, and trends are expressed or discharged. Such a distinction is arbitrary insofar as the strength, direction, and goal of a trend and the obstacles which it encounters, both in the outside world and

in conflicting trends within the personality, are closely related to the
manner in which the trend is channeled, expressed, and satisfied, and
to the total personality structure.

EMOTIONAL LABILITY

Emotional lability refers to the way in which affect (emotion)
is discharged and manifested and not to the general fluidity or sta-

Table 45 (XVIII-37). EMOTIONAL LABILITY

(Categories: Marked and Slight)

Percentages of the Respective Physique Type Totals

Physique Types	Delinquents		Non-Delinquents		Difference in Percentages between Delinquents and Non-Delinquents	Probability (Based on X^2 Test)
	No.	%	No.	%		
TOTAL	189	43.1	85	19.1	24.0	.01
Mesomorph	126	47.7	24	17.9	29.8	
Endomorph	23	41.8	11	16.7	25.1	
Ectomorph	21	33.4	36	20.0	13.4	
Balanced	19	34.0	14	21.6	12.4	

Significance of Differences between Physique Types

Mesomorph-Endomorph	-	-	-
Mesomorph-Ectomorph	-	-	-
Mesomorph-Balanced	-	-	-
Endomorph-Ectomorph	-	-	-
Endomorph-Balanced	-	-	-
Ectomorph-Balanced	-	-	-

bility of a person. It pertains to qualities in the affective reactions of
an individual which permit his inner drives, urges, and feelings to
take their course and which allow tensions to explode, thus leading
to certain emotions and moods which are more or less independent
of consequences and of the objective requirements of a situation.

(a) It is clear that *emotional lability* is significantly associated
with delinquency (Table 45). (b) In the breakdown of the total

group into physique types a significant difference in the influence of this trait on the delinquency of the four body types does not emerge, despite what appears to be a heavier impact on the delinquency of the mesomorphs and endomorphs than on ectomorphs and boys of balanced physique. (c) Nor does the incidence of *emotional lability* vary significantly among the four body types of the delinquents. (d) And further, *emotional lability* is not seen to differ significantly among the physique types of the non-delinquents. Therefore an inference of its essentially constitutional orientation cannot be drawn from the table.

In brief, *emotional lability* is significantly related to delinquency both in the mass and in the four body types, but it cannot be deemed to exert a differential criminogenic impact on the physique types.

SELF-CONTROL

Self-control is the opposite of emotional lability. It is the faculty of controlling the discharge and expression of affectivity, but is not identical with the faculty of the healthy and mature person of determining the direction of his life and of what he wants to get out of it within the limits of his surrounding circumstances.

(a) Correlative to the finding of greater emotional lability among the delinquents than the non-delinquents, *self-control* was found in *Unraveling* to be *negatively* associated with delinquency (Table 46). (b) In the analysis of body types, a significant variation in the criminogenic impact of this trait fails to emerge, despite the appearance of a lesser influence of *self-control* on the delinquency of boys of balanced physique. (c) The difference in the incidence of *self-control* between mesomorphic delinquents and those of balanced physique type is at the .10 level of significance; but because a significant divergence was not disclosed in the criminogenic impact of this trait on the four body types, the difference noted cannot be accepted with confidence. (d) *Self-control* is not found to vary in incidence among the body types of the non-delinquents and can therefore not be said to have a constitutional emphasis.

To recapitulate, *self-control,* a trait which cannot on our evidence be said to incline toward the constitutional end of the biosocial spectrum, is negatively related to delinquency in the mass and within the four physique types, on whose delinquency it does not, however, exert a varied impact. Despite what appears to be a significant diversity in its incidence among the delinquents (centered in a difference between mesomorphs and the balanced type), other findings in the table fail to justify a definitive conclusion that *lack* of

Table 46 (XVIII-38). SELF-CONTROL

(Categories: Marked and Slight)

Percentages of the Respective Physique Type Totals

Physique Types	Delinquents		Non-Delinquents		Difference in Percentages between Delinquents and Non-Delinquents	Probability (Based on X^2 Test)
	No.	%	No.	%		
TOTAL	184	38.9	295	66.0	−27.1	.01
Mesomorph	120	42.3	86	64.6	−22.3	
Endomorph	22	37.2	46	69.7	−32.5	
Ectomorph	24	36.9	117	64.6	−27.7	
Balanced	18	27.7	46	68.7	−41.0	

Significance of Differences between Physique Types

Mesomorph–Endomorph	-	-	-
Mesomorph–Ectomorph	-	-	-
Mesomorph–Balanced	.10	-	-
Endomorph–Ectomorph	-	-	-
Endomorph–Balanced	-	-	-
Ectomorph–Balanced	-	-	-

self-control has more to do with embroiling boys of balanced type in delinquency than mesomorphs. Because of the ambiguity of the findings, it would be worth while to reassess this trait on another and larger sample of cases.

VIVACITY

Vivacity has to do with "liveliness" of behavior.

(a) *Vivacity* is seen to be significantly associated with delinquency, the delinquents as a group being more vivacious than the non-delinquents (Table 47). (b) In the analysis of the physique types, a sufficiently significant divergence in the criminogenic impact of this trait on their delinquency fails to emerge, despite the seemingly greater influence of this characteristic on the delinquency of endo-

Table 47 (XVIII-39). VIVACITY

(Categories: Marked and Slight)

Percentages of the Respective Physique Type Totals

Physique Types	Delinquents		Non-Delinquents		Difference in Percentages between Delinquents and Non-Delinquents	Probability (Based on X^2 Test)
	No.	%	No.	%		
TOTAL	108	50.2	43	23.6	26.6	.01
Mesomorph	76	51.3	11	20.4	30.9	
Endomorph	9	50.0	3	9.1	40.9	
Ectomorph	15	50.0	20	29.0	21.0	
Balanced	8	42.1	9	34.6	7.5	

Significance of Differences between Physique Types

Mesomorph–Endomorph	-	-	-
Mesomorph–Ectomorph	-	-	-
Mesomorph–Balanced	-	-	-
Endomorph–Ectomorph	-	.05	-
Endomorph–Balanced	-	.10	-
Ectomorph–Balanced	-	-	-

morphs. (c) The incidence of *vivacity* is not found to vary significantly among the four body types of the delinquents. (d) There is sufficient diversity in the distribution of this trait among the physique types of the non-delinquents, however, to justify an inference of its constitutional orientation, the endormorphs being less vivacious as a group than the ectomorphs and boys of balanced physique.

Despite appearances to the contrary, then, the probably constitutionally oriented trait of *vivacity* is not found to have a significantly varied influence on the delinquency of the physique types. There is, however, a suggestion of a possibly greater role of this trait in the delinquency of endomorphs which warrants further exploration. It looks as if, among endomorphs, those boys who atypically are vivacious are more likely to become delinquents.

COMPULSORY TRENDS

Compulsory trends, which include not only typical neurotic compulsions but the less evident cases of a rigidity not permitting of

Table 48 (XVIII-40). COMPULSORY TRENDS

(Categories: Marked and Slight)

Percentages of the Respective Physique Type Totals

Physique Types	Delinquents		Non-Delinquents		Difference in Percentages between Delinquents and Non-Delinquents	Probability (Based on X^2 Test)
	No.	%	No.	%		
TOTAL	96	20.7	135	30.7	-10.0	.01
Mesomorph	57	20.2	39	29.1	-8.9	
Endomorph	15	26.3	19	31.2	-4.9	
Ectomorph	14	21.5	59	33.0	-11.5	
Balanced	10	16.4	18	27.2	-10.8	

Significance of Differences between Physique Types

Mesomorph-Endomorph	-	-	-
Mesomorph-Ectomorph	-	-	-
Mesomorph-Balanced	-	-	-
Endomorph-Ectomorph	-	-	-
Endomorph-Balanced	-	-	-
Ectomorph-Balanced	-	-	-

flexible adaptation to changing situations, reflect attempts to defend the self against conscious or, more often, unconscious anxiety.

(a) *Compulsory trends* were found in *Unraveling* to be negatively associated with delinquency (Table 48). (b) In the breakdown of the total group into physique types, a significant difference is not found in the influence of this trait on the delinquency of the four body types. (c) Nor is the incidence of *compulsory trends* found to vary significantly among delinquents of the four body types. (d) The trait does not differ significantly in incidence among the physique types of the non-delinquents, so an inference of essentially constitutional orientation is not, on this evidence, justified.

Briefly, *compulsory trends* cannot be deemed to exert a differential criminogenic impact on the physique types.

EXTROVERSIVE TRENDS

A preponderance of *extroversive trends* in the personality structure means a tendency to discharge tensions in emotion or in motoric action.

Table 49 (XVIII-41). PREPONDERANCE OF EXTROVERSIVE TRENDS

(Categories: Marked and Slight)

Percentages of the Respective Physique Type Totals

Physique Types	Delinquents		Non-Delinquents		Difference in Percentages between Delinquents and Non-Delinquents	Probability (Based on X^2 Test)
	No.	%	No.	%		
TOTAL	194	54.3	124	35.7	18.6	.01
Mesomorph	132	58.2	33	33.3	24.9	
Endomorph	20	48.8	21	33.8	15.0	
Ectomorph	20	43.5	49	36.8	6.7	
Balanced	22	51.2	21	38.9	12.3	

Significance of Differences between Physique Types

Mesomorph-Endomorph	-	-	-
Mesomorph-Ectomorph	-	-	-
Mesomorph-Balanced	-	-	-
Endomorph-Ectomorph	-	-	-
Endomorph-Balanced	-	-	-
Ectomorph-Balanced	-	-	-

(a) This tendency was found in *Unraveling* to be significantly associated with delinquency (Table 49). (b) In the breakdown of the total group into physique types a significant difference does not emerge in the influence of this trait in the delinquency of the four body types. (c) Nor does the incidence of *extroversive trends* vary significantly among the four body types of the delinquents. (d) Preponderance of *extroversive trends* does not differ significantly in incidence among the physique types of the non-delinquents, and therefore an inference of the essentially constitutional orientation of this tendency is not justified on the evidence.

In brief, the presence of *extroversive trends* in the character structure is significantly related to delinquency both in the mass and in the four physique types, but this dynamism cannot be deemed to exert a differential criminogenic impact on the latter.

INTROVERSIVE TRENDS

A preponderance of *introversive trends* reflects the tendency to pile up tensions by an emphasis on the creative mental processes, a living more "within one's self," and by difficulty in relating oneself emotionally to others.

(a) Significant association was not found in *Unraveling* between preponderance of *introversive trends* in the personality structure and delinquency, the incidence of such trends among delinquents and non-delinquents as a whole being quite similar (Table 50). (b) Neither is a significant difference in criminogenic influence on the body types found. Thus this trait cannot be said to have any important etiologic role. (c) There is, however, some variation in the incidence of this trait among the delinquents, the endomorphs as a group being significantly less introverted than the mesomorphs. (d) Since a reliable variation in preponderance of *introversive trends* does not emerge among the four body types of the non-delinquents, there is no adequate evidence for an inference that this trait has an essentially constitutional orientation.

To summarize, since *introversive trends* do not vary significantly in incidence among the physique types of the non-delinquents, it cannot be concluded that they are essentially of constitutional orientation. Nor is there definitive proof that introversiveness is criminogenic either in general or within any body type.

Table 50 (XVIII–42). PREPONDERANCE OF INTROVERSIVE TRENDS

(Categories: Marked and Slight)

Percentages of the Respective Physique Type Totals

Physique Types	Delinquents		Non-Delinquents		Difference in Percentages between Delinquents and Non-Delinquents	Probability (Based on X^2 Test)
	No.	%	No.	%		
TOTAL	99	27.6	86	24.3	3.3	.50
Mesomorph	66	28.7	24	23.6	5.1	
Endomorph	6	14.3	12	19.7	–5.4	
Ectomorph	15	33.4	33	23.9	9.5	
Balanced	12	28.6	17	32.1	–3.5	

Significance of Differences between Physique Types

Mesomorph–Endomorph	.10	–	–
Mesomorph–Ectomorph	–	–	–
Mesomorph–Balanced	–	–	–
Endomorph–Ectomorph	–	–	–
Endomorph–Balanced	–	–	–
Ectomorph–Balanced	–	–	–

Analysis of the tables in the present chapter confirms the basic impression already gained from the two prior chapters that body structure is somehow associated with the etiologic dynamics of delinquency. In other words, in addition to those traits which had been shown in *Unraveling Juvenile Delinquency* to set apart delinquents from non-delinquents in the mass, certain traits and characteristics seemingly operate with special delinquency-inducing selectivity on one or another physique type.

VI

Personality and Temperament

Supplementing the information derived from the Rorschach Test, we analyze in this chapter a series of personality and temperamental traits and dynamics which were derived by the staff psychiatrist in his interviews with the boys.

To the skillful psychiatrist, children reveal themselves much more readily than do adults. Through long experience in interviewing boys, the psychiatrist of *Unraveling,* Dr. Bryant E. Moulton, had developed a special flair for gaining quick rapport with youngsters.

Since our aim was to obtain as objective an assessment as possible of the personality of each boy by a psychiatrically-orientated investigator, we did not make accessible to the psychiatrist the findings of the Rorschach Test or of any of the other tests and examinations that were given to each boy. However, on the whole, his assessments, independently arrived at, paralleled closely the findings of the Rorschach experts.[1] This fact enhances the reliability of both sets of data.

Here, as in *Unraveling,* we present the psychiatric findings under the general rubrics of deep-rooted emotional dynamics, appetitive-aesthetic tendencies, personality orientation, and some aspects of mental pathology (see *Unraveling Juvenile Delinquency,* Chapter XIX, for details).

DEEP-ROOTED EMOTIONAL DYNAMICS

Any classification of dynamic tendencies involves perplexing problems of definition. Certain readers might prefer their inclusion in some category other than the one in which we placed them. The difficulties of classification in the field of instinct, emotion, temperament, personality, and character are too well known to require elaboration. They spring largely from the fact that knowledge of the structure and dynamics of human personality is as yet far from complete, and description involves fundamental differences in points of view. Moreover, any attempt to separate cognitive processes from conative or affective must involve some distortion of reality, because of the subtle and pervasive interrelationship of all mental dynamics and the essential unity of mental activity.

SENSITIVITY

The first trait in the area now under scrutiny is *sensitivity,* that is, the acute awareness of conflicting situations and stimuli and of their implications, resulting in some inhibition of action.

(a) An association between the trait of *sensitivity* and delinquency in general was not found in *Unraveling Juvenile Delinquency* (Table 51). (b) Significant differences are not revealed in the influence of this characteristic on the delinquency of the physique types. It can therefore not be said that there is an association between delinquency and *sensitivity* in any of the four body types. (c) A significant variation occurs in the incidence of *sensitivity* among the physique types of the delinquents, its incidence being greater in ectomorphs than in mesomorphs and endomorphs. (d) Since a significant difference is found in the incidence of *sensitivity* among the physique types of the non-delinquents, the mesomorphs and endomorphs being the least sensitive and the ectomorphs and balanced type the most, there is ground for the inference that this trait is of constitutional orientation.

By way of summary and comment, the following points should be noted: Since the constitutionally oriented trait of *sensitivity* is not found to be associated with delinquency either in general or within any of the four body types, it cannot be concluded that it is criminogenic in any obvious sense. It is, however, to be noted that *sensitivity* most highly characterizes both non-delinquent and delinquent ectomorphs as compared with mesomorphs and endomorphs. This finding is in keeping with the respective morphologies of the body types as expressed in the definition of the ectomorphic physique which is characterized not only by linearity and fragility, but also by having "the greatest surface area and hence relatively the greatest sensory exposure to the outside world,"[2] and the defini-

Table 51 (XIX-1). SENSITIVITY

Percentages of the Respective Physique Type Totals

Physique Types	Delinquents		Non-Delinquents		Difference in Percentages between Delinquents and Non-Delinquents	Probability (Based on X^2 Test)
	No.	%	No.	%		
TOTAL	157	31.9	175	36.2	-4.3	.20
Mesomorph	78	26.2	31	20.8	5.4	
Endomorph	16	28.1	16	22.2	5.9	
Ectomorph	37	52.1	96	50.5	1.6	
Balanced	26	39.4	32	44.4	-5.0	

Significance of Differences between Physique Types

Mesomorph-Endomorph	-	-	-
Mesomorph-Ectomorph	.02	.01	-
Mesomorph-Balanced	-	.05	-
Endomorph-Ectomorph	.05	.02	-
Endomorph-Balanced	-	.05	-
Ectomorph-Balanced	-	-	-

tion of the mesomorphic body type as having prominent bone and muscle, with "the skin made thick by a heavy underlying connective tissue."[3]

The great *sensitivity* of ectomorphs, though not found to be directly associated with delinquency, may well underlie other criminogenic traits and thereby indirectly contribute to delinquency. It is a characteristic that should be kept in mind in connection with the analysis of the differential response of the physique types to environmental stimuli (Chapters VIII and IX).

SUGGESTIBILITY

To be suggestible is to be easily swayed by an appeal to one's feelings, despite one's better judgment.

Table 52 (XIX-1). SUGGESTIBILITY

Percentages of the Respective Physique Type Totals

Physique Types	Delinquents		Non-Delinquents		Difference in Percentages between Delinquents and Non-Delinquents	Probability (Based on X^2 Test)
	No.	%	No.	%		
TOTAL	295	60.0	127	26.3	33.7	.01
Mesomorph	182	61.1	33	22.1	39.0	
Endomorph	38	66.7	26	36.1	30.6	
Ectomorph	37	52.1	42	22.1	30.0	
Balanced	38	57.6	26	36.1	21.5	

Significance of Differences between Physique Types

Mesomorph-Endomorph	-	-	-
Mesomorph-Ectomorph	-	-	-
Mesomorph-Balanced	-	-	-
Endomorph-Ectomorph	-	-	-
Endomorph-Balanced	-	-	-
Ectomorph-Balanced	-	-	-

(a) *Suggestibility* was found in *Unraveling* significantly to differentiate delinquents from non-delinquents, the former as a group being far more *suggestible* than the non-delinquents (Table 52). (b) Breakdown into physique types fails to reveal a significant variation in the influence of this trait on delinquency. (c) Nor is a divergence found in the incidence of *suggestibility* among the body types of the delinquents. (d) Since a variance in the incidence of this trait among the non-delinquent body types is not established at a sufficiently significant level, it cannot safely be inferred that this trait has constitutional orientation. Inspection of the distribution would seem to show a difference in incidence distinguishing meso-morphs and ectomorphs, on the one hand, from endomorphs and boys of balanced physique, on the other, the latter two appearing to be more suggestible as a group than the former; but the levels of significance are not sufficient to establish this as a trustworthy fact.

To summarize, *suggestibility* is an etiologic trait not differentially associated with the delinquency of the body types. Variation in its incidence among the physique types of the non-delinquents does not occur at a sufficiently high level of significance to warrant an infer-ence that it has a constitutional emphasis; but the possibility of a true variation is worth checking.

INADEQUACY

Inadequacy is the inability to express or conduct oneself, in most aspects of life, with a fair degree of efficiency.

(a) As is shown in Table 53 this characteristic is significantly associated with delinquency. (b) This association continues among the physique types, but there is variation in the role which *inadequacy* plays in their misconduct. When it occurs in an ectomorph it has less potency for delinquency than when it occurs in a mesomorph. (c) *Inadequacy* is also found to vary in incidence among the body types of the delinquents, the mesomorphic group containing a significantly lower proportion of boys who possess this trait than the endomorphs or the boys of balanced physique and possibly, though not defini-tively, than the ectomorphs. (d) Since the trait is found to vary significantly in incidence among the body types of the non-delinquents, it is possible to infer that it has a constitutional orienta-tion. Mesomorphic non-delinquents are, as a group, not as inadequate as are ectomorphs or those of balanced physique.

To summarize, the probably constitutionally oriented trait of *inadequacy,* although more characteristic of ectomorphs than of mesomorphs, has less to do with their delinquency than it does with that of mesomorphs who, as a group, are not as inadequate. The greater influence of *inadequacy* on the delinquency of mesomorphs is not due to any excess of this trait in that body type, as is shown by the fact that its incidence among non-delinquent mesomorphs is

Table 53 (XIX-1). INADEQUACY

Percentages of the Respective Physique Type Totals

Physique Types	Delinquents		Non-Delinquents		Difference in Percentages between Delinquents and Non-Delinquents	Probability (Based on X^2 Test)
	No.	%	No.	%		
TOTAL	419	85.2	335	69.4	15.8	.01
Mesomorph	241	80.9	81	54.4	26.5	
Endomorph	53	93.0	48	66.7	26.3	
Ectomorph	64	90.1	152	80.0	10.1	
Balanced	61	92.4	54	75.0	17.4	

Significance of Differences between Physique Types

Mesomorph-Endomorph	.05	–	–
Mesomorph-Ectomorph	–	.01	.10
Mesomorph-Balanced	.05	.05	–
Endomorph-Ectomorph	–	–	–
Endomorph-Balanced	–	–	–
Ectomorph-Balanced	–	–	–

lower than among the ectomorphs and boys of bolanced physique. The result is rather attributable to the fact that when this, to them uncommon, trait does exist among mesomorphs, it exerts (perhaps compensatorily) a specially heavy delinquency-inducing pressure.

STUBBORNNESS

Stubbornness is probably the result of thwarted dynamic qualities.

(a) The trait of *stubbornness* is shown to be significantly associated with delinquency, the delinquents being far more stubborn as a group than the non-delinquents (Table 54). (b) In the breakdown of the total group into physique types, a significant variation is not found in the delinquency-related impact of this trait on the four body types. (c) Nor is the incidence of *stubbornness* found to vary

Table 54 (XIX-1). STUBBORNNESS

Percentages of the Respective Physique Type Totals

Physique Types	Delinquents		Non-Delinquents		Difference in Percentages between Delinquents and Non-Delinquents	Probability (Based on χ^2 Test)
	No.	%	No.	%		
TOTAL	204	41.5	38	7.9	33.6	.01
Mesomorph	133	44.6	13	8.7	35.9	
Endomorph	21	36.8	6	8.3	28.5	
Ectomorph	27	38.0	16	8.4	29.6	
Balanced	23	34.8	3	4.2	30.6	

Significance of Differences between Physique Types

Mesomorph–Endomorph	-	-	-
Mesomorph–Ectomorph	-	-	-
Mesomorph–Balanced	-	-	-
Endomorph–Ectomorph	-	-	-
Endomorph–Balanced	-	-	-
Ectomorph–Balanced	-	-	-

significantly among the physique types of the delinquents. (d) The incidence of *stubbornness* does not differ significantly between the physique types of the non-delinquents, and therefore an inference of essentially constitutional orientation is, on the evidence, not justified.

Briefly, *stubbornness* is significantly related to delinquency both in the mass and in the four physique types, but it cannot be deemed to exert a differential criminogenic impact on the body types.

ADVENTUROUSNESS

Adventurousness has to do with an exceptional need for change, excitement, or risk.

(a) The trait of *adventurousness* is seen to be significantly associated with a tendency to misconduct, delinquents being far more adventurous as a group than non-delinquents (Table 55). (b) The breakdown of the totals into physique types fails to uncover a significant difference in the criminogenic impact of this trait on the four body types. (c) Nor does the incidence of *adventurousness* differ

Table 55 (XIX-1). ADVENTUROUSNESS

Percentages of the Respective Physique Type Totals

Physique Types	Delinquents		Non-Delinquents		Difference in Percentages between Delinquents and Non-Delinquents	Probability (Based on X^2 Test)
	No.	%	No.	%		
TOTAL	272	55.3	88	18.2	37.1	.01
Mesomorph	173	58.1	33	22.1	36.0	
Endomorph	30	52.6	8	11.1	41.5	
Ectomorph	32	45.1	31	16.3	28.8	
Balanced	37	56.1	16	22.2	33.9	

Significance of Differences between Physique Types

Mesomorph-Endomorph	-	-	-
Mesomorph-Ectomorph	-	-	-
Mesomorph-Balanced	-	-	-
Endomorph-Ectomorph	-	-	-
Endomorph-Balanced	-	-	-
Ectomorph-Balanced	-	-	-

significantly among the body types of the delinquents. (d) *Adventurousness* does not vary significantly among the physique types of the non-delinquents, precluding an inference of its essentially constitutional orientation.

To summarize, *adventurousness* is significantly related to delinquency both in the mass and in the four physique types, but it cannot be deemed to exert a differential criminogenic impact on the latter.

UNINHIBITED MOTOR RESPONSES TO STIMULI

In contrast to extroversive trends (obtained by means of the Rorschach Test) encompassing emotion as well as action, *uninhibited motor responses to stimuli* deals only with extroversiveness of action and refers to a direct, behavioral resolution of tension.

Table 56 (XIX-1). UNINHIBITED MOTOR RESPONSES TO STIMULI

Percentages of the Respective Physique Type Totals

Physique Types	Delinquents		Non-Delinquents		Difference in Percentages between Delinquents and Non-Delinquents	Probability (Based on X^2 Test)
	No.	%	No.	%		
TOTAL	278	56.5	139	28.8	27.7	.01
Mesomorph	184	61.7	67	45.0	16.7	
Endomorph	30	52.6	14	19.4	33.2	
Ectomorph	28	39.4	39	20.5	18.9	
Balanced	36	54.5	19	26.4	28.1	

Significance of Differences between Physique Types

Mesomorph–Endomorph	–	.02	–
Mesomorph–Ectomorph	.05	.02	–
Mesomorph–Balanced	–	.05	–
Endomorph–Ectomorph	–	–	–
Endomorph–Balanced	–	–	–
Ectomorph–Balanced	–	–	–

(a) *Uninhibited motor responses to stimuli* were found to be greater among the delinquents than the non-delinquents (Table 56).

(b) Despite what may appear from mere inspection to be an

excessive delinquency-inducing influence of this characteristic on endomorphs and boys of balanced physique, as contrasted with mesomorphs and ectomorphs, statistically significant variation is not found in the impact of this trait on the boys of the four physique types. (c) Significant diversity in trait-incidence is found among the body types of the delinquents, the major contrast occurring between mesomorphs and ectomorphs. The mesomorphs are less inhibited in motor responses to stimuli than the ectomorphs. (d) *Uninhibited motor responses to stimuli* is a characteristic which varies significantly in incidence among the body types of the non-delinquents, permitting a deduction that this trait is probably oriented toward the constitutional border of the biosocial spectrum. The chief variance is between the mesomorphs, on the one hand, and the three remaining body types, on the other, the tendency to uninhibited motor response being most characteristic of mesomorphs.

Despite appearances to the contrary, it cannot be said that this essentially constitutional trait is more heavily involved in the delinquency of boys of any one physique type than in that of any other.

EMOTIONAL INSTABILITY

The trait of *emotional instability* is reflected in a lack of harmonious, integrated, and appropriate feelings and reactions.

(a) *Emotional instability* was found in *Unraveling* to be associated with delinquency in general, as shown by the very considerable difference in incidence of this trait among the totals of delinquents and non-delinquents, the former being far more unstable than the latter (Table 57). (b) Comparison of differences between delinquents and non-delinquents among the four physique types reveals some variation in the association of *emotional instability* with delinquency. The divergence is established between the mesomorphs and the ectomorphs, the trait being found to play a significantly greater role in the delinquency of mesomorphs than of ectomorphs (which was likewise the case as regards destructiveness and destructive-sadistic trends). (c) Significant variation is not, however, found in the incidence of *emotional instability* among the body types of the delinquents. (d) This trait varies in incidence among the physique types of the non-delinquents, making it reasonable to infer that it has a constitutional orientation. It is found to be more characteristic of ectomorphs than of the other physique types.

Table 57 (XIX-1). EMOTIONAL INSTABILITY

Percentages of the Respective Physique Type Totals

Physique Types	Delinquents		Non-Delinquents		Difference in Percentages between Delinquents and Non-Delinquents	Probability (Based on X^2 Test)
	No.	%	No.	%		
TOTAL	402	81.7	241	49.9	31.8	.01
Mesomorph	237	79.5	53	35.6	43.9	
Endomorph	47	82.5	33	45.8	36.7	
Ectomorph	63	88.7	121	63.7	25.0	
Balanced	55	83.3	34	47.2	36.1	

Significance of Differences between Physique Types

Mesomorph-Endomorph	-	-	-
Mesomorph-Ectomorph	-	.01	.05
Mesomorph-Balanced	-	-	-
Endomorph-Ectomorph	-	.05	-
Endomorph-Balanced	-	-	-
Ectomorph-Balanced	-	.10	-

To summarize and interpret: this probably constitutionally oriented trait is clearly less influential in bringing about delinquency among ectomorphs than among mesomorphs. The result may be attributable, not to the lesser selective influence of this trait on ectomorphs, but rather to the fact that it is more common among ectomorphs generally (regardless of whether they are delinquents or non-delinquents) and therefore its presence among them is not a disturbing psychologic novelty tending to bring about maladjustment and delinquency. This situation is in marked contrast to that existing among mesomorphs, where emotional instability, uncommon in this physique type, plays an especially heavy criminogenic role when it does occur.

APPETITIVE-AESTHETIC TENDENCIES

We turn next to the traits of aestheticism, sensuousness, and acquisitiveness.

AESTHETICISM

Aestheticism is the impulse for the more refined, discriminating, and artistic.

Table 58 (XIX-2). AESTHETICISM

Percentages of the Respective Physique Type Totals

Physique Types	Delinquents		Non-Delinquents		Difference in Percentages between Delinquents and Non-Delinquents	Probability (Based on X^2 Test)
	No.	%	No.	%		
TOTAL	84	17.1	182	37.7	-20.6	.01
Mesomorph	39	13.1	41	27.5	-14.4	
Endomorph	7	12.3	21	29.2	-16.9	
Ectomorph	23	32.4	93	48.9	-16.5	
Balanced	15	22.7	27	37.5	-14.8	

Significance of Differences between Physique Types

Mesomorph-Endomorph	-	-	-
Mesomorph-Ectomorph	.05	.02	-
Mesomorph-Balanced	-	-	-
Endomorph-Ectomorph	.05	.05	-
Endomorph-Balanced	-	-	-
Ectomorph-Balanced	-	-	-

(a) In the comparison of the total of delinquents and non-delinquents, the former were found to be significantly less aesthetic than the latter (Table 58). (b) The breakdown of the total into physique types reveals no significant differences in the delinquency-inducing impact of the trait on boys of any one physique type in contrast to those of other body types. (c) *Aestheticism* is found to vary significantly in incidence among the four physique types of the delinquents, the delinquent ectomorphs being as a group more aesthetic than mesomorphs and endomorphs. (d) Since a significant variation is found in the incidence of *aestheticism* among the four body types of the non-delinquents—the ectomorphs (like the delinquent ectomorphs) being as a group more aesthetic than the mesomorphs and endomorphs—it may be inferred that the trait is essentially of constitutional orientation.

From the evidence in the table, it cannot be concluded that the essentially constitutionally oriented trait of *aestheticism* exerts a greater influence on the delinquency of any particular body type than of the others. This is true despite the fact that *aestheticism* is more characteristic of both non-delinquent and delinquent ectomorphs than of mesomorphs and endomorphs.

SENSUOUSNESS

As was true of aestheticism, so as regards *sensuousness* (which is the inclination to free indulgence of appetites), (a) significantly more of our delinquents than of the non-delinquents were found to possess the trait. (b) Inspection of the differences between delinquents and controls of the four body types indicates variation in the impact of this trait on delinquency. A significant difference is found between the delinquency-inducing influence of *sensuousness* in the ectomorphs and boys of balanced physique. Among the former, the trait exerts little, if any, criminogenic influence; among the latter, its role is clearly predominant. (c) The trait is found to vary significantly in incidence among the body types of the delinquents, the endomorphs containing a higher proportion of sensuous boys than there are among the mesomorphic or ectomorphic delinquents. (d) This trait is found to vary significantly in incidence among the body types of the non-delinquents also, which makes reasonable the inference that *sensuousness* has a constitutional emphasis. As is to be expected, endomorphs (boys of the soft, round body type) are, as a group, more sensuous than boys of the other physique types.

In brief, this constitutionally oriented trait has a significantly

Table 59 (XIX-2). SENSUOUSNESS

Percentages of the Respective Physique Type Totals

Physique Types	Delinquents		Non-Delinquents		Difference in Percentages between Delinquents and Non-Delinquents	Probability (Based on x^2 Test)
	No.	%	No.	%		
TOTAL	99	20.1	27	5.6	14.5	.01
Mesomorph	54	18.1	4	2.7	15.4	
Endomorph	23	40.4	15	20.8	19.6	
Ectomorph	7	9.9	8	4.2	5.7	
Balanced	15	22.7	0	0.0	22.7	

Significance of Differences between Physique Types

Mesomorph–Endomorph	.05	.02	—
Mesomorph–Ectomorph	—	—	—
Mesomorph–Balanced	—	—	—
Endomorph–Ectomorph	.02	.05	—
Endomorph–Balanced	—	.02	—
Ectomorph–Balanced	—	.05	.05

greater influence on the delinquency of boys of balanced physique than of ectomorphs.

ACQUISITIVENESS

Acquisitiveness (held by some psychologists to be instinctual) refers to the inclination to acquire material things, money, or objects, over and above any desire for their immediate use. It is interesting to note that *acquisitiveness,* taken for granted as a chief motive for theft, is not found to be excessively common either among delinquents or non-delinquents.

(a) In our mass comparison of the two groups, *acquisitiveness* was, however, found to be significantly associated with antisocial

Table 60 (XIX-2). ACQUISITIVENESS

Percentages of the Respective Physique Type Totals

Physique Types	Delinquents		Non-Delinquents		Difference in Percentages between Delinquents and Non-Delinquents	Probability (Based on χ^2 Test)
	No.	%	No.	%		
TOTAL	101	20.5	67	13.9	6.6	.01
Mesomorph	55	18.5	21	14.1	4.4	
Endomorph	9	15.8	4	5.6	10.2	
Ectomorph	23	32.4	38	20.0	12.4	
Balanced	14	21.2	4	5.6	15.6	

Significance of Differences between Physique Types

Mesomorph–Endomorph	-	-	-
Mesomorph–Ectomorph	.10	-	-
Mesomorph–Balanced	-	-	-
Endomorph–Ectomorph	-	.02	-
Endomorph–Balanced	-	-	-
Ectomorph–Balanced	-	.02	-

behavior, delinquents being more acquisitive than their matched non-delinquents (Table 60). (b) In the breakdown of the total group of delinquents and non-delinquents into physique types no significant differences emerge in the criminogenic impact of the trait on boys of any type in contrast to the others. (c) A significant variation is found in the incidence of this trait among the delinquents, the ectomorphic offenders being, as a group, more acquisitive than the mesomorphic; and possibly also than the endomorphic. (d) Since a significant variation occurs in the incidence of *acquisitiveness* among the four body types of the non-delinquents, ectomorphs being found to be more acquisitive than endomorphs and boys of balanced type, it may be inferred that the trait is essentially of constitutional orientation.

In brief, the essentially constitutional trait of *acquisitiveness,* although a part of the criminogenic syndrome of traits and factors, is not found to play a heavier role in the delinquency of any particular body type than in that of the others.

Personality Orientation

We turn now to a group of traits which may be regarded as reflecting a basic personality orientation: namely, conventionality, lack of self-criticism, conscientiousness, and practicality.

CONVENTIONALITY

Conventionality is a preference for the safe and familiar.

(a) In our mass comparison of delinquents and non-delinquents, *lack of conventionality* was found to be significantly and markedly associated with delinquency (Table 61). (b) Despite what appears from simple inspection to be an excessive impact of the absence of this trait on the delinquency of endomorphs, the statistical evidence for this is not sufficiently conclusive to permit of a positive assertion. (c) *Conventionality* is found to vary in incidence among the physique types of the delinquents. Here, the ectomorphic delinquents, like their non-delinquent counterparts, are as a group less conventional than the endomorphs or the mesomorphs. (d) Significant variation is established in the incidence of *conventionality* among the four body types of the non-delinquents, the trait being clearly more characteristic of endomorphs than of boys of the other physiques. The ectomorphs are found to be not only significantly less conventional as a group than the mesomorphs, but also than the endomorphs. Because of this variation in the incidence of this trait among the non?delinquents, the inference is warranted that it is essentially focused in constitution, although of course sociocultural influences participate in its formation.

To summarize, despite appearances, it cannot be definitely concluded on this evidence that the constitutionally oriented trait of

Table 61 (XIX-3). CONVENTIONALITY

Percentages of the Respective Physique Type Totals

Physique Types	Delinquents		Non-Delinquents		Difference in Percentages between Delinquents and Non-Delinquents	Probability (Based on X^2 Test)
	No.	%	No.	%		
TOTAL	123	25.0	234	48.4	-23.4	.01
Mesomorph	83	27.9	77	51.7	-23.8	
Endomorph	19	33.3	54	75.0	-41.7	
Ectomorph	9	12.7	69	36.3	-23.6	
Balanced	12	18.2	34	47.2	-29.0	

Significance of Differences between Physique Types

Mesomorph-Endomorph	-	.02	-
Mesomorph-Ectomorph	.05	.05	-
Mesomorph-Balanced	-	-	-
Endomorph-Ectomorph	.05	.01	-
Endomorph-Balanced	-	.02	-
Ectomorph-Balanced	-	-	-

conventionality is more heavily involved in the misconduct of endomorphs than in that of other body types. It is, in other words, not found to have a selective criminogenic impact on the delinquency of one or another body type.

LACK OF SELF-CRITICISM

Lack of self-criticism is an inability and unwillingness to assay one's own faults and virtues, abilities, and liabilities.

(a) *Lack of self-criticism* was found in *Unraveling* to be significantly associated with delinquency (Table 62). (b) The present breakdown of the total groups of delinquents and non-delinquents into physique types does not reveal any significant variation in the influence of this trait on the delinquency of the four body types. (c) Nor is the incidence of *lack of self-criticism* found to vary

Table 62 (XIX-3). LACK OF SELF-CRITICISM

Percentages of the Respective Physique Type Totals

Physique Types	Delinquents		Non-Delinquents		Difference in Percentages between Delinquents and Non-Delinquents	Probability (Based on X^2 Test)
	No.	%	No.	%		
TOTAL	143	29.1	52	10.8	18.3	.01
Mesomorph	85	28.5	19	12.8	15.7	
Endomorph	20	35.1	10	13.9	21.2	
Ectomorph	19	26.8	13	6.8	20.0	
Balanced	19	28.8	10	13.9	14.9	

Significance of Differences between Physique Types

Mesomorph-Endomorph	-	-	-
Mesomorph-Ectomorph	-	-	-
Mesomorph-Balanced	-	-	-
Endomorph-Ectomorph	-	-	-
Endomorph-Balanced	-	-	-
Ectomorph-Balanced	-	-	-

significantly among the body types of the delinquents. (d) The proportionate incidence of *lack of self-criticism* does not vary significantly among the physique types of the non-delinquents either, and therefore an inference of its essentially constitutional orientation cannot be supported on the evidence at hand.

The foregoing analysis adds up to the conclusion that *lack of self-criticism* is significantly related to delinquency both in the mass and in the four physique types, but cannot be deemed to exert a varied criminogenic impact on the body types.

CONSCIENTIOUSNESS

Conscientiousness has to do with scrupulousness about achieving one's aims.

(a) There was found in *Unraveling* a substantial difference in incidence of this trait between delinquents and non-delinquents, the

Table 63 (XIX-3). CONSCIENTIOUSNESS

Percentages of the Respective Physique Type Totals

Physique Types	Delinquents		Non-Delinquents		Difference in Percentages between Delinquents and Non-Delinquents	Probability (Based on X^2 Test)
	No.	%	No.	%		
TOTAL	43	8.7	261	54.0	-45.3	.01
Mesomorph	27	9.1	73	49.0	-39.9	
Endomorph	5	8.8	41	56.9	-48.1	
Ectomorph	5	7.0	105	55.3	-48.3	
Balanced	6	9.1	42	58.3	-49.2	

Significance of Differences between Physique Types

Mesomorph–Endomorph	-	-	-
Mesomorph–Ectomorph	-	-	-
Mesomorph–Balanced	-	-	-
Endomorph–Ectomorph	-	-	-
Endomorph–Balanced	-	-	-
Ectomorph–Balanced	-	-	-

former being, as a group, far *less* conscientious. It is evident therefore that *conscientiousness* is negatively associated with delinquency (Table 63). (b) The breakdown of the total group into physique types fails to establish a significant variance in the operation of this trait on the delinquency of the four body types. (c) The incidence of *conscientiousness* does not vary significantly among the body types of the delinquents. (d) Nor is this trait found to differ significantly in incidence among the physique types of the non-delinquents, and therefore an opinion that it is essentially constitutional in origin cannot be justified.

In brief, the trait of *conscientiousness* is negatively related to delinquency both in the mass and in the four physique types, but cannot be deemed to exert a differential criminogenic impact on the latter. (See note 23, Chap. 1.)

PRACTICALITY

Practicality is the inclination to consider the feasibility of any contemplated course.

(a) As in respect to conscientiousness, the delinquents as a group

Table 64 (XIX-3). PRACTICALITY

Percentages of the Respective Physique Type Totals

Physique Types	Delinquents		Non-Delinquents		Difference in Percentages between Delinquents and Non-Delinquents	Probability (Based on x^2 Test)
	No.	%	No.	%		
TOTAL	92	18.7	168	34.8	-16.1	.01
Mesomorph	65	21.8	64	43.0	-21.2	
Endomorph	4	7.0	24	33.3	-26.3	
Ectomorph	10	14.1	56	29.5	-15.4	
Balanced	13	19.7	24	33.3	-13.6	

Significance of Differences between Physique Types

Mesomorph-Endomorph	.02	-	-
Mesomorph-Ectomorph	-	.10	-
Mesomorph-Balanced	-	-	-
Endomorph-Ectomorph	-	-	-
Endomorph-Balanced	-	-	-
Ectomorph-Balanced	-	-	-

were found to be less practical than their non-delinquent counter-parts (Table 64). (b) Examination of the differences between the delinquents and non-delinquents of each body type does not show that this characteristic exerts a divergent criminogenic influence on the physique types. (c) The trait is found to vary in incidence among the body types of the delinquents, however, a significantly higher proportion of mesomorphic offenders than of endomorphic being practical. (d) Sufficiently significant variation exists in the incidence of this trait among the non-delinquent physique types (in the contrast between mesomorphs and ectomorphs) to permit of an inference that *practicality* is probably constitutional in orientation, mesomorphs as a group being more practical than ectomorphs.

To sum up, this probably constitutionally oriented criminogenic trait does not contribute selectively to the delinquency of the four body types. Delinquents are found to be uniformly *less* practical than non-delinquents regardless of body type.

Some Aspects of Mental Pathology

Both the psychiatrist and the Rorschach analysts contributed information about the mental pathology of the boys under study. Any interested reader may refer to *Unraveling Juvenile Delinquency*,[4] where we described how we resolved those few differences in diagnoses arrived at independently and by different investigators through psychiatric examination, on the one hand, and the Rorschach Test, on the other. Although our data on mental pathology are not as comprehensive as we would desire, there is some value in presenting a few of the more relevant findings.

EMOTIONAL CONFLICTS

The term *emotional conflict* as here used refers to an inability to reconcile opposing feelings, or attitudes, or contradictory goals, not only in respect to those most intimately related to the boy (mother, father, siblings, companions) but also as regards more generalized emotion-arousing objects or institutions (e.g., religion, the community) and their standards (e.g., sexual conventions). These were noted by the psychiatrist only if it could be established that they resulted in a change in a boy's conduct.

(a) *Emotional conflicts* were found in *Unraveling* to be associated with antisocial conduct, a far higher proportion of delinquents manifesting such conflicts than of non-delinquents (Table 65). (b)

Table 65 (XIX-4). EMOTIONAL CONFLICTS

Percentages of the Respective Physique Type Totals

Physique Types	Delinquents		Non-Delinquents		Difference in Percentages between Delinquents and Non-Delinquents	Probability (Based on X^2 Test)
	No.	%	No.	%		
TOTAL	336	75.0	159	37.7	37.3	.01
Mesomorph	192	71.1	30	22.7	48.4	
Endomorph	45	84.9	25	36.8	48.1	
Ectomorph	55	80.9	85	52.5	28.4	
Balanced	44	77.2	19	31.7	45.5	

Significance of Differences between Physique Types

Mesomorph-Endomorph	.10	–	–
Mesomorph-Ectomorph	–	.01	.05
Mesomorph-Balanced	–	–	–
Endomorph-Ectomorph	–	–	–
Endomorph-Balanced	–	–	–
Ectomorph-Balanced	–	.05	–

Although conflicts are found to be related to the delinquency of all the body types, a significant variation in its delinquency-inducing impact now emerges. The presence of *emotional conflicts* has significantly more to do with the delinquency of mesomorphs than of ectomorphs. (c) Want of uniformity is established also in the incidence of *emotional conflicts* among the physique types of the delinquents, endomorphic delinquents being more characterized by conflicts than mesomorphs. (d) Since the presence of *emotional conflicts* is found to vary in incidence among the body types of the non-delinquents, it may be reasonably concluded that the tendency to develop conflicts is of constitutional orientation. As might be anticipated, *emotional conflicts* exist more frequently in an ectomorphic habitus than among mesomorphs or boys of balanced physique.

To summarize and interpret, the tendency to *emotional conflicts* has a constitutional orientation, being more characteristic of ectomorphs than of mesomorphs and boys of balanced type. However, *emotional conflicts* are significantly less influential in the delinquency of ectomorphs than of mesomorphs. Since this lesser criminogenic influence among ectomorphs is not attributable to any deficiency of conflicts in that body type (conflicts being, on the contrary, excessively present among ectomorphic *non-delinquents*), a reasonable explanation would seem to be that, as in the case of emotional instability, the fact that the tendency to *emotional conflicts* is normally more common among ectomorphs makes their presence in that body type not as disturbing a psychologic strain as when occurring in others; and therefore conflicts have less of a tendency to impel ectomorphs toward delinquency than other body types. Ectomorphs evidently express their conflicts in other ways.

NEUROTICISM

Next we are concerned with both *marked and mild neuroticism*. If a neurosis interfered with efficient adaptation, the boy was classified as a marked neurotic, otherwise as mild. *Marked neuroticism* is a condition in which the individual suffers from more than average insecurity and anxiety (conscious or unconscious) against which he develops protective devices differing quantitatively or qualitatively from the culturally accepted ones and leading to conflicts which are, as a rule, not solvable by him for the time being. *Mild neuroticism* is a condition that does not prevent the individual from relatively efficient adaptation. In addition to the boys who were diagnosed as marked or mild neurotics are included boys who could not be clearly placed in one or the other category but who evidenced distinct neurotic trends.

Despite the fact that, as we have just seen, our delinquents as a group were more conflict-ridden than the non-delinquents, they were found on the whole to be less neurotic than the non-de-

Table 66 (XVIII-43). NEUROTICISM

(Categories: Marked, Mild, and Trends)

Percentages of the Respective Physique Type Totals

Physique Types	Delinquents		Non-Delinquents		Difference in Percentages between Delinquents and Non-Delinquents	Probability (Based on X² Test)
	No.	%	No.	%		
TOTAL	120	25.1	173	37.0	-11.9	.01
Mesomorph	68	23.7	53	36.0	-12.3	
Endomorph	17	28.8	25	37.9	-9.1	
Ectomorph	19	28.7	69	37.1	-8.4	
Balanced	16	24.3	26	37.7	-13.4	

Significance of Differences between Physique Types

Mesomorph-Endomorph	-	-	-
Mesomorph-Ectomorph	-	-	-
Mesomorph-Balanced	-	-	-
Endomorph-Ectomorph	-	-	-
Endomorph-Balanced	-	-	-
Ectomorph-Balanced	-	-	-

linquents. This would appear to mean that the boys who became delinquents tended to express their conflicts in external behavior ("acting out") rather than through "bottling up" of feeling, with resultant neurotic symptoms.

(a) *Neuroticism* was found in *Unraveling* to be negatively associated with delinquency, delinquents as a group being less neurotic than non-delinquents (Table 66). (b) Breakdown of the total group of delinquents and non-delinquents by physique types .fails to disclose a significant divergence in the influence of *neuroticism* on the delinquency of the four body types. (c) Nor is the proportion of this condition found to vary significantly among the four body types of the delinquents. (d) It is clear from the table that *neuroticism* does not differ significantly in its incidence among the physique types of the non-delinquents. An inference of its essentially constitutional orientation is therefore not supportable on the evidence at hand.

Briefly, although the *absence of neuroticism* is significantly related to delinquency both in the mass and in the four body types, it cannot be deemed to exert a differential criminogenic impact on boys of different physiques.

PSYCHOPATHY

Among psychopaths are included not only the boys who were diagnosed as "psychopathic personalities" but also those labelled "asocial," "primitive," "poorly adjusted," or "unstable." *Psychopathy* is not a uniform and definite concept. As employed by our Rorschach consultant, Ernest G. Schachtel, it refers (following Bleuler and others) to all marked mental and emotional deviations that do not clearly belong in any one of the other diagnostic groupings. "Often a difference in degree of a disorder rather than of kind places a person in this category. This may be illustrated by saying that the psychopath is less ill than the psychotic and more ill than the neurotic. He is distinguished from the neurotic also by the fact that he is much more often openly destructive and antisocial or asocial. He is also usually less amenable than the neurotic to therapeutic or educative efforts. The most important trait of the psychopath is the fleeting, non-integrative, superficial quality of his personal relations."

(a) *Psychopathy* was found in *Unraveling* to be significantly associated with delinquency, a far higher proportion of delinquents than of non-delinquents being psychopathic (Table 67). (b) In the present breakdown of the totals of delinquents and of non-delinquents into physique types, a significant difference fails to emerge in the role of this trait in the delinquency of the four body types. (c) Nor does the incidence of *psychopathy* vary significantly among the four body types of the delinquents. (d) *Psychopathy* is not found

Table 67 (XVIII-43). PSYCHOPATHY

Percentages of the Respective Physique Type Totals

Physique Types	Delinquents		Non-Delinquents		Difference in Percentages between Delinquents and Non-Delinquents	Probability (Based on x^2 Test)
	No.	%	No.	%		
TOTAL	118	24.7	31	6.5	18.2	.01
Mesomorph	79	27.5	12	8.2	19.3	
Endomorph	12	20.3	4	6.1	14.2	
Ectomorph	13	19.7	9	4.8	14.9	
Balanced	14	21.2	6	8.7	12.5	

Significance of Differences between Physique Types

Mesomorph-Endomorph	-	-	-
Mesomorph-Ectomorph	-	-	-
Mesomorph-Balanced	-	-	-
Endomorph-Ectomorph	-	-	-
Endomorph-Balanced	-	-	-
Ectomorph-Balanced	-	-	-

to differ significantly in incidence among the physique types of the non-delinquents and therefore an inference of its essentially constitutional orientation is not justified so far as our evidence is concerned. This may, however, be a condition which is hereditary but does not vary with body type.

In brief, *psychopathy* is significantly related to delinquency both in the mass and in the four physique types, but it cannot be deemed to exert a differential criminogenic impact on the latter.

We have now completed the analysis of the traits encompassed in this portion of the inquiry and pointed out which ones were found to exert a special influence in the totality of the dynamic processes that are involved in the delinquency of boys of the four physique types.

The prime fact that emerges is that *bodily structure in relation to traits of temperament and character must be taken into account when assessing etiologic influences in delinquency.* When we pull together the various strands of the analysis in the next chapter, the reader should gain a clearer picture of the role of physique in delinquency.

NOTES

1. See *Unraveling,* note 1, pp. 252-3.
2. W. H. Sheldon, with the collaboration of S. S. Stevens and W. B. Tucker, *The Varieties of Human Physique* (New York: Harper & Brothers, 1940), p. 5.
3. *Ibid.*
4. *Unraveling,* Chapter XVIII, pages 242-3, note 8, or Appendix F of this volume.

VII

Traits, Delinquency, and Physique Types

In the preceding four chapters we have analyzed in detail each of 67 tables dealing with selected traits of the delinquents and non-delinquents. In order to have a clearer picture of how these traits affect the delinquency of the physique types, we present in this chapter a summary which synthesizes the findings in accordance with a criminogenic-morphologic typology that has developed inductively from our data.

CRIMINOGENIC-CONSTITUTIONAL TYPOLOGY

It will be recalled that there are two sets of strands in the analysis of the tables in Chapters III-VI. One refers to the crimi-nogenic dimension, and the other to the constitutional.

As regards the *criminogenic* aspect, the traits distribute themselves into the four following groups:

Group 1: Traits which in *Unraveling* were *not* found to be associated with delinquency (that is, did not distinguish delinquents *as a group* from non-delinquents *as a group*) and in the present study are also *not* found to differentiate the delinquents from the non-delinquents of *any body type.*

Group 2: Traits which were *not* found in *Unraveling* to distinguish delinquents as a *whole* from non-delinquents as a *whole,* but are now found to differentiate the delinquents from the non-delinquents of *one or more body types.*

Group 3: Traits which were found in *Unraveling* to differentiate delinquents from non-delinquents *in the mass,* but do *not* now show a significantly *different* impact on *any body type.*

Group 4: Traits which were found in *Unraveling* to distinguish delinquents from non-delinquents *in the mass,* but are now found to exert a significantly *varied* influence on the delinquency of the *body types.*

As regards the *constitutional* (anthropologic) aspect of the analysis, the following four types of traits have evolved from our data:

Type A: Traits that *vary* significantly in incidence among the body types of the *non-delinquents,* but not among the body types of the delinquents.

Type B: Traits that *vary* significantly among the body types of *both the non-delinquents and the delinquents.*

Type C: Traits that *do not vary* significantly among the body types of the *non-delinquents* but *do vary* among those of the *delinquents.*

Type D: Traits that *do not vary* significantly among the body types of either the non-delinquents or the delinquents.

GROUP-TYPES

On the basis of the two dimensions of the analysis (the criminogenic and the morphologic), the traits combine into the following *group-types:* 1-A, 1-B, 1-C, 1-D; 2-A, 2-C; 3-A, 3-B, 3-C, 3-D; 4-A, 4-B, 4-C.[1] What these group-types signify and which of the traits belong in each will be described in detail. First, however, it might be helpful to the reader to consult the chart below for the combined Groups (criminogenic dimension of the analysis) and Types (morphologic dimension of the analysis).

GROUP-TYPE 1-A

In Group-Type 1-A (a) the delinquents as a class were not found in *Unraveling* to differ significantly from their non-delinquent counterparts in the incidence of a particular trait; (b) a significant variation has not been established in the differences in percentage incidence between the delinquents and non-delinquents of the body types; (c) the delinquents of the four body types do not differ significantly from each other in size of trait incidence; (d) the

Group-Types	Presence of Difference Significant Between *Totals* of Dels. and Non-Dels. (*a*)	Presence of Significant Variation Among *Differences* Between Dels. and Non-Dels. of *Body Types* (*b*)	Presence of Significant Variation in *Trait Incidence* Among Body Types of *Dels.* (*c*)	Presence of Significant Variation in *Trait Incidence* Among Body Types of *Non-Dels.* (*d*)	No. of Traits
1-A	No	No	No	Yes	1
1-B	No	No	Yes	Yes	2
1-C	No	No	Yes	No	1
1-D	No	No	No	No	5
2-A	No	Yes	No	Yes	1
2-C	No	Yes	Yes	No	2
3-A	Yes	No	No	Yes	3
3-B	Yes	No	Yes	Yes	7
3-C	Yes	No	Yes	No	4
3-D	Yes	No	No	No	24
4-A	Yes	Yes	No	Yes	5
4-B	Yes	Yes	Yes	Yes	5
4-C	Yes	Yes	Yes	No	7

non-delinquents of the four body types do, however, differ significantly in the incidence of the trait, permitting of an inference that the trait is constitutionally oriented.

Thus, traits in Group-Type 1-A are not associated with delinquency either generally or in any of the physique types, but they probably have a constitutional orientation.

Only one characteristic falls into this category, namely the neurologically-related condition of tremors (Table 8).

GROUP-TYPE 1-B

Group-Type 1-B resembles Group-Type 1-A in aspects (a), (b), and (d) described above, but differs from Group-Type 1-A in that, in aspect (c), the trait incidence does differ significantly among the body types of the delinquents.

Only two traits have been found in Group-Type 1-B: genital underdevelopment (Table 9) and sensitivity (Table 51).

Since these traits differ in incidence among the body types of the delinquents, on the one hand, and of the non-delinquents, on the other, and since variation has not been found among the percentage *differences* between the delinquents and non-delinquents of the body types, it must be concluded that *the traits in Group-Type 1-B, though probably constitutionally oriented are not directly associated with delinquency either in the mass or in any of the body types*. However, because they characterize certain body types more than others, they may play an *indirect* role in delinquency. This will become clearer later.

GROUP-TYPE I-C

In Group-Type 1-C (a) delinquents as a group do not differ significantly from non-delinquents in the incidence of a trait and (b) delinquents of each of the four body types do not differ significantly in trait incidence from their corresponding non-delinquents; (c) the body types among the delinquents do vary significantly from each other in the incidence of the traits, and (d) the traits do not differ in incidence among the body types of the non-delinquents.

Thus, traits in Group-Type 1-C are not criminogenic either generally or in any physique type and are not constitutionally oriented, but do influence a varied response among the body types of those who become delinquent.

Only one trait is found in this Group-Type: preponderance of introversive trends (Table 50).

GROUP-TYPE I-D

In Group-Type 1-D (a) delinquents as a group do not differ significantly from non-delinquents in the incidence of a trait; (b) delinquents of each of the four body types do not differ significantly from their corresponding non-delinquents; and (c) the body types among the delinquents do not differ significantly from each other in the incidence of the traits; and (d) the traits do not vary in incidence among the body types of the non-delinquents, making impossible, on this evidence alone, any inference that they are of constitutional inclination.

Thus, traits in Group-Type 1-D are not criminogenic either generally or in any physique type, do not exert a varied influence on the delinquency of the body types, and are probably not constitutionally oriented.

The following traits fall into Group-Type 1-D: irregular reflexes (Table 5), originality (Table 13), banality (Table 14), intuition (Table 16), and marked feeling of not being wanted or loved (Table 26).

GROUP-TYPE 2-A

In Group-Type 2-A, as in 1-A, 1-B, 1-C, and 1-D (a) a significant difference between the total groups of delinquents and non-delinquents in the incidence of a trait was not found; (b) however, unlike all the Group-Types already described, a significant variation between delinquents and non-delinquents has been revealed, indicating a greater criminogenic influence on one or another body type; (c) the body types among the delinquents do not, however, differ significantly in the incidence of the trait; but (d) body types among the non-delinquents do vary in trait incidence, justifying an inference that such traits are probably of constitutional orientation.

Thus, traits in Group-Type 2-A, though not associated with delinquency in the mass, are revealed in a breakdown by physique type to be significantly related to the delinquency of one or another body type. They are probably of constitutional orientation and their delinquency-inducing impact evidently derives from their atypical occurrence in a body type in which their incidence is generally less prevalent than in other body types. Cyanosis (Table 6) is such a trait.

GROUP-TYPE 2-C

In Group-Type 2-C (a) a significant difference between the totals
of delinquents and of non-delinquents in the incidence of a trait was
not found; (b) comparison of the differences between delinquents
and non-delinquents has, however, revealed an association of the
traits with the delinquency of one or another of the body types; (c)
the traits differ in incidence among the body types of the delinquents;
but (d) have not been found to vary in incidence among the body
types of the non-delinquents and can therefore not be said to have
a constitutional orientation.

*Thus, traits in Group-Type 2-C, though not found to be generally
associated with delinquency and not found to have a constitutional
orientation, are, in a breakdown by physique type, revealed to be
associated with the delinquency of one or another body type.*

There are two such traits: namely, high performance intelligence
(Table 12) and feeling of not being taken care of (Table 27). As
regards the former, its occurrence in boys of balanced type evidently
makes them more prone to delinquency than when it occurs in
mesomorphs; the second trait is more likely to lead to delinquency
when present in mesomorphs than when it exists among boys of
other body types.

GROUP-TYPE 3-A

In Group-Type 3-A (a) the traits were found to differ significantly in incidence between the total groups of delinquents and
non-delinquents; (b) the incidence of such traits probably continues to be significantly different between the delinquents and non-
delinquents of all body types, but such traits do not have a greater
bearing on the delinquency of any particular body type than on that
of any other; (c) nor is a variation found in the incidence of the
traits among the body types of the delinquents; (d) but a significant divergence in the incidence of the traits does occur among
the body types of the non-delinquents, making reasonable an
inference that such traits are of constitutional orientation.

The traits in Group-Type 3-A are: tendency to phantasy (Table 17), marked submissiveness (Table 23), and vivacity (Table 47).

The mechanisms of the criminogenic influence of these traits are not clearly discernible from analysis of the tables. Although the incidence of the traits varies among the body types of the non-delinquents (reflecting their probably constitutional orientation), an expectable variation in the impact of such traits on the delinquency of the body types is not found. This may be a statistical artifact, to be resolved only by study of other samples of cases.

For the present, we must conclude that traits in Group-Type 3-A are probably oriented toward the constitutional end of the biosocial continuum and are associated with delinquency in the mass and with the delinquency of all the body types, but are not found to have a greater influence on the delinquency of one body type than of any of the others.

GROUP-TYPE 3-B

Traits in Group-Type 3-B differ from those in Group-Type 3-A only in that the incidence of the traits varies not only among the body types of the non-delinquents but also of the delinquents. Although such traits were found in *Unraveling* to be associated with delinquency in general, and continue to be associated with the delinquency of the four physique types, they do not appear to have a significantly greater bearing on the delinquency of any one body type than on that of the others.

Thus, the traits in Group-Type 3-B have a probably constitutional orientation and are associated with delinquency in the mass and with the delinquency of the body types, but are not found to have a greater bearing on the misconduct of one body type than of any of the others. The traits in Group-Type 3-B are:

Social assertiveness (Table 21)
Masochistic trends (Table 43)
Uninhibited motor responses to stimuli (Table 56)
Aestheticism (Table 58)

Acquisitiveness (Table 60)
Conventionality (Table 61)
Practicality (Table 64)

GROUP-TYPE 3-C

In Group-Type 3-C, as in 3-A and 3-B, the traits (a) differ significantly in incidence between the total groups of delinquents and non-delinquents; (b) are not found to have a greater bearing on the delinquency of any body type as compared to any other, although the incidence of the trait significantly differentiates the delinquents from the non-delinquents among the four physique types. However, traits in Group-Type 3-C differ from those in 3-A in that (c) they vary in incidence among the body types of the delinquents, and (d) do not vary among the body types of the non-delinquents, ruling out an inference that they are oriented in constitution.

Although the criminogenic influence of a trait in Group-Type 3-C does not vary significantly among the body types and such traits cannot be assigned to the constitutional pole of the biosocial continuum, there is nevertheless some evidence (from inspection of the data) that their presence may in fact have a special influence on the delinquency of one or another body type. However, the evidence is not definitive, in view of the absence of a finding of significant variation in the size of the differences between the delinquents and non-delinquents of each body type. Exploration of another sample of cases might prove more revealing.

There are four traits in this Group-Type: enuresis in childhood (Table 4), unmethodical approach to problems (Table 19), defiance (Table 22), and self-control (Table 46).

GROUP-TYPE 3-D

In Group-Type 3-D the traits resemble those in 3-C except for the fact that (c) a variation in the incidence of the traits is not found among the body types of the delinquents.

The traits in Group-Type 3-D are more numerous than those

in any other category. They cannot be said to be of constitutional orientation. They are associated with delinquency in the mass and in all the body types but are not found to have a greater bearing on the delinquency of one body type than of any other.

There are 24 traits in Group-Type 3-D:

Poor health in infancy (Table 1)
Marked power of observation (Table 15)
Common sense (Table 18)
Potential capacity for objective interests (Table 20)
Enhanced feelings of insecurity (Table 25)
Marked feeling of not being taken seriously (Table 28)
Feeling of helplessness (Table 29)
Feeling of not being appreciated (Table 30)
Feeling of resentment (Table 32)
Hostility (Table 34)
Marked suspiciousness (Table 35)
Feeling of isolation (Table 37)
Defensive attitude (Table 38)
Narcissistic trends (Table 41)
Emotional lability (Table 45)
Compulsory trends (Table 48)
Preponderance of extroversive trends (Table 49)
Suggestibility (Table 52)
Stubbornness (Table 54)
Adventurousness (Table 55)
Lack of self-criticism (Table 62)
Conscientiousness (Table 63)
Neuroticism (Table 66)
Psychopathy (Table 67)

GROUP-TYPE 4-A

As to traits falling into Group-Type 4-A, (a) a significant difference is found in their incidence among the delinquents and non-delinquents in the mass; (b) significant variation indicating a greater criminogenic influence in one or another body type is revealed; (c) the incidence of the traits does not differ among the physique types of the delinquents; (d) it does differ, however, among the body types of the non-delinquents, making possible the inference that the traits are of constitutional orientation.

Thus, the probably constitutionally oriented traits of Group-Type 4-A are generally criminogenic and vary in their impact on the delinquency of the physique types, although they do not differ in incidence among the body types of the delinquents. This would seem to indicate that their greater bearing on the delinquency of some body structures is attributable to their occurrence in a physique in which their incidence is generally less prevalent than in other morphologic types.

The heavier role of such traits in the delinquency of a particular body type appears to be explainable by the fact that, being normally less characteristic of that body type than of others, they create more stress or disharmony when they do occur, with resultant maladapted behavior. Such traits are: lack of fear of failure and defeat (Table 31), destructiveness (Table 36), lack of marked dependence on others (Table 39), destructive-sadistic trends (Table 44), and emotional instability (Table 57).

GROUP-TYPE 4-B

Traits falling in Group-Type 4-B resemble those in 4-A except for the fact that (c) the incidence of the trait varies among the body types of the delinquents.

Thus, the traits of Group-Type 4-B are generally criminogenic, vary in impact on the delinquency of the physique types, and differ in incidence among the body types of the delinquents and non-delinquents.

In traits of this kind, the difference in their criminogenic influence on the body types seems reasonably attributable to their normally lesser incidence among non-delinquents irrespective of body type than among delinquents; but the effect of this on delinquency varies among the body types. Such traits are: susceptibility to contagion (Table 2), strength of hand grip (Table 10), inadequacy

(Table 53), sensuousness (Table 59), and emotional conflicts (Table 65).

GROUP-TYPE 4-C

Traits falling into Group-Type 4-C differ from those in 4-B in that (d) a variation is not found among the body types of the non-delinquents, rendering insupportable an inference of constitutional orientation.

Thus, traits in Group-Type 4-C, although varying in incidence among the four body types of the delinquents, cannot be said to have a constitutional orientation. It would nevertheless appear that certain body types possessing such traits are more vulnerable to delinquency than are other body types which have such traits.

The traits in Group-Type 4-C are:

Extreme restlessness in early childhood (Table 3)
Dermographia (Table 7)
Low verbal intelligence (Table 11)
Ambivalence to authority (Table 24)
Good surface contact with others (Table 33)
Feeling of being able to manage own life (Table 40)
Receptive trends (Table 42)

TRAITS WITH VARIED INFLUENCE ON DELINQUENCY OF PHYSIQUE TYPES

We have now completed the summary of the 67 traits encompassed by this inquiry. For the moment we shall lay aside (1) the 38 traits not found to vary in incidence among the body types of the non-delinquents on the one hand, or of the delinquents on the other; (2) the seven traits which, though associated with delinquency and found to vary in incidence among the body types of both the delinquents and non-delinquents, are, nevertheless, not found to exert a *differential* impact on the delinquency of the body types; and (3) the two traits which vary in incidence among the body types of the delinquents and non-delinquents but are not related to delinquency generally and not found to exert an influence on the delinquency of any body type. They will all be adverted to in Chapter X, "Common Ground of Criminogenesis."

We are interested in stressing now only the 20 traits among the 67 that have been clearly found to vary in their relationship to the delinquency of the body types:

Susceptibility to contagion (Table 2)
Extreme restlessness in early childhood (Table 3)
Cyanosis (Table 6)
Dermographia (Table 7)
Strength of hand grip (Table 10)
Verbal intelligence (Table 11)
Performance intelligence (Table 12)
Ambivalence to authority (Table 24)
Feeling of not being taken care of (Table 27)
Fear of failure and defeat (Table 31)
Good surface contact with others (Table 33)
Destructiveness (Table 36)
Inadequacy (Table 53)
Emotional instability (Table 57)
Sensuousness (Table 59)
Emotional conflicts (Table 65)

While not ignoring those traits that have been found to be generally associated with delinquency, it is these 20 traits involving a *varied* impact on the delinquency of the physique types that largely command our attention.

In this chapter, we have summarized the traits analyzed in the tables in Chapters III-VI. Before the significance of the findings can be brought out more clearly, it will be necessary to summarize them by *physique types* with particular emphasis on the varied impact of the traits on their delinquency. This will be accomplished in Chapters XI-XIV. In the meantime, we invite the reader's attention to the selective influence of certain *sociocultural* factors on the delinquency of the physique types.

NOTE

1. No traits were found to combine into Group-Types 2-B, 2-D, 4-D.

VIII

Effect of Family and Home Environment on the Delinquency of Four Physique Types

INTRODUCTORY

In the prior chapters, we discovered those physical, characterial, and personality traits that appear to have exerted a specially selective influence on the delinquency of one or another of the physique types, and we determined which of the traits vary significantly among the physique types of the non-delinquents so that it may reasonably be inferred that they are of constitutional orientation. Now it is our purpose to examine the influence of factors in the home and family environment on the delinquency of the boys of each physique type.

One of the commonest fallacies, in the study not only of delinquency but of other social problems, is the implicit assumption that "environment" or "culture" exercises a *uniform* effect upon, and brings forth a like response from, the great variety of persons subjected to sociocultural stimuli. But inasmuch as the aspect of behavior under scrutiny is always the result of the interplay of the organism and the environment, and since organisms differ markedly in original endowment, one cannot conclude that responses to like stimuli will necessarily be uniform; for example, that all or even most boys living in "delinquency areas" will become delinquent, or that all or most of them living in a region where gangs flourish will *ipso facto* become gang members, or that all, or most, boys who "differentially associate" with delinquents will become delinquent. The same may be said about a great many influences to which brothers and sisters may be subjected in the under-the-roof culture of the home they share.

One of the most important points stressed in *Unraveling Juvenile Delinquency* is that many elements of the environment operate *selectively* on persons subjected to them. Given a similar sociocultural *milieu,* the response to some of its elements may be uniform, to others varied and selective.[1] A chief contribution of *Unraveling* was to point out a few of the ways in which the sociocultural matrix of the community exercised a significantly varied effect on the delinquents as a whole as opposed to the non-delinquents.[2]

In the present work we seek to determine the *variations* in influence for delinquency (as reflected in divergence of response) which are exerted on the *four physique types* by certain aspects of their environment.

In this chapter we deal with the selective effect on the delinquency of boys of the four predominant physique types, of the pathology of parents (delinquency, alcoholism, emotional disturbances, and serious physical ailments); the economic circumstances in which the boys were reared; the physical aspects of their homes; the instability of their homes; and the unwholesomeness of the family atmosphere in which they were brought up.

The method of analysis is somewhat different from that employed in Chapters III through VI in considering physical and mental traits. In the analysis of *traits*, the incidence of a trait among *non-delinquents* played an important role not merely as a control to the delinquents of the four physique types, but also as a basis for determining the probable constitutional orientation of a trait. Here we focus attention only on *delinquents*. The question of constitutional orientation is obviously irrelevant in considering social factors. The reasonableness of employing variation in the incidence of social factors among the *delinquents* only, as a criterion of the influence of the factors on the delinquency of boys of the four body types, is supported by the fact that in the tables analyzed in the present and succeeding chapters there was hardly ever found a significant variation in incidence of sociocultural factors among the body types of the *non-delinquents.* Certainly there can be no reasonable explanation of any variation in the incidence of sociocultural factors among non-delinquents of the four body types other than pure chance. The basic body type of a boy is obviously not determined by the environmental circumstances by which he happens to be surrounded years after his birth. But body type may well have some bearing on how a boy *reacts* to environmental stress in terms of delinquency or some other conduct phenomenon. Although in the tables we present the incidence of the social factors among the body types of both the delinquents and the non-delinquents, our focus is on their incidence among the *delinquents* of each body type as contrasted with every other body type.

NATIVITY OF PARENTS

NATIVITY OF PARENTS

Before turning to the first area of our discussion, namely, the effect on the delinquency of the physique types of pathology among the parents of the boys, the reader is again reminded that the 500 delinquents and 500 non-delinquents who are the subjects of *Unraveling Juvenile Delinquency* were matched, case by case, by ethnic origin— Italian with Italian, Irish with Irish, and so on.[3] Therefore, it is of course to be expected that, as Table 68 shows, the incidence of foreign-born parents and the general cultural matrix of the early life of the boys were quite similar among our delinquents and non-delinquents.

In breaking the total of delinquents down into body types, a significant difference is not found in the incidence of boys of the four physique types who are the sons of one or two foreign-born parents. It cannot be said, therefore, that being the son of parents born abroad is more of a factor in the delinquency of boys of one body build than those of another.

Table 68 (IX-2). NATIVITY OF PARENTS

(One or Both Parents Foreign Born)

Percentages of the Respective Physique Type Totals

Physique Types	Delinquents		Non-Delinquents		Difference in Percentages between Delinquents and Non-Delinquents	Probability (Based on X^2 Test)
	No.	%	No.	%		
TOTAL	277	57.9	293	61.3	–3.4	.30
Mesomorph	179	61.9	100	68.5	–6.6	
Endomorph	29	51.8	39	54.9	–3.1	
Ectomorph	37	54.5	114	60.3	–5.8	
Balanced	32	49.3	40	55.6	–6.3	

Significance of Differences between Physique Types for Delinquents

Mesomorph–Endomorph	–
Mesomorph–Ectomorph	–
Mesomorph–Balanced	–
Endomorph–Ectomorph	–
Endomorph–Balanced	–
Ectomorph–Balanced	–

PATHOLOGY OF PARENTS

We next consider a few factors which throw some light on the differences in impulsion to delinquent behavior of boys whose parents were handicapped by their own antisocial behavior, alcoholism, emotional disturbances, and serious physical ailments, in performing the functions of daily life and in fulfilling the many obligations and responsibilities of parenthood. Later in this chapter, and also in the next one, we shall see more clearly how the inadequacies of parents differentially affect the conduct of boys of the various physique types.

DELINQUENCY OF FATHER

Although a far higher proportion of the fathers of the delinquent boys than of those in the control group were persistently and seriously antisocial (we are not concerned here with occasional violations of traffic regulations, license laws, and similar sporadic or minor offenses), this does not appear to have had more of an impact on the delinquency of boys of any one physique type than of any other (Table 69). The antisocial behavior of the father, who is the obvious

Table 69 (IX-10). DELINQUENCY OF FATHER

Percentages of the Respective Physique Type Totals

Physique Types	Delinquents		Non-Delinquents		Difference in Percentages between Delinquents and Non-Delinquents	Probability (Based on x^2 Test)
	No.	%	No.	%		
TOTAL	328	66.3	155	32.0	34.3	.01
Mesomorph	198	66.2	50	33.6	32.6	
Endomorph	36	61.0	19	26.4	34.6	
Ectomorph	51	71.8	63	33.0	38.8	
Balanced	43	65.2	23	31.9	33.3	

Significance of Differences between Physique Types for Delinquents

Mesomorph-Endomorph	–
Mesomorph-Ectomorph	–
Mesomorph-Balanced	–
Endomorph-Ectomorph	–
Endomorph-Balanced	–
Ectomorph-Balanced	–

object of the growing boy's identification with an adult pattern, is quite uniformly criminogenic irrespective of the constitutional morphology of the son.

ALCOHOLISM OF FATHER

The fathers of our delinquents were also generally more alcoholic than those of the non-delinquents (Table 70); but as was true of the criminal behavior of the fathers, their excessive drinking is not found to have exerted a greater influence on the delinquency of boys of any one physique type than of the others. Here again it would appear that the pervasiveness of the unwholesome effect of a disappointing father symbol transcends morphologic differences in body structure.

Table 70 (IX-10). ALCOHOLISM OF FATHER

Percentages of the Respective Physique Type Totals

Physique Types	Delinquents		Non-Delinquents		Difference in Percentages between Delinquents and Non-Delinquents	Probability (Based on X^2 Test)
	No.	%	No.	%		
TOTAL	309	62.4	187	38.6	23.8	.01
Mesomorph	178	59.5	54	36.2	23.3	
Endomorph	37	62.7	25	34.7	28.0	
Ectomorph	50	70.4	76	39.8	30.6	
Balanced	44	66.7	32	44.4	22.3	

Significance of Differences between Physique Types for Delinquents

Mesomorph-Endomorph	–
Mesomorph-Ectomorph	–
Mesomorph-Balanced	–
Endomorph-Ectomorph	–
Endomorph-Balanced	–
Ectomorph-Balanced	–

EMOTIONAL DISTURBANCE IN FATHER

Table 71 shows that, as was true of antisociality and excessive drinking, so it is a fact that a considerably higher proportion of the fathers of the delinquents than of the non-delinquents were seriously disturbed emotionally (psychotic, psychopathic, psychoneurotic, sexually abnormal, markedly unstable). However, unlike the non-differentiated influence of paternal criminalism or alcoholism on the delinquency of boys of the different body types, emotional disturbances in a father appear to affect ectomorphs somewhat more adversely than mesomorphs. At least the trend is in this direction. One can only speculate that identification with and emulation of the father has been perhaps disrupted or made less attractive by his emotional illness and that ectomorphs, being more sensitive than

Table 71 (IX-10). EMOTIONAL DISTURBANCE IN FATHER

Percentages of the Respective Physique Type Totals

Physique Types	Delinquents		Non-Delinquents		Difference in Percentages between Delinquents and Non-Delinquents	Probability (Based on X^2 Test)
	No.	%	No.	%		
TOTAL	219	44.2	88	18.2	26.0	.01
Mesomorph	118	39.5	21	14.1	25.4	
Endomorph	27	45.8	17	23.6	22.2	
Ectomorph	40	56.3	38	19.9	36.4	
Balanced	34	51.5	12	16.7	34.8	

Significance of Differences between Physique Types for Delinquents

Mesomorph-Endomorph	-
Mesomorph-Ectomorph	.10
Mesomorph-Balanced	-
Endomorph-Ectomorph	-
Endomorph-Balanced	-
Ectomorph-Balanced	-

others, react more to this situation in terms of delinquency because they particularly require a stable adult as a source of security.

PHYSICAL AILMENT IN FATHER

In Table 72 we consider the effect on delinquency of some serious physical ailments of the fathers of the delinquents (cancer, tuberculosis, diabetes; diseases of the cardio-vascular and renal systems; arthritis, syphilis; certain glandular disturbances; diseases of the nervous system, such as chorea). Although the incidence of such diseases among them is not very much greater than among the fathers of the non-delinquents, it is nevertheless statistically significant.

However, no evidence has come to light in the breakdown into
physique types to indicate that serious physical ailments among the

Table 72 (IX-10). SERIOUS PHYSICAL AILMENT IN FATHER

Percentages of the Respective Physique Type Totals

Physique Types	Delinquents		Non-Delinquents		Difference in Percentages between Delinquents and Non-Delinquents	Probability (Based on X^2 Test)
	No.	%	No.	%		
TOTAL	197	39.8	139	28.7	11.1	.01
Mesomorph	121	40.5	50	33.6	6.9	
Endomorph	26	44.1	16	22.2	21.9	
Ectomorph	24	33.8	56	29.3	4.5	
Balanced	26	39.4	17	23.6	15.8	

Significance of Differences between Physique Types for Delinquents

Mesomorph-Endomorph	-
Mesomorph-Ectomorph	-
Mesomorph-Balanced	-
Endomorph-Ectomorph	-
Endomorph-Balanced	-
Ectomorph-Balanced	-

fathers has a varied influence on the delinquency of boys of the
four physique types.

DELINQUENCY OF MOTHER

As was the case regarding the persistent antisocial behavior of
their fathers, so in respect to maternal misconduct, a much higher
proportion of delinquents' mothers were found to be antisocial than
of the non-delinquents' (Table 73). It will be recalled that no varied
influence was found on the delinquency of boys of the four physique
types as a result of paternal misconduct. This is also the case as regards the antisocial behavior of the mothers, which evidently does
not contribute with special force to the delinquency of any one body
type as opposed to the others.

Table 73 (IX–10). DELINQUENCY OF MOTHER

Percentages of the Respective Physique Type Totals

Physique Types	Delinquents		Non-Delinquents		Difference in Percentages between Delinquents and Non-Delinquents	Probability (Based on X^2 Test)
	No.	%	No.	%		
TOTAL	221	44.6	75	15.5	29.1	.01
Mesomorph	136	45.5	30	20.1	25.4	
Endomorph	21	35.6	9	12.5	23.1	
Ectomorph	38	53.5	23	12.0	41.5	
Balanced	26	39.4	13	18.1	21.3	

Significance of Differences between Physique Types for Delinquents

Mesomorph–Endomorph	–
Mesomorph–Ectomorph	–
Mesomorph–Balanced	–
Endomorph–Ectomorph	–
Endomorph–Balanced	–
Ectomorph–Balanced	–

ALCOHOLISM OF MOTHER

Although the mothers of the delinquents and non-delinquents were not found to be nearly as alcoholic as the fathers of the boys, the delinquents' mothers were more so than the non-delinquents'. Here, as is true of the effect on boys of the four physique types of the alcoholic habits of their fathers, maternal inebriety is not found to have any greater delinquency-inducing force on boys of any particular physique type than on those of any other.

EMOTIONAL DISTURBANCE IN MOTHER

As was true of emotional disturbance of the fathers, so in the case of the mothers, a greater proportion of the delinquents' than of the non-delinquents' mothers showed evidences of affective disorganization (Table 75). Emotional derangement in the mothers evidently does not exert any especially selective pressure to delinquency on any body type.

Table 74 (IX-10). ALCOHOLISM OF MOTHER

Percentages of the Respective Physique Type Totals

Physique Types	Delinquents		Non-Delinquents		Difference in Percentages between Delinquents and Non-Delinquents	Probability (Based on X^2 Test)
	No.	%	No.	%		
TOTAL	114	23.0	35	7.2	15.8	.01
Mesomorph	68	22.7	10	6.7	16.0	
Endomorph	12	20.3	3	4.2	16.1	
Ectomorph	21	29.6	17	8.9	20.7	
Balanced	13	19.7	5	6.9	12.8	

Significance of Differences between Physique Types for Delinquents

Mesomorph-Endomorph	−
Mesomorph-Ectomorph	−
Mesomorph-Balanced	−
Endomorph-Ectomorph	−
Endomorph-Balanced	−
Ectomorph-Balanced	−

Table 75 (IX-10). EMOTIONAL DISTURBANCE IN MOTHER

Percentages of the Respective Physique Type Totals

Physique Types	Delinquents		Non-Delinquents		Difference in Percentages between Delinquents and Non-Delinquents	Probability (Based on X^2 Test)
	No.	%	No.	%		
TOTAL	201	40.6	85	17.6	23.0	.01
Mesomorph	116	38.8	22	14.8	24.0	
Endomorph	26	44.1	14	19.4	24.7	
Ectomorph	32	45.1	37	19.4	25.7	
Balanced	27	40.9	12	16.7	24.2	

Significance of Differences between Physique Types for Delinquents

Mesomorph-Endomorph	−
Mesomorph-Ectomorph	−
Mesomorph-Balanced	−
Endomorph-Ectomorph	−
Endomorph-Balanced	−
Ectomorph-Balanced	−

PHYSICAL AILMENT IN MOTHER

As was the case among the fathers, serious physical ailments were found in *Unraveling* to be more prevalent in the medical history of

Table 76 (IX-10). SERIOUS PHYSICAL AILMENT IN MOTHER

Percentages of the Respective Physique Type Totals

Physique Types	Delinquents		Non-Delinquents		Difference in Percentages between Delinquents and Non-Delinquents	Probability (Based on X^2 Test)
	No.	%	No.	%		
TOTAL	239	48.3	160	33.1	15.2	.01
Mesomorph	140	46.8	57	38.3	8.5	
Endomorph	33	55.9	23	31.9	24.0	
Ectomorph	36	50.7	65	34.0	16.7	
Balanced	30	45.5	15	20.8	24.7	

Significance of Differences between Physique Types for Delinquents

Mesomorph-Endomorph	-
Mesomorph-Ectomorph	-
Mesomorph-Balanced	-
Endomorph-Ectomorph	-
Endomorph-Balanced	-
Ectomorph-Balanced	-

the mothers of the delinquents than in that of the non-delinquents. As was true likewise of the etiologic impact on the boys of the illness of the father, serious illness of the mother does not reveal a significant variation as a delinquency-inducing influence on boys of the four body types (Table 74).

ECONOMIC CONDITIONS

The reader is reminded that when the 500 delinquents and the 500 matched non-delinquents were originally selected from underprivileged neighborhoods of Boston, the external sociocultural conditions surrounding both groups were similar. All came from families of low socio-economic status. In *Unraveling* we reported that 65% of both groups of families were living in slum tenements; that the average monthly rental per room was $4.77 among the families of the delinquents and $4.90 among the families of the non-delinquents; and that the furnishings of both groups of homes were equally sparse. And it is a fact that, almost without exception, all the boys, whether delinquent or non-delinquent, grew up in homes in which the families had practically no savings to tide them over periods of unemployment and emergency; they lived "from day to day" and from "hand to mouth."

FINANCIAL DEPENDENCE OF FAMILY

Despite this objective similarity of both groups of families in economic level, it was found in *Unraveling* that a significantly higher proportion of the families of the delinquent boys than of the controls were continuously dependent for support either on public or private

Table 77 (IX-14). FINANCIAL INDEPENDENCE OF FAMILY

Percentages of the Respective Physique Type Totals

Physique Types	Delinquents		Non-Delinquents		Difference in Percentages between Delinquents and Non-Delinquents	Probability (Based on X^2 Test)
	No.	%	No.	%		
TOTAL	181	36.6	73	15.1	21.5	.01
Mesomorph	112	37.5	27	18.1	19.4	
Endomorph	23	39.0	7	9.7	29.3	
Ectomorph	23	32.4	30	15.7	16.7	
Balanced	23	34.9	9	12.5	22.4	

Significance of Differences between Physique Types for Delinquents

Mesomorph-Endomorph	−
Mesomorph-Ectomorph	−
Mesomorph-Balanced	−
Endomorph-Ectomorph	−
Endomorph-Balanced	−
Ectomorph-Balanced	−

charities or on relatives (Table 77). Since the groups were originally matched for residence in economically and culturally underprivileged urban areas, the material disparity mentioned is probably more reflective of a diversity of attitude toward and management of money than of any fundamental differences in income. This is established in the next table.

MANAGEMENT OF FAMILY INCOME

As was true of the effect of economic dependency on antisocial behavior, so as regards poor management of the family income, a significant difference was found to exist between the delinquents and the non-delinquents as a whole, the former having been more largely reared in homes in which funds were carelessly handled (Table 78). Income was spent without careful planning of the

Table 78 (X-1). POOR MANAGEMENT OF FAMILY INCOME

(Categories: Partially Planned and Haphazard)

Percentages of the Respective Physique Type Totals

Physique Types	Delinquents		Non-Delinquents		Difference in Percentages between Delinquents and Non-Delinquents	Probability (Based on X^2 Test)
	No.	%	No.	%		
TOTAL	324	66.0	211	44.1	21.9	.01
Mesomorph	196	66.2	65	44.5	21.7	
Endomorph	34	57.6	27	37.5	20.1	
Ectomorph	50	71.4	88	46.6	24.8	
Balanced	44	66.7	31	43.7	23.0	

Significance of Differences between Physique Types for Delinquents

Mesomorph-Endomorph	−
Mesomorph-Ectomorph	−
Mesomorph-Balanced	−
Endomorph-Ectomorph	−
Endomorph-Balanced	−
Ectomorph-Balanced	−

family's needs and often diverted to uses which, although providing some luxuries on a "dollar down, dollar a week" basis (as a car, or a television set, or a washing machine, or a new bedroom set), neglected the obvious and regularly-needed essentials (rent, food, clothing, medical care) with the resultant imposition on community welfare resources of the task of providing or supplementing the basic needs of daily life.

However, as in the case of financial dependency, there is no trustworthy evidence that rearing in homes in which the income was poorly managed had a worse effect on boys of one physique type than of any other, as mirrored in the degree of association of this factor with delinquency.

GAINFUL EMPLOYMENT OF MOTHER

Partially reflective of the economic needs of the families of both the

Table 79 (X-9). GAINFUL EMPLOYMENT OF MOTHER

(Categories: Regularly and Occasionally Employed)

Percentages of the Respective Physique Type Totals

Physique Types	Delinquents		Non-Delinquents		Difference in Percentages between Delinquents and Non-Delinquents	Probability (Based on X^2 Test)
	No.	%	No.	%		
TOTAL	230	46.9	159	33.1	13.8	.01
Mesomorph	128	43.0	52	34.9	8.1	
Endomorph	24	42.1	27	37.5	4.6	
Ectomorph	44	62.8	58	30.3	32.5	
Balanced	34	51.5	22	31.8	19.7	

Significance of Differences between Physique Types for Delinquents

Mesomorph-Endomorph	–
Mesomorph-Ectomorph	.05
Mesomorph-Balanced	–
Endomorph-Ectomorph	.10
Endomorph-Balanced	–
Ectomorph-Balanced	–

delinquents and non-delinquents is the gainful employment of the mothers, usually outside the home. This means that to some extent the children were deprived of maternal supervision and advice at a stage when they needed it most. The types of work in which the mothers engaged were cleaning and scrubbing, domestic service by the hour or day, factory work, running a store or lodging house or helping their husbands do so, waiting on table, or entertaining in cafés and restaurants. Almost half of the mothers of the delinquents and a third of the mothers of the non-delinquents were employed part or full time (Table 78). A breakdown by body type now shows that a mother's absence from home had its greatest effect in the resultant delinquency of boys of ectomorphic physique as contrasted with its significantly lesser delinquency-inducing influence on the mesomorphs and endomorphs. The effect of rearing in a home in which a youngster is deprived of his mother's presence is most obviously critical for ectomorphs who, as has been emphasized, are more sensitive.

PHYSICAL ASPECTS OF THE HOME

We turn now to a consideration of certain physical aspects of the homes in which the boys were reared—overcrowding, disorderliness, uncleanliness, careless household routine, and lack of cultural refinement. An overcrowded, disorderly, unclean, unpleasant home gives the lie to the familiar sentiment that "there's no place like home." To modern youth, it tends to be expulsive, adding indirectly to the attractions of the city streets. It also tends to multiply the hazards of unwholesome sex expression and other traumatic experiences.

CROWDING OF HOME

Crowding of the home was determined by the number of occupants per room, exclusive of an infant; if there were more than two occupants per bedroom, the home was considered crowded. In view of the fact that both our delinquents and non-delinquents were selected from the underprivileged areas of a large city, it is not surprising to find that there was actually only a small (albeit significant) difference in the proportion of crowded homes between the delinquents and non-delinquents (Table 80).

In breaking down the total group of delinquents into physique types, a significant dissimilarity is not found among the four body types of the delinquents in the incidence of living in crowded quarters. It can therefore not be concluded that overcrowding exerts a greater influence to delinquency on one physique type than on any other.

Table 80 (VIII-7). CROWDED HOME

(Category: More than Two Occupants per Bedroom)

Percentages of the Respective Physique Type Totals

Physique Types	Delinquents		Non-Delinquents		Difference in Percentages between Delinquents and Non-Delinquents	Probability (Based on X^2 Test)
	No.	%	No.	%		
TOTAL	162	33.0	122	25.3	7.7	.01
Mesomorph	104	35.0	42	28.2	6.8	
Endomorph	20	34.5	10	13.9	20.6	
Ectomorph	22	31.4	51	26.7	4.7	
Balanced	16	24.2	19	26.8	-2.6	

Significance of Differences between Physique Types for Delinquents

Mesomorph-Endomorph	-
Mesomorph-Ectomorph	-
Mesomorph-Balanced	-
Endomorph-Ectomorph	-
Endomorph-Balanced	-
Ectomorph-Balanced	-

CLEANLINESS AND ORDERLINESS OF HOME

Next we are concerned with the effect on delinquency of rearing in homes that are unclean and/or disorderly. The findings must again be considered in the light of the fact that the delinquents and non-delinquents lived in uniformly underprivileged areas, in similar types of houses, and in conditions of not very different degrees of crowding.

This makes all the more important the finding in *Unraveling* that a significantly higher proportion of the homes of delinquents than of non-delinquents were unclean and/or disorderly (Table 81), probably reflecting less self-respect and diligence in homemaking on the part of the mothers of the delinquents. However, the slipshod way of life that especially characterizes the households of the delinquents is not found to have a significantly greater bearing on the delinquency of boys of any particular physique type than on that of the others.

Table 81 (VIII-8). UNCLEAN AND DISORDERLY HOME

(Categories: Sporadically and Habitually)

Percentages of the Respective Physique Type Totals

Physique Types	Delinquents		Non-Delinquents		Difference in Percentages between Delinquents and Non-Delinquents	Probability (Based on X^2 Test)
	No.	%	No.	%		
TOTAL	254	51.6	167	34.7	16.9	.01
Mesomorph	159	53.5	50	33.6	19.9	
Endomorph	26	44.1	28	38.9	5.2	
Ectomorph	33	47.1	65	34.4	12.7	
Balanced	36	54.5	24	33.8	20.7	

Significance of Differences between Physique Types for Delinquents

Mesomorph-Endomorph	–
Mesomorph-Ectomorph	–
Mesomorph-Balanced	–
Endomorph-Ectomorph	–
Endomorph-Balanced	–
Ectomorph-Balanced	–

HOUSEHOLD ROUTINE

Considering next the matter of planlessness or carelessness in household routine, this was more pervasive in the homes of the

Table 82 (X-2). CARELESS HOUSEHOLD ROUTINE

(Categories: Partially Planned and Haphazard)

Percentages of the Respective Physique Type Totals

Physique Types	Delinquents		Non-Delinquents		Difference in Percentages between Delinquents and Non-Delinquents	Probability (Based on X^2 Test)
	No.	%	No.	%		
TOTAL	368	75.6	243	51.2	24.4	.01
Mesomorph	236	80.6	79	53.7	26.9	
Endomorph	35	59.3	32	44.4	14.9	
Ectomorph	50	71.4	96	52.2	19.2	
Balanced	47	72.3	36	50.0	22.3	

Significance of Differences between Physique Types for Delinquents

Mesomorph-Endomorph	.05
Mesomorph-Ectomorph	-
Mesomorph-Balanced	-
Endomorph-Ectomorph	-
Endomorph-Balanced	-
Ectomorph-Balanced	-

delinquents than of the non-delinquents (Table 82), but is significantly more disastrous in terms of its relationship to delinquency among mesomorphs than among endomorphs.

CULTURAL REFINEMENT IN HOME

Since the homes of the delinquents and non-delinquents are in the group of the lowest socio-economic status, it is not too surprising that there was in them almost no evidence of appreciation of "the finer things of life," such as harmony of decoration, interest in music, art, literature, and the like. Despite the general similarity in their socio-economic background, the homes of the delinquents showed as a whole even less refinement of taste and harmony of surroundings than those of the non-delinquents (Table 83).

Apparently, however, poor cultural surroundings have more of a criminogenic impact on the sensitive ectomorphic boys than on the rugged mesomorphs.

Table 83 (X-3). LACK OF CULTURAL REFINEMENT IN HOME

Percentages of the Respective Physique Type Totals

Physique Types	Delinquents		Non-Delinquents		Difference in Percentages between Delinquents and Non-Delinquents	Probability (Based on X^2 Test)
	No.	%	No.	%		
TOTAL	448	91.6	386	81.3	10.3	.01
Mesomorph	263	88.9	126	85.1	3.8	
Endomorph	55	94.8	58	81.7	13.1	
Ectomorph	67	97.1	151	81.7	15.4	
Balanced	63	95.5	51	71.8	23.7	

Significance of Differences between Physique Types for Delinquents

Mesomorph–Endomorph	–
Mesomorph–Ectomorph	.05
Mesomorph–Balanced	–
Endomorph–Ectomorph	–
Endomorph–Balanced	–
Ectomorph–Balanced	–

STABILITY OF HOME AND NEIGHBORHOOD

As was pointed out in *Unraveling,* the *stability of the home* is perhaps the most significant single factor to be explored from the point of view of the mental hygiene of the members of the family, since insecurities, confusions about standards of conduct, and problems of emotional and ideational identification of the growing child with the parent figures are all more or less involved.

It will be obvious from the tables about to be analyzed that the delinquent boys had been the victims of many more unsettling experiences (often related to their own aberrant behavior) than those who managed to remain non-delinquent. These experiences are of a kind that require unusual demands upon powers of adaptation.

They raise or reflect fears and doubts regarding parental understanding, affection, protection, and the relationship of the growing child to the authoritarian world.

In *Unraveling Juvenile Delinquency* we presented ample evidence that, despite the matching of delinquents and non-delinquents as to residence in underprivileged areas, the home conditions under which the delinquents were reared were in fact far less wholesome and stable than those of the non-delinquents. We are interested now to see whether this situational instability played an especially *selective* role in impelling any one of the physique types into delinquency beyond its effect on delinquency in general.

BROKEN HOMES

It is important to determine whether the fact that the home of a boy was broken (as a result of death, desertion, separation, divorce, or prolonged absence of one or both parents) exerted any special delin-

Table 84 (XI-8). BROKEN HOME

Percentages of the Respective Physique Type Totals

Physique Types	Delinquents		Non-Delinquents		Difference in Percentages between Delinquents and Non-Delinquents	Probability (Based on x^2 Test)
	No.	%	No.	%		
TOTAL	299	60.4	166	34.3	26.1	.01
Mesomorph	164	54.8	53	35.6	19.2	
Endomorph	38	64.4	24	33.3	31.1	
Ectomorph	52	73.2	62	32.5	40.7	
Balanced	45	68.2	27	37.5	30.7	

Significance of Differences between Physique Types for Delinquents

Mesomorph–Endomorph	–
Mesomorph–Ectomorph	.05
Mesomorph–Balanced	–
Endomorph–Ectomorph	–
Endomorph–Balanced	–
Ectomorph–Balanced	–

quency-inducing influence on one or another of the body types. It was already evident from the general comparison in *Unraveling* that rearing in a broken home, with its attendant emotional disruptions, is one important element in the constellation of delinquency-related factors (Table 84). It now appears that while the homes of some 60 per cent of our delinquents were fractured as compared with a third of the homes of the non-delinquents, growing up in a broken home exerts more than the usual influence on the delinquency of ecto-morphic boys as contrasted with mesomorphs.

REARING BY PARENT SUBSTITUTE

The impact of an unstable home situation on delinquency is further reflected in boys who were reared by step- or foster-parents. (Not included for consideration here are instances in which the boy

Table 85 (XI-12). REARING BY PARENT SUBSTITUTE

(Categories: One Step-Parent, Foster Parents, Relatives)

Percentages of the Respective Physique Type Totals

Physique Types	Delinquents		Non-Delinquents		Difference in Percentages between Delinquents and Non-Delinquents	Probability (Based on X^2 Test)
	No.	%	No.	%		
TOTAL	227	45.9	59	12.2	33.7	.01
Mesomorph	126	42.1	14	9.4	32.7	
Endomorph	26	44.1	14	19.4	24.7	
Ectomorph	42	59.2	18	9.4	49.8	
Balanced	33	50.0	13	18.1	31.9	

Significance of Differences between Physique Types for Delinquents

Mesomorph-Endomorph	-
Mesomorph-Ectomorph	.05
Mesomorph-Balanced	-
Endomorph-Ectomorph	-
Endomorph-Balanced	-
Ectomorph-Balanced	-

spent only brief periods in foster homes or in the care of relatives.)
As might be expected, considerably more of the delinquents than of
the other boys had substitute parents (Table 85). And, as in respect
to the heavier criminogenic impact of broken homes on the ectomorphs, so as regards rearing by parent substitutes it is found that
the sensitive ectomorphs react excessively to this difficult family
situation, especially in contrast to the mesomorphs.

FREQUENCY OF MOVING

Not only was there less stability in the home life of our delinquents but also in their neighborhood ties, as reflected in the more

Table 86 (XIII-2). FREQUENCY OF MOVING

(Category: 8 or More Moves)

Percentages of the Respective Physique Type Totals

Physique Types	Delinquents		Non-Delinquents		Difference in Percentages between Delinquents and Non-Delinquents	Probability (Based on X^2 Test)
	No.	%	No.	%		
TOTAL	266	53.7	91	18.8	34.9	.01
Mesomorph	151	50.5	24	16.1	34.4	
Endomorph	31	52.5	14	19.5	33.0	
Ectomorph	44	62.0	36	18.9	43.1	
Balanced	40	60.6	17	23.6	37.0	

Significance of Differences between Physique Types for Delinquents

Mesomorph-Endomorph	-
Mesomorph-Ectomorph	-
Mesomorph-Balanced	-
Endomorph-Ectomorph	-
Endomorph-Balanced	-
Ectomorph-Balanced	-

frequent moving (eight or more times) of the families of the delinquents than of the non-delinquents (Table 86). Whatever the effect
of excessive mobility may be upon the tendency to be uninfluenced

by the opinion of neighbors as a guide to conduct, frequent changing of residence operated more powerfully on the boys who became delinquent than on the others.

There is, however, no clear evidence that repeated uprooting of neighborhood ties has any greater delinquency-inducing force on boys of any one physique type than of any other.

Atmosphere of Family Life

Our interest is now focused on the effect of the home atmosphere on the delinquency of boys of the various body structures. The elements of the family drama included in this analysis are domination of the home by the mother, lack of self-respect and ambition of the parents, and low standards of conduct among the members of the family.

It may be said at the outset that a finding that the atmosphere of the homes of the delinquents was far less wholesome than that of the non-delinquents would hardly be a matter for surprise in view of the findings already presented which reflect the greater inadequacy of the mothers and fathers for assumption of family responsibilities.

DOMINANCE OF MOTHER IN FAMILY AFFAIRS

Much has been said recently about the increasingly important place of the mother in American family life, in the guidance of family affairs, and in the general assumption of leadership in the home— for example, in disciplining the children, controlling expenditures, and making decisions for the family. In *Unraveling Juvenile Delinquency* we found that in half of the homes of both the delinquents and the non-delinquents the mother played this dominant role. There being no significant difference in the incidence of this factor among delinquents and the control group, it cannot be inferred that maternal domination of family life is especially criminogenic (Table 87).

In breaking down the group of delinquents into physique types, it does not appear that boys of any body type are more likely to become delinquent than the others as a result of being reared in a mother-dominated home.

Table 87 (X-8). DOMINANCE OF MOTHER IN FAMILY AFFAIRS

Percentages of the Respective Physique Type Totals

Physique Types	Delinquents		Non-Delinquents		Difference in Percentages between Delinquents and Non-Delinquents	Probability (Based on X² Test)
	No.	%	No.	%		
TOTAL	233	50.4	234	51.9	-1.5	.70
Mesomorph	136	48.7	69	48.6	0.1	
Endomorph	29	54.7	37	56.9	-2.2	
Ectomorph	33	49.3	90	51.4	-2.1	
Balanced	35	55.6	38	55.1	0.5	

Significance of Differences between Physique Types for Delinquents

Mesomorph-Endomorph	-
Mesomorph-Ectomorph	-
Mesomorph-Balanced	-
Endomorph-Ectomorph	-
Endomorph-Balanced	-
Ectomorph-Balanced	-

SELF-RESPECT OF PARENTS

Lack of self-respect of parents is reflected in their shamelessness about being dependent on others for support, in approval of delinquency among the members of the family, in lack of embarrassment about irregularity in the behavior of any members of the family, in indifference to the opinion of others about them. Table 88 shows that a far higher proportion of the parents of the delinquents than of the non-delinquents were found to be lacking in self-respect. However, there is no reliable evidence that this has any more to do with the delinquency of boys of any one physique type than of any other.

AMBITION OF PARENTS

The great majority of the parents of both the delinquents and non-delinquents showed little or no ambition as reflected in desire for improvement in their status, higher education for their children, efforts to enhance their economic status, serious intent to move to

Table 88 (X-4). SELF-RESPECT OF PARENTS LACKING

Percentages of the Respective Physique Type Totals

Physique Types	Delinquents		Non-Delinquents		Difference in Percentages between Delinquents and Non-Delinquents	Probability (Based on X^2 Test)
	No.	%	No.	%		
TOTAL	214	43.2	48	10.2	33.0	.01
Mesomorph	134	44.8	18	12.2	32.6	
Endomorph	19	32.2	4	5.6	26.6	
Ectomorph	34	47.9	20	10.9	37.0	
Balanced	27	40.9	6	8.5	32.4	

Significance of Differences between Physique Types for Delinquents

Mesomorph-Endomorph	-
Mesomorph-Ectomorph	-
Mesomorph-Balanced	-
Endomorph-Ectomorph	-
Endomorph-Balanced	-
Ectomorph-Balanced	-

Table 89 (X-5). AMBITION OF PARENTS LACKING

Percentages of the Respective Physique Type Totals

Physique Types	Delinquents		Non-Delinquents		Difference in Percentages between Delinquents and Non-Delinquents	Probability (Based on X^2 Test)
	No.	%	No.	%		
TOTAL	442	89.5	331	70.1	19.4	.01
Mesomorph	270	90.3	106	72.6	17.7	
Endomorph	47	79.7	46	67.6	12.1	
Ectomorph	66	93.0	134	72.0	21.0	
Balanced	59	90.8	45	62.5	28.3	

Significance of Differences between Physique Types for Delinquents

Mesomorph-Endomorph	-
Mesomorph-Ectomorph	-
Mesomorph-Balanced	-
Endomorph-Ectomorph	-
Endomorph-Balanced	-
Ectomorph-Balanced	-

better neighborhoods or into more adequate homes. However, parents of the delinquents were as a group less ambitious than those of the non-delinquents (Table 89).

It cannot be definitively said, however, that lack of ambition had more to do with the delinquency of one body type than of the others, although there is an indication (at the .15 level of probability) that endomorphs are less affected by this than ectomorphs.

CONDUCT STANDARDS OF FAMILY

Not only were the parents of the delinquents less self-respecting and ambitious than those of the non-delinquents, but the standards

Table 90 (X-6). LOW CONDUCT STANDARDS OF FAMILY

Percentages of the Respective Physique Type Totals

Physique Types	Delinquents		Non-Delinquents		Difference in Percentages between Delinquents and Non-Delinquents	Probability (Based on X^2 Test)
	No.	%	No.	%		
TOTAL	447	90.3	262	54.1	36.2	.01
Mesomorph	265	88.6	83	55.7	32.9	
Endomorph	55	93.2	30	41.7	51.5	
Ectomorph	70	98.6	107	56.1	42.5	
Balanced	57	86.3	42	58.4	27.9	

Significance of Differences between Physique Types for Delinquents

Mesomorph-Endomorph	-
Mesomorph-Ectomorph	.02
Mesomorph-Balanced	-
Endomorph-Ectomorph	-
Endomorph-Balanced	-
Ectomorph-Balanced	.05

of conduct were lower in the homes in which the delinquents were reared (as reflected in delinquency, alcoholism, and/or immorality among one or more members of the family, exclusive of the boy under study). The delinquents to a far greater extent than the non-delinquents were the products of such a generally undesirable home atmosphere (Table 90); but again it is among the ectomorphs, in contrast to the lesser effect on mesomorphs and boys of balanced physique, that deleterious environmental influences take their heaviest toll, as seen by the fact that low behavior standards of the family exert the greatest influence in connection with their delinquency.

In the next chapter we shall continue with the consideration of the effect of unwholesome family life on the delinquency of the various physique types.

NOTES

1. *Unraveling,* pp. 167-8. "The area-studies establish that a region of economic and cultural disorganization tends to have a criminogenic effect on people residing therein; but the studies fail to emphasize that this influence affects only a selected group comprising a relatively small proportion of all the residents. They do not reveal why the deleterious influences of even the most extreme delinquency area fail to turn the great majority of its boys into persistent delinquents. They do not disclose whether the children who do not succumb to the evil and disruptive neighborhood influence differ from those who become delinquents and if so, in what respects . . . The true significance of the factors dealt with by the area sociologist can be determined only through close study of the points of impact of social forces upon individuals and classes of varying biologic make-up and childhood conditioning." *Ibid.,* pp. 5-6. The crucial issue raised by this statement has not yet been met by sociologically oriented criminologists.

2. *Ibid.,* p. 155. See, generally, Chapters X, XI, XII, XIII of *Unraveling.*

3. Chapter I, pp. 16, 17, note 5.

IX

Effect of Family and Home Environment on the Delinquency of Four Physique Types (Continued)

INTRODUCTORY

In this chapter we continue the exploration of the selective influence on the delinquency of the physique types of certain aspects of their home environment. In general, our concern is now with factors that reflect disunity of the family, weak affectional ties between parents and boy, and the poor supervisory and disciplinary practices of the parents.

In *Unraveling Juvenile Delinquency* it had come to light that in a great many of the factors of the home life and intra-family relationships, a marked difference existed between the delinquents and non-delinquents, the former being considerably less advantaged than the latter. These findings assume particular significance for the understanding and prediction of delinquency because the boys had been matched not only for residence in underprivileged areas but by ethnic origins.

EVIDENCES OF FAMILY DISUNITY

We shall first consider a few aspects of family life which reflect weakness in the family ties—incompatibility of the parents, lack of recreations for the family as a group, lack of interest in the children's friends, meager provision of recreational facilities for them, and lack of family cohesiveness.

What special influence did this kind of disorganized and uninterested home environment have on the delinquent behavior of the four major physique types?

COMPATIBILITY OF PARENTS

Table 91 shows that a far higher proportion of the parents of the delinquent boys than of the non-delinquent were found to be incompatible, as reflected either in obvious and continuous tensions

Table 91 (X-7). INCOMPATIBILITY OF PARENTS

(Categories: Fair and Poor)

Percentages of the Respective Physique Type Totals

Physique Types	Delinquents		Non-Delinquents		Difference in Percentages between Delinquents and Non-Delinquents	Probability (Based on X^2 Test)
	No.	%	No.	%		
TOTAL	309	63.2	167	34.8	28.4	.01
Mesomorph	179	60.4	44	29.5	30.9	
Endomorph	33	56.9	23	32.4	24.5	
Ectomorph	57	81.4	73	38.8	42.6	
Balanced	40	61.5	27	38.0	23.5	

Significance of Differences between Physique Types for Delinquents

Mesomorph-Endomorph	-
Mesomorph-Ectomorph	.02
Mesomorph-Balanced	-
Endomorph-Ectomorph	.05
Endomorph-Balanced	-
Ectomorph-Balanced	.05

between them even though they continued to live together, or in an open breach (desertion, separation, divorce). The unwholesome influence of such conditions on the sound development of children need not be labored. It is seen in numerous clinical case histories. In breaking down the delinquents into physique types, it becomes evident that there is a greater association of this factor with the delinquency of the ectomorphs than with that of the other physique types. It is again to be remembered that ectomorphs have been found to be more sensitive than boys of the other physique types. Evidently the incompatibility of their parents affects them more deeply and is more likely to result in delinquency than when it occurs among boys of the other body types.

FAMILY GROUP RECREATIONS

Another evidence of family disunity is found in the lack of family group recreations such as picnicking or going to the beach together, taking automobile rides, visiting relatives, or going to the movies together. In general, far fewer of the families of the delinquents than of the non-delinquents were in the habit of having such joint

Table 92 (X-11). FAMILY GROUP RECREATION LACKING

Percentages of the Respective Physique Type Totals

Physique Types	Delinquents		Non-Delinquents		Difference in Percentages between Delinquents and Non-Delinquents	Probability (Based on X^2 Test)
	No.	%	No.	%		
TOTAL	329	67.2	185	38.5	28.7	.01
Mesomorph	207	70.4	62	41.9	28.5	
Endomorph	32	54.2	24	34.3	19.9	
Ectomorph	48	68.6	68	35.8	32.8	
Balanced	42	63.7	31	43.1	20.6	

Significance of Differences between Physique Types for Delinquents

Mesomorph-Endomorph	.10
Mesomorph-Ectomorph	-
Mesomorph-Balanced	-
Endomorph-Ectomorph	-
Endomorph-Balanced	-
Ectomorph-Balanced	-

recreations (Table 92). Failure of parents to foster recreational outlets in which all family members can participate reflects less cohesiveness in the families of delinquents as a group than of non-delinquents. Now we find evidence that lack of group recreations contributes most heavily to the delinquency of mesomorphs, at least in contrast to endomorphs. Muscular, energetic mesomorphs no doubt seek recreational outlets for their drives outside the home.

PARENTS' INTEREST IN CHILDREN'S FRIENDS

The need for the children who became delinquent to rely more on their own interests and companionships for recreational expres-

Table 93 (X-12). PARENTS UNINTERESTED IN CHILDREN'S FRIENDS

(Categories: Indifferent and Inhospitable)

Percentages of the Respective Physique Type Totals

Physique Types	Delinquents		Non-Delinquents		Difference in Percentages between Delinquents and Non-Delinquents	Probability (Based on X^2 Test)
	No.	%	No.	%		
TOTAL	387	79.8	297	61.9	17.9	.01
Mesomorph	241	82.0	82	55.0	27.0	
Endomorph	42	72.4	51	70.8	1.6	
Ectomorph	54	80.6	120	63.8	16.8	
Balanced	50	75.8	44	62.0	13.8	

Significance of Differences between Physique Types for Delinquents

Mesomorph-Endomorph	-
Mesomorph-Ectomorph	-
Mesomorph-Balanced	-
Endomorph-Ectomorph	-
Endomorph-Balanced	-
Ectomorph-Balanced	-

sion was further aggravated by the failure of their parents to give any serious thought to making the homes attractive to the boys and to encourage them to bring their playmates home. The parents were in fact indifferent and even downright inhospitable to them. Whether because of more crowded home conditions and other hardships or the character of the parents, the mothers and fathers of the delinquents were more indifferent or inhospitable to their children's friends than were the parents of the non-delinquents (Table 93). Despite appearances to the contrary, statistical computation does not show this factor to have more of a criminogenic influence on boys of some particular physique type than on the others.

RECREATIONAL FACILITIES IN HOME

Not only did the parents of the delinquent boys not welcome their children's friends into their homes, but they made far less provision

Table 94 (X-13). MEAGER RECREATIONAL FACILITIES IN HOME

Percentages of the Respective Physique Type Totals

Physique Types	Delinquents		Non-Delinquents		Difference in Percentages between Delinquents and Non-Delinquents	Probability (Based on X^2 Test)
	No.	%	No.	%		
TOTAL	261	53.2	177	36.6	16.6	.01
Mesomorph	164	55.2	50	33.6	21.6	
Endomorph	23	39.0	25	34.7	4.3	
Ectomorph	37	54.4	77	40.5	13.9	
Balanced	37	56.1	25	34.7	21.4	

Significance of Differences between Physique Types for Delinquents

Mesomorph-Endomorph	.10
Mesomorph-Ectomorph	-
Mesomorph-Balanced	-
Endomorph-Ectomorph	-
Endomorph-Balanced	-
Ectomorph-Balanced	-

for the play-time of their sons than did the parents of the non-delinquents (Table 94). Certainly they did not set aside any special space for play; nor did they provide more than an occasional toy or book.

Lack of suitable recreational facilities at home is found to have more to do with impelling the energetic, muscular mesomorphic type of boy to delinquency than the easygoing, "comfortable," obese endomorph.

FAMILY COHESIVENESS

Among the most striking findings of *Unraveling,* and one found to be of considerable predictive power in distinguishing potential delinquents from non-delinquents, is the marked difference in in-

Table 95 (X-14). LACK OF FAMILY COHESIVENESS

(Categories: Some and None)

Percentages of the Respective Physique Type Totals

Physique Types	Delinquents		Non-Delinquents		Difference in Percentages between Delinquents and Non-Delinquents	Probability (Based on X^2 Test)
	No.	%	No.	%		
TOTAL	414	81.8	185	38.2	43.6	.01
Mesomorph	240	80.5	50	33.5	47.0	
Endomorph	51	76.4	24	33.3	43.1	
Ectomorph	67	94.4	81	42.4	52.0	
Balanced	56	84.8	30	41.7	43.1	

Significance of Differences between Physique Types for Delinquents

Mesomorph–Endomorph	–
Mesomorph–Ectomorph	.02
Mesomorph–Balanced	–
Endomorph–Ectomorph	.05
Endomorph–Balanced	–
Ectomorph–Balanced	–

cidence of family cohesiveness between delinquents and non-delinquents.[1] As Table 95 shows, lack of unity of family life (home being "just a place to hang your hat," where the self-interest of each member exceeds his group interest) is much more common in the delinquent group than in the non-delinquent. The breakdown into body types reveals that such haphazard family ties exert a more damaging effect on the sensitive ectomorphs than on the sturdy mesomorphs and easygoing endomorphs.

AFFECTION OF FAMILY FOR BOY

What of the effect on the boys of lack of affection from their fathers, mothers, and brothers and sisters in inducing or impelling those of different physique types to delinquency?

RANK OF BOY AMONG SIBLINGS

First, a word about the ordinal rank of a boy among the children in the family. It has often been said that an only child, a first-born

Table 96 (XI-5). RANK OF BOY AMONG SIBLINGS

(Categories: Only Child, First-born, or Youngest)

Percentages of the Respective Physique Type Totals

Physique Types	Delinquents		Non-Delinquents		Difference in Percentages between Delinquents and Non-Delinquents	Probability (Based on X^2 Test)
	No.	%	No.	%		
TOTAL	196	39.6	254	52.5	-12.9	.01
Mesomorph	109	36.4	60	40.2	-3.8	
Endomorph	24	40.7	48	66.7	-26.0	
Ectomorph	33	46.5	112	58.6	-12.1	
Balanced	30	45.4	34	47.1	-1.7	

Significance of Differences between Physique Types for Delinquents

Mesomorph-Endomorph	-
Mesomorph-Ectomorph	-
Mesomorph-Balanced	-
Endomorph-Ectomorph	-
Endomorph-Balanced	-
Ectomorph-Balanced	-

child, or the youngest child in the family has a "preferred" position among his brothers and sisters, that is, that he is generally more favored, receives more affection and attention and more spoiling than the "middle" children; and, the argument runs, he is, therefore, more likely to be the delinquent member of the family. In *Unraveling Juvenile Delinquency* this was not found to be so; actually, a lower proportion of our delinquents than of our non-delinquents had such a "preferred" status among their siblings (Table 96). From a breakdown into body types, there is no sufficiently trustworthy evidence that a preferred status in birth rank has more to do with the delinquency of any physique type than with that of any other. (The significant variation in incidence that occurs among the physique types in the non-delinquent control group must be regarded as fortuitous.)

ATTACHMENT OF FATHER TO BOY

In *Unraveling* we emphasized that a warm relationship between father and son is of prime significance in helping a boy to develop

Table 97 (XI-13). FATHER NOT ATTACHED TO BOY

(Categories: Indifferent and Hostile)

Percentages of the Respective Physique Type Totals

Physique Types	Delinquents		Non-Delinquents		Difference in Percentages between Delinquents and Non-Delinquents	Probability (Based on X^2 Test)
	No.	%	No.	%		
TOTAL	290	59.5	90	19.3	40.2	.01
Mesomorph	168	57.5	25	17.7	39.8	
Endomorph	34	58.6	15	21.1	37.5	
Ectomorph	45	63.4	37	20.3	43.1	
Balanced	43	65.2	13	18.6	46.6	

Significance of Differences between Physique Types for Delinquents

Mesomorph–Endomorph	–
Mesomorph–Ectomorph	–
Mesomorph–Balanced	–
Endomorph–Ectomorph	–
Endomorph–Balanced	–
Ectomorph–Balanced	–

a wholesome set of ideals through the process of emotional identification, provided, of course, the father himself has wholesome
ideals. If the bond is not close, the growing boy may seek substitute
satisfactions in companionship with older delinquents; or he may
pass through a stage of grave insecurity, frustration, and resentment,
with resultant psychoneurotic symptoms difficult to eliminate in later
years. Parental affection, like family cohesiveness, has been found
to have marked predictive significance for potential delinquency.
We saw in *Unraveling* that a considerably higher proportion of the
fathers of the delinquents than of the non-delinquents had no affectional attachment to their sons (Table 97). Since the incidence of
this factor is not found to vary significantly among the four physique
types of the delinquents, it cannot be said that a father's indifference
or hostility has any greater effect on delinquency in the case of any
particular physique type than among the others.

ATTACHMENT OF MOTHER TO BOY

A considerably higher proportion of mothers than of fathers of
both delinquents and non-delinquents were warmly attached
to the boys. However, as was true of the fathers, a much greater
proportion of the mothers of the delinquents than of the non-
delinquents were typically indifferent or hostile to their sons (Table
98). Deprivation of mother-love is found to exert the most extensive
damage in contributing toward the delinquency of the sensitive ectomorphs in clear contrast to its lesser impact on the sturdy mesomorphs.

ATTACHMENT OF SIBLINGS TO BOY

As was the case in regard to the fathers and the mothers of the
delinquents, so in respect to their siblings a considerably higher
proportion of the delinquents than of the control group were deprived of the warm regard of their brothers and sisters (Table 99).
Again it is on the ectomorphs, as well as the endomorphs, that such
deprivation has the greatest impact in contributing to their delinquency in contrast with its lesser influence on mesomorphs and boys
of balanced type.

Table 98 (XI-14). MOTHER NOT ATTACHED TO BOY

(Categories: Indifferent and Hostile)

Percentages of the Respective Physique Type Totals

Physique Types	Delinquents		Non-Delinquents		Difference in Percentages between Delinquents and Non-Delinquents	Probability (Based on X^2 Test)
	No.	%	No.	%		
TOTAL	136	27.7	21	4.3	23.4	.01
Mesomorph	72	24.2	7	4.8	19.4	
Endomorph	19	32.8	2	2.8	30.0	
Ectomorph	27	39.1	7	3.8	35.3	
Balanced	18	27.7	5	6.9	20.8	

Significance of Differences between Physique Types for Delinquents

Mesomorph-Endomorph	-
Mesomorph-Ectomorph	.10
Mesomorph-Balanced	-
Endomorph-Ectomorph	-
Endomorph-Balanced	-
Ectomorph-Balanced	-

Table 99 (XI-18). SIBLINGS NOT ATTACHED TO BOY

(Categories: Indifferent and Hostile)

Percentages of the Respective Physique Type Totals

Physique Types	Delinquents		Non-Delinquents		Difference in Percentages between Delinquents and Non-Delinquents	Probability (Based on X^2 Test)
	No.	%	No.	%		
TOTAL	131	28.4	31	7.2	21.2	.01
Mesomorph	70	24.9	8	5.9	19.0	
Endomorph	22	39.3	4	6.9	32.4	
Ectomorph	28	41.2	13	7.8	33.4	
Balanced	11	19.3	6	8.8	10.5	

Significance of Differences between Physique Types for Delinquents

Mesomorph-Endomorph	-
Mesomorph-Ectomorph	.10
Mesomorph-Balanced	-
Endomorph-Ectomorph	-
Endomorph-Balanced	.10
Ectomorph-Balanced	.05

FEELING OF BOY FOR PARENTS

So much for affectional warmth from members of the immediate family. Now we look at the current of feeling of the boys toward their parents and the relationship of this to the delinquency of boys of the different physique types.

ATTACHMENT OF BOY TO FATHER

Correlative to the lesser warmth of feeling of the fathers of the delinquents for them is the fact that the delinquents themselves

Table 100 (XI-15). BOY NOT ATTACHED TO FATHER

(Categories: Indifferent, Hostile, and Noncommittal)

Percentages of the Respective Physique Type Totals

Physique Types	Delinquents		Non-Delinquents		Difference in Percentages between Delinquents and Non-Delinquents	Probability (Based on X^2 Test)
	No.	%	No.	%		
TOTAL	332	67.5	170	35.2	32.3	.01
Mesomorph	201	67.4	52	34.9	32.5	
Endomorph	36	63.1	22	30.6	32.5	
Ectomorph	47	66.2	67	35.2	31.0	
Balanced	48	72.8	29	40.4	32.4	

Significance of Differences between Physique Types for Delinquents

Mesomorph-Endomorph	–
Mesomorph-Ectomorph	–
Mesomorph-Balanced	–
Endomorph-Ectomorph	–
Endomorph-Balanced	–
Ectomorph-Balanced	–

were found in *Unraveling* to be far less attached to their fathers than were the non-delinquents (Table 100). In the breakdown into body types it does not emerge that this factor plays any greater role in impelling boys of one body type to delinquency than of any others.

ACCEPTABILITY OF FATHER TO BOY FOR EMULATION

In interviewing the boys, the psychiatrist interpreted expressions of criticism of their fathers and a desire not to pattern themselves after their fathers as indicating the unacceptability of the father as a person with whom to identify emotionally. Almost a third of the delinquent boys, as compared with a much smaller group of the non-delinquents, made it clearly evident that their fathers were unacceptable to them as persons to admire and emulate (Table 101). As was true in regard to the lesser attachment of the delinquent boys to their fathers, so with respect to the lesser acceptability of their fathers as patterns for emulation a significant variation in the incidence of this factor is not found among the four physique types. It cannot be concluded, therefore, that unacceptability of the father as a symbol for emulation and identification has a more pervasive

Table 101 (XI-16). FATHER UNACCEPTABLE TO BOY FOR EMULATION

Percentages of the Respective Physique Type Totals

Physique Types	Delinquents		Non-Delinquents		Difference in Percentages between Delinquents and Non-Delinquents	Probability (Based on X^2 Test)
	No.	%	No.	%		
TOTAL	123	30.8	31	7.3	23.5	.01
Mesomorph	73	30.7	7	5.6	25.1	
Endomorph	18	34.0	8	12.1	21.9	
Ectomorph	15	26.3	11	6.5	19.8	
Balanced	17	32.7	5	7.9	24.8	

Significance of Differences between Physique Types for Delinquents

Mesomorph–Endomorph	–
Mesomorph–Ectomorph	–
Mesomorph–Balanced	–
Endomorph–Ectomorph	–
Endomorph–Balanced	–
Ectomorph–Balanced	–

effect on the delinquency of boys of any one physique type than of any other.

ATTACHMENT OF BOY TO MOTHER

A much higher proportion of both delinquents and non-delinquents expressed attachment to their mothers than to their fathers.

Table 102 (XI-17). BOY NOT ATTACHED TO MOTHER

(Categories: Indifferent, Hostile, and Noncommittal)

Percentages of the Respective Physique Type Totals

Physique Types	Delinquents		Non-Delinquents		Difference in Percentages between Delinquents and Non-Delinquents	Probability (Based on x^2 Test)
	No.	%	No.	%		
TOTAL	171	34.7	50	10.4	24.3	.01
Mesomorph	103	34.6	16	10.8	23.8	
Endomorph	18	31.7	4	5.6	26.1	
Ectomorph	28	39.4	25	13.2	26.2	
Balanced	22	33.3	5	6.9	26.4	

Significance of Differences between Physique Types for Delinquents

Mesomorph–Endomorph	–
Mesomorph–Ectomorph	–
Mesomorph–Balanced	–
Endomorph–Ectomorph	–
Endomorph–Balanced	–
Ectomorph–Balanced	–

However, as was true of lack of attachment of the boys to their fathers, a considerably higher proportion of the delinquents than of the non-delinquents voiced no love for their mothers (Table 102). And just as in the case of lack of attachment of the boys to their fathers and of the unacceptability of their fathers as patterns for emulation, no significant difference is found to exist in the incidence of this factor among the four physique types. It can therefore not be said that a boy's indifference or hostility to his mother has a greater influence on the delinquency of any particular physique type than on that of the others.

SUPERVISION AND DISCIPLINE OF BOY

We consider next the question of whether careless supervision of the boy and faulty disciplinary practices by his parents played any special role in the delinquency of any particular physique type. These two factors were also found in *Unraveling* to have strong prognostic force in distinguishing between potential delinquents and non-delinquents.

SUPERVISION BY MOTHER

As a group, the mothers of our delinquents were far more careless in their supervision of the boys than the mothers of the non-

Table 103 (X-10).   UNSUITABLE SUPERVISION BY MOTHER

Percentages of the Respective Physique Type Totals

Physique Types	Delinquents		Non-Delinquents		Difference in Percentages between Delinquents and Non-Delinquents	Probability (Based on X^2 Test)
	No.	%	No.	%		
TOTAL	315	63.9	63	13.3	50.6	.01
Mesomorph	179	60.3	17	11.6	48.7	
Endomorph	36	61.0	10	13.9	47.1	
Ectomorph	54	76.1	25	13.4	62.7	
Balanced	46	69.7	11	15.7	54.0	

Significance of Differences between Physique Types for Delinquents

Mesomorph–Endomorph	–
Mesomorph–Ectomorph	.05
Mesomorph–Balanced	–
Endomorph–Ectomorph	–
Endomorph–Balanced	–
Ectomorph–Balanced	–

delinquents, leaving them more largely to their own devices without guidance or in the care of irresponsible children or adults (Table 103). It is on the ectomorphs, however, that inadequate supervision of a boy exerts more of a propulsive inclination to delinquency than on the mesomorphs. Thus again we have an instance of the greater reactivity of the sensitive ectomorphs to the various aspects of unwholesome family life.

Turning now to disciplinary methods, it will be seen from the next few tables that on the whole the most marked difference between the disciplinary practices of the parents of the delinquents and those of the control group is found in the considerably greater extent to which the former resorted to physical punishment, and the consequent lesser extent to which they dealt with the boys in a consistently fair, albeit firm, manner. Of course the outcome is influenced by the fact that the delinquent boys, being so continually involved in misbehavior, may have called forth either more punitive or more exasperation-induced erratic action on the part of their parents. Nevertheless, the tables furnish a fairly reliable commentary on the ineffectiveness of punishment as opposed to more reasoned and consistent efforts to control the conduct of children.

DISCIPLINE BY FATHER

We are first concerned with lax, overstrict, or inconsistent discipline as opposed to firm and kindly discipline which a boy accepts because of its fairness and consistency and because he feels that, despite the punishment, his father cares about him. As might be expected, the disciplinary practices of the fathers of the delinquent boys were far less suitable than those of the fathers of the nondelinquents (Table 104). Here, too, as in so many other factors reflecting unwholesome home and family life, it is found that inconsistent, lax, or overstrict discipline has a more deleterious influence on ectomorphs than on one or another body type, this time, the endomorphs.

Table 104 (XI-22). UNSUITABLE DISCIPLINE BY FATHER

(Categories: Lax, Over-strict, and Erratic)

Percentages of the Respective Physique Type Totals

Physique Types	Delinquents		Non-Delinquents		Difference in Percentages between Delinquents and Non-Delinquents	Probability (Based on X^2 Test)
	No.	%	No.	%		
TOTAL	430	94.5	201	45.2	49.3	.01
Mesomorph	260	94.9	66	47.8	47.1	
Endomorph	49	87.5	30	44.8	42.7	
Ectomorph	62	98.4	76	43.7	54.7	
Balanced	59	95.2	29	44.6	50.6	

Significance of Differences between Physique Types for Delinquents

Mesomorph-Endomorph	-
Mesomorph-Ectomorph	-
Mesomorph-Balanced	-
Endomorph-Ectomorph	.10
Endomorph-Balanced	-
Ectomorph-Balanced	-

PHYSICAL PUNISHMENT BY FATHER

That pain-inflicting discipline is not very effective in preventing delinquency seems to be a reasonable inference from the fact that two-thirds of the fathers of our delinquents resorted to physical punishment in handling the disciplinary problems presented by the boy, as compared with a third of the fathers of the non-delinquents (Table 105). Although there is no clearcut evidence that physical punishment is more influential a factor in the delinquency of one body type than another, there is some possibility that it is on boys of the soft, round, comfort-loving endomorphic physique that this harsh method of discipline plays an excessive role in connection with delinquency, in contrast at least with boys of balanced physique. We may speculate that the naturally "easygoing" kind of a young-

Table 105 (XI-23). PHYSICAL PUNISHMENT BY FATHER

Percentages of the Respective Physique Type Totals

Physique Types	Delinquents		Non-Delinquents		Difference in Percentages between Delinquents and Non-Delinquents	Probability (Based on X² Test)
	No.	%	No.	%		
TOTAL	296	67.7	153	35.3	32.4	.01
Mesomorph	179	67.8	50	38.2	29.6	
Endomorph	42	76.4	17	25.8	50.6	
Ectomorph	39	70.9	63	36.6	34.3	
Balanced	36	57.1	23	35.9	21.2	

Significance of Differences between Physique Types for Delinquents

Mesomorph-Endomorph	–
Mesomorph-Ectomorph	–
Mesomorph-Balanced	–
Endomorph-Ectomorph	–
Endomorph-Balanced	–
Ectomorph-Balanced	–

ster is more resentful of physical punishment than boys of other body builds.

SCOLDING OR THREATENING BY FATHER

A significant difference was not found in *Unraveling Juvenile Delinquency* in the proportion of our delinquents and non-delinquents whose fathers resorted to scolding or to threats of punishing them for their misdeeds (Table 106). In breaking down the delinquent group into physique types, no significant evidence emerges of any variation in the reaction of the boys in terms of delinquent behavior resulting from this particular disciplinary method.

DISCIPLINE BY MOTHER

As was true of unsuitable discipline by the fathers, so, in respect to such practices on the part of the mothers, a far higher proportion of the delinquents than of the non-delinquents were subjected to

Table 106 (XI-23). SCOLDING OR THREATENING BY FATHER

Percentages of the Respective Physique Type Totals

Physique Types	Delinquents		Non-Delinquents		Difference in Percentages between Delinquents and Non-Delinquents	Probability (Based on X^2 Test)
	No.	%	No.	%		
TOTAL	140	32.0	134	30.9	1.1	.80
Mesomorph	82	31.1	46	35.1	-4.0	
Endomorph	21	38.2	18	27.3	10.9	
Ectomorph	20	36.4	53	30.8	5.6	
Balanced	17	27.0	17	26.6	0.4	

Significance of Differences between Physique Types for Delinquents

Mesomorph-Endomorph	–
Mesomorph-Ectomorph	–
Mesomorph-Balanced	–
Endomorph-Ectomorph	–
Endomorph-Balanced	–
Ectomorph-Balanced	–

Table 107 (XI-22). UNSUITABLE DISCIPLINE BY MOTHER

(Categories: Lax, Over-strict, and Erratic)

Percentages of the Respective Physique Type Totals

Physique Types	Delinquents		Non-Delinquents		Difference in Percentages between Delinquents and Non-Delinquents	Probability (Based on X^2 Test)
	No.	%	No.	%		
TOTAL	471	95.7	169	35.3	60.4	.01
Mesomorph	284	95.3	43	29.2	66.1	
Endomorph	56	96.6	28	38.9	57.7	
Ectomorph	68	97.1	79	42.1	55.0	
Balanced	63	95.5	19	26.4	69.1	

Significance of Differences between Physique Types for Delinquents

Mesomorph-Endomorph	–
Mesomorph-Ectomorph	–
Mesomorph-Balanced	–
Endomorph-Ectomorph	–
Endomorph-Balanced	–
Ectomorph-Balanced	–

lax, overstrict, or erratic disciplinary practices (Table 107). However, this is not clearly found to have affected boys of the four physique types differently insofar as delinquency is concerned.

PHYSICAL PUNISHMENT BY MOTHER

As in the case of their fathers, the mothers of our delinquents resorted to physical punishment to a greater extent than did the mothers

Table 108 (XI-23). PHYSICAL PUNISHMENT BY MOTHER

Percentages of the Respective Physique Type Totals

Physique Types	Delinquents		Non-Delinquents		Difference in Percentages between Delinquents and Non-Delinquents	Probability (Based on X^2 Test)
	No.	%	No.	%		
TOTAL	264	55.3	165	34.9	20.4	.01
Mesomorph	161	55.7	54	37.5	18.2	
Endomorph	34	58.6	22	31.0	27.6	
Ectomorph	33	50.8	62	33.3	17.5	
Balanced	36	55.4	27	37.5	17.9	

Significance of Differences between Physique Types for Delinquents

Mesomorph–Endomorph	–
Mesomorph–Ectomorph	–
Mesomorph–Balanced	–
Endomorph–Ectomorph	–
Endomorph–Balanced	–
Ectomorph–Balanced	–

of the non-delinquents (Table 108). And, again, in the breakdown of the delinquents into physique types there is no trustworthy evidence that boys of any one physique type are any more or any less influenced for delinquency by physical punishment than are boys of the other body types.

SCOLDING OR THREATENING BY MOTHER

Only a slightly higher but nevertheless significantly greater proportion of the mothers of our delinquents than of the non-delinquents resorted to threatening or scolding of the boys (Table 109). It is not now found that the reaction to this kind of discipline is any greater in terms of delinquency on the part of boys of any one physique type than of any other.

In reflecting upon the findings pertaining to unwholesome disciplinary practices on the part of the parents, the point that stands

Table 109 (XI-23). SCOLDING OR THREATENING BY MOTHER

Percentages of the Respective Physique Type Totals

Physique Types	Delinquents		Non-Delinquents		Difference in Percentages between Delinquents and Non-Delinquents	Probability (Based on X^2 Test)
	No.	%	No.	%		
TOTAL	223	46.8	177	37.4	9.4	.01
Mesomorph	135	46.7	59	41.0	5.7	
Endomorph	25	43.1	18	25.4	17.7	
Ectomorph	34	52.3	70	37.6	14.7	
Balanced	29	44.6	30	41.7	2.9	

Significance of Differences between Physique Types for Delinquents

Mesomorph-Endomorph	–
Mesomorph-Ectomorph	–
Mesomorph-Balanced	–
Endomorph-Ectomorph	–
Endomorph-Balanced	–
Ectomorph-Balanced	–

out is that the impact of such an approach to the annoying antics of growing children is not shown to vary significantly with body type. One may tentatively conclude, then, that bad discipline is so pervasively damaging that its leveling influence overrides even marked differences of bodily morphology and temperament. As was pointed out, this is a factor which, in checking on the validity of the social prediction table presented in *Unraveling,* has been demonstrated to have a high power of forecasting delinquency.[2] The same is true of poor supervision by the mother and lack of family unity.

SUMMARY

Analysis of the 42 sociocultural factors encompassed in this and the preceding chapter has revealed three factors not found in *Unraveling Juvenile Delinquency* to be associated with delinquency in general, and that are likewise not found to have any influence on the delinquency of the body types.[3] They can be laid aside.

Those sociocultural factors among the 42 studied which, though associated with delinquency in general, are not found to exert a significantly varied influence on the delinquency of the body types, will be adverted to in the next chapter, "Common Ground of Criminogenesis." Now we wish only to focus on those factors which exert a *varied* influence on the delinquency of the body types. There are 15 such factors:

Emotional disturbance in father (Table 71)
Gainful employment of mother (Table 79)
Careless household routine (Table 82)
Lack of cultural refinement in home (Table 83)
Broken home (Table 84)
Rearing by parent substitute (Table 85)
Low conduct standards of family (Table 90)
Incompatibility of parents (Table 91)
Lack of family group recreations (Table 92)
Meager recreational facilities in home (Table 94)
Lack of family unity (Table 95)
Lack of attachment of mother to boy (Table 98)
Lack of attachment of siblings to boy (Table 99)
Careless supervision by mother (Table 103)
Unsuitable discipline by father (Table 104)

In addition to these 15 factors, there are two which, from inspection at least, appear to have a varying impact on the delinquency of the physique types, but as such differences are expressed by a probability of .15 (instead of .01 — .10) we merely mention them in passing. Examination of another sample of cases would be needed in order to clarify their status. The factors are: lack of ambition of parents (Table 89) and physical punishment of boy by father (Table 105).

We have now completed an analysis of the impact of 42 sociocultural factors (largely reflective of family relationships and home background) on the delinquency of the boys of the four body types. The major finding of the analysis is that the effect on delinquency of certain environmental circumstances is *not uniform* in all the body types. A variation occurs that "makes sense" and which must be taken into account in preventive and therapeutic programs. This will become more evident in Chapters XI-XIV in which we will distinguish each physique type from the others in terms of those traits and factors that have the greatest effect on the delinquency of each body type as contrasted with the others.

Before proceeding to this, however, we shall call attention to those traits and sociocultural factors that are associated with delinquency but are not found to vary in their impact on the delinquency of the body types.

NOTES

1. The predictive table based on social data which was presented in *Unraveling* (pp. 260-262) is founded on the factors of *discipline of boy by father, supervision of boy by mother, affection of father for boy, affection of mother for boy, and family cohesiveness.* It has been successfully validated on several occasions on varied samples of cases other than those on which it was constructed. Thus Thompson, in 1952, analyzing 100 cases randomly gathered from the files of the Cambridge-Somerville (Massachusetts) Youth Study, found that actual delinquency or non-delinquency corresponded with predicted behavior in 91 per cent of the cases. See R. E. Thompson, "A Validation of the Glueck Social Prediction Scale for Proneness to Delinquency," *Journal of Criminal Law, Criminology and Police Science,* Vol. 43, No. 4 (1952), pp. 451-470. Again, Axelrad and Glick, in 1953, applying the prediction table to a

random sample of 100 boys committed•to the Hawthorne-Cedar Knolls School of the Jewish Board of Guardians, to which they were committed on delinquency petitions by the children's courts of New York City, also found that in 91 per cent of the group the delinquent behavior could have been predicted. See S. Axelrad and S. J. Glick, "Application of the Glueck Social Prediction Table to 100 Jewish Delinquent Boys," *The Jewish Social Quarterly,* Vol. 30, No. 2 (1953), pp. 127-136. For other validations, see Note 6, Chap. I.

2. See note 1.

3. Foreign birth of one or both parents (Table 68), domination of family affairs by mother (Table 87), scolding or threatening of boy by father (Table 106).

X

Common Ground of Criminogenesis

The focus of this work is on those traits and environmental pressures that exert a *differential* influence on the delinquency of the body types. Yet it has already become evident that certain traits and sociocultural factors do not have a varied effect. These must not be lost sight of in the *totality* of influences, internal and external, that exert sufficient pressure to impel certain boys to become persistent delinquents. It is obvious that these traits and factors, in combination with those affecting body types *varyingly,* determine which boys of each type are likely to become delinquent.

A word of explanation about these non-differentiative traits. Statistically speaking, the failure to find a significant variation in the difference in trait incidence between delinquents and non-delinquents of the various physique types does not necessarily rule out the actual existence of such variation; the situation as to such traits remains ambiguous.[1] But it does not seem probable, in the light of the statistical computations, that variance in etiologic association does in fact exist in the majority of traits in which a significant difference in impact was not found to exist.[2] Until studies are made on larger samples we may, then, tentatively accept the traits which have not shown significant variance in the extent of their association with the delinquency of the body types as constituting the "common ground" of etiology.

TRAITS

The 38 traits that are associated with delinquency but are *not* found to have a *significantly varied* effect on the delinquency of the body types are the following:[3]

Poor health in infancy (Table 1)
Enuresis in childhood (Table 4)
Absence of marked power of observation (Table 15)
Tendency to phantasy (Table 17)
Lack of common sense (Table 18)
Unmethodical approach to problems (Table 19)
Absence of potential capacity for objective interests (Table 20)
Social assertiveness (Table 21)
Defiance (Table 22)
Absence of marked submissiveness (Table 23)
Absence of enhanced feeling of insecurity (Table 25)
Absence of marked feeling of not being taken seriously (Table 28)
Absence of feeling of helplessness and powerlessness (Table 29)
Feeling of not being appreciated (Table 30)
Feeling of resentment (Table 32)
Hostility (Table 34)
Marked suspiciousness (Table 35)
Feeling of isolation (Table 37)
Defensive attitude (Table 38)
Narcissistic trends (Table 41)
Absence of masochistic trends (Table 43)
Emotional lability (Table 45)
Absence of self-control (Table 46)
Vivacity (Table 47)
Absence of compulsory trends (Table 48)
Preponderance of extroversive trends (Table 49)
Suggestibility (Table 52)
Stubbornness (Table 54)
Adventurousness (Table 55)
Uninhibited motor response to stimuli (Table 56)

Absence of aestheticism (Table 58)
Acquisitiveness (Table 60)
Absence of conventionality (Table 61)
Absence of self-criticism (Table 62)
Absence of conscientiousness (Table 63)
Absence of practicality (Table 64)
Absence of neuroticism (Table 66)
Psychopathy (Table 67)

The fact that the attitudes, feelings, and dynamisms reflected in these 38 traits, though related to delinquency, are not found to exert a significantly different criminogenic influence on one body type than on any others is of itself a noteworthy finding.

SOCIOCULTURAL FACTORS

What now of the sociocultural influences associated with delinquency but *not* found to have a *varied* impact on the body types? There are 24 such factors in the total of 42 studied:

Delinquency of father (Table 69)
Alcoholism of father (Table 70)
Serious physical ailment of father (Table 72)
Delinquency of mother (Table 73)
Alcoholism of mother (Table 74)
Emotional disturbance of mother (Table 75)
Serious physical ailment of mother (Table 76)
Financial dependence of family (Table 77)
Poor management of family income (Table 78)
Crowded home (Table 80)
Unclean or disorderly home (Table 81)
Frequent moving (Table 86)
Lack of self-respect in parents (Table 88)
Lack of ambition in parents (Table 89)
Lack of interest of parents in children's friends (Table 93)
Boy not a youngest, first-born, or only child (Table 96)
Father not attached to boy (Table 97)

Boy not attached to father (Table 100)
Father unacceptable to boy for emulation (Table 101)
Boy not attached to mother (Table 102)
Father physically punishes boy (Table 105)
Mother's discipline unsuitable (Table 107)
Mother physically punishes boy (Table 108)
Mother scolds or threatens boy (Table 109)

Significance of Common Ground of Criminogenesis

The fact that many striking traits and also numerous home and family pressures and provocations are at the bottom of delinquency of our group of boys, *irrespective of their body structure,* is as important to note as the fact that other traits and sociocultural influences play a *differential* role among the body types. This suggests that there may be an underlying combination of internal and external influences in delinquency so pervasive and potent as to transcend that of morphologic and temperamental-emotional *differences* between physique types. In the exciting, stimulating, uncontrolled, and culturally divisive milieu of the underprivileged urban area, this general admixture of attitudes, dynamisms, and home influences is obviously an unwholesome brew, whether for the muscular mesomorphs, the soft endomorphs, the fragile ectomorphs, or boys of the balanced type.

Without resort to psychoanalytic explanations of the bad effects of these non-differentiative internal and external pressures on the development of a strong but not tyrannical ego, a well-integrated, consistent, and not overly punishing conscience, and a satisfactory apparatus for sublimation of instinctual drives, it is obvious that the traits and family pressures assembled in this chapter, could in themselves largely account for the delinquency of the boys in question. Surely it is not surprising that there is a considerably greater likelihood that boys will get into trouble if they lack common sense; if they feel that they are not appreciated; if they are resentful, hostile, and markedly suspicious; if they are emotionally impulsive, extroversive, and suggestible; if they are stubborn, adventurous, and acquisitive; if they do not adhere to conventional patterns of thinking and acting; if they are not critical of themselves; if they are not conscientious; if they are impractical.

This syndrome of feelings, attitudes, and dynamic tendencies could in itself account for the delinquency of a large segment of the boys, even though some of them may have been more affected by certain elements in the mosaic of internal pressures than by others. But when to this system of internal influences the external are added— particularly those in the intimate and emotion-laden relations between parents and children—the reason for the delinquency of many of the boys becomes all the more apparent.

Again, therefore, without resort to psychoanalytic mechanisms (which must be left to the clinician), it is not surprising that many delinquents are boys who, irrespective of their body structure, become offenders against society as a result of a multiplicity of pathologic family pressures, among which are rearing by criminalistic and alcoholic parents, by emotionally disturbed (neurotic, psychopathic, or psychotic) mothers, by fathers who are not warmly attached to their sons and who are not acceptable to the youngsters as persons to emulate; in families lacking self-respect and ambition; by parents who are uninterested in their children's friends; in unattractive, unclean, disorderly homes; and in deprivation of close neighborhood ties, as the result of frequent moving of the family.

Yet with all this, a striking finding of *Unraveling Juvenile Delinquency* has yet to be explained; namely, that despite the original matching of each delinquent boy with a non-delinquent by ethnic derivation (among other bases of matching), 60 per cent of our delinquents proved, on anthropologic examination, to be *mesomorphs* as compared with 12 to 14 per cent of each of the other body types. (See Chap. 1, p. 9 of the present work.) Since the control group of non-delinquent mesomorphs was found to comprise only 30 per cent, the excessive proportion of mesomorphic delinquents cannot be attributed to an excess of boys of that physique type in the underprivileged urban population from which our samples were drawn. Actually, the proportion of ectomorphs in the non-delinquent control group (39.6%) proved to be greater than of mesomorphs (30.7%).

Part of the explanation must therefore rest in the selective operation of certain traits and sociocultural pressures on boys of the four body types.

It is to these *distinctive* influences as they make a pattern of differentiation of impact on the delinquency of boys of each physique type, especially on the mesomorphs (who, as we have learned, constitute the most numerous or "core type" among the delinquents), that we now turn our attention.

NOTES

1. Seven of these traits would appear from inspection to be differentially associated with the delinquency of the body types, but as the statistical findings are not definitive we have included them among the above 38: enuresis in childhood, tendency to phantasy, unmethodical approach to problems, defiance, absence of marked submissiveness, absence of self-control, and vivacity.

2. In a communication to the authors (March 17, 1955) John W. Tukey, Professor of Mathematics at Princeton, whose method of "multiple comparisons" is used in this inquiry, has commented regarding the traits and sociocultural factors that have not been found to vary in their impact on the delinquency of the body types that "it is not too likely" [that other investigators would, with data of comparable extent, find significant variations] "but is not to be excluded."

3. Among them are two—lack of ambition in parents and father physically punishes boy—which appear to be differentially associated with the delinquency of the body types, but, as was true of a few of the traits, the statistical findings are not definitive and must await evidence in other samples of cases.

XI

Mesomorphs and Delinquency

Having reviewed the traits and factors that underlie the delinquency of all our boys—irrespective of physique type—we are now ready to integrate by physique type those influences that play a special role in the delinquency of the various body types. We recognize the tentative nature of these conclusions pending a check against other samples.

This chapter is devoted to the mesomorphs who, because of their large proportion in the total of delinquents, may be deemed the "core" of the delinquent group. In arriving at this integration we will focus on (a) the traits that have been found to differentiate the non-delinquent mesomorphs from the other body types, these comprising what may be called, in one sense, their *delinquency potential;* (b) the traits that exert a special influence on the delinquency of the mesomorphs in contrast with the other body types; (c) the sociocultural factors that exert a special influence on the delinquency of the mesomorphs as compared with their effect on the delinquency of the other physique types.

This tripartite analysis will also be applied in the succeeding chapters dealing with endomorphs, ectomorphs, and the balanced type. Although the resultant portraits will necessarily be imperfect because of the limitations of the inquiry to a selected group of traits assembled originally for the more general purposes of *Unraveling*

Juvenile Delinquency without thought of a later breakdown of the data by body types, the findings should be at least suggestive concerning the implications of body structure in the prevention and control of juvenile delinquency.

TRAITS DISTINGUISHING MESOMORPHS FROM OTHER PHYSIQUE TYPES

Mesomorphy, says Sheldon, "means relative predominance of muscle, bone, and connective tissue. The mesomorphic physique is normally heavy, hard, and rectangular in outline. Bone and muscle are prominent and the skin is made thick by a heavy underlying connective tissue. The entire bodily economy is dominated, relatively, by tissues derived from the *mesodermal* embryonic layer."[1]

Exhibit 1.   TRAITS DISTINGUISHING NON-DELINQUENT MESOMORPHS
FROM OTHER PHYSIQUE TYPES

Table	Highest (H) or Lowest (L) as Compared with		
	Endo-morphs	Ecto-morphs	Balanced Type
2. Susceptibility to Contagion		L	
8. Tremors		L	
9. Genital Under-development	L	L	
10. Strength of Hand Grip	H	H	H
17. Tendency to Phantasy		L	L
21. Social Assertiveness	H		
23. Marked Submissiveness	L		
31. Fear of Failure and Defeat			H
36. Destructiveness		L	
44. Destructive-Sadistic Trends		L	
51. Sensitivity		L	L
53. Inadequacy		L	L
56. Uninhibited Motor Responses to Stimuli	H	H	H
57. Emotional Instability		L	
58. Aestheticism		L	
59. Sensuousness	L		
61. Conventionality	L	H	
64. Practicality		H	
65. Emotional Conflicts		L	

This description of the mesomorphic body type or norm suggests physical strength. Has evidence of this emerged from our inquiry?

As far as clinical indications permit, it is reasonable to infer that mesomorphs are in fact more vigorous than the other body types. This conclusion is based on the fact that, as compared with other physiques, mesomorphs are as a group found to have been less susceptible to contagion in childhood, less burdened by disorders of which tremors are symptomatic, have better developed genitals, and have more strength in their hands. Certain of their characteristics are, then, in accord with the underlying organismal pattern of this physique type.

Turning to psychologic traits (some derived from Rorschach Tests and some from psychiatric interviews), it is evident from Exhibit 1[2] that mesomorphic non-delinquents are strikingly different from one or more of the other physique types. They are less sensitive, less aesthetic, and less sensuous; they have less of a tendency to phantasy, suffer less from feelings of inadequacy, and are less destructive and destructive-sadistic. Further, they are more practical, more socially assertive, markedly less submissive to authority, and not as convention-bound as the endomorphs, but less so than the ectomorphs, and they are more fearful of failure and defeat than boys of balanced physique.

In dynamisms, mesomorphic non-delinquents as opposed to one or more of the other physique types are found to be less unstable emotionally, less burdened by emotional conflicts, and less inhibited in motor responses to stimuli (i.e., more likely to express their tensions in action rather than to bottle them up). In this latter regard they differ from all the other body types.

It should already be somewhat obvious that unless channeled toward socially acceptable goals, such traits might well furnish the strength, daring, and enterprise, together with the dynamic tendency to unrestrained action, that are involved in much delinquency, and may hence explain the high proportion of mesomorphs in our delinquent group. In brief, the mesomorphs apparently have a higher delinquency *potential* than the other body types.

Traits Contributing Selectively to Delinquency of Mesomorphs

The reader is reminded that a determination of the body types on which a particular trait has a greater delinquency-propelling force than on another was arrived at by comparing the quantum of difference in percentages of the incidence of a particular trait between the delinquents and the non-delinquents of each body type (by the method of multiple comparisons, described on pp. 33, 278–83).

There are in fact 9 traits in all among the 67 we studied that have been found to exert a greater influence on the delinquency of mesomorphs than on that of one or more of the other body types: susceptibility to contagion, low verbal intelligence, feeling of not

Exhibit 2. TRAITS CONTRIBUTING SELECTIVELY TO DELINQUENCY OF MESOMORPHS

Table	Highest (H) or Lowest (L) as Compared with		
	Endo-morphs	Ecto-morphs	Balanced Type
2. Susceptibility to Contagion		H	
3. Extreme Restlessness in Early Childhood		L	
6. Cyanosis	L		
7. Dermographia		L	
10. Strength of Hand Grip			L
11. Low Verbal Intelligence		H	
12. High Performance Intelligence	L		L
24. Ambivalence to Authority	L		
27. Feeling of Not Being Taken Care of	H	H	H
33. Good Surface Contact with Others	L		
36. Destructiveness		H	
40. Feeling of Being Able to Manage Own Life	L		
42. Receptive Trends			H
44. Destructive-Sadistic Trends		H	
53. Inadequacy		H	
57. Emotional Instability		H	
65. Emotional Conflicts		H	

being taken care of, destructiveness, destructive-sadistic trends, receptive trends, feelings of inadequacy, emotional instability, and emotional conflicts.

Exhibit 2 makes it evident at a glance that, in the considerable majority of instances, the greater impact of certain traits on the conduct of the sturdy mesomorphs contrasts most sharply with their lesser impact on the delinquency of the fragile ectomorphs. In fact, in only one trait—receptive trends (the more or less unconscious expectation that others—people, society, God—will take care of one)—is the contrast exclusively with another physique type, the balanced, while in the feeling of not being taken care of, it is with all three of the other body types.

Comparison of Exhibit 2 with Exhibit 1 reveals that six of the nine traits, though significantly *less* characteristic of *non-delinquent* mesomorphs than of one or more of the other body types (largely ectomorphs), emerge now as more markedly associated with the delinquency of mesomorphs. Susceptibility to the contagious diseases of childhood is one such trait. It constitutes more of a danger signal of delinquency when atypically occurring in mesomorphs than in ectomorphs. Destructiveness (the tendency to hurt, to destroy) and destructive-sadistic drives, both of which are likewise *less* character-istic of mesomorphic youngsters than of ectomorphs, are also more likely to result in antisocial behavior when occurring in mesomorphs than in ectomorphs. This is the case, too, as regards feelings of inadequacy, emotional instability, and emotional conflicts. All six traits are *less* characteristic of non-delinquent mesomorphs than of one or more of the other body types, notably of ectomorphs, yet exert a greater criminogenic influence.

A reasonable hypothesis to account for the excessive association of such traits with the delinquency of mesomorphs would appear to be that traits *atypical of this constitutional "host,"* when they do exist in mesomorphs, tend to bring about some sort of internal disharmony. This (together with traits that are generally crim-inogenic) leads reactively or indirectly to delinquency. Some such hypothesis is worthy of exploration on larger samples of cases of each physique type.

So much for the six traits that are atypical of the mesomorphic norm.

The greater involvement of the three remaining traits in the de-linquency of mesomorphs than in that of one or another body type, namely, low verbal intelligence, feeling of not being taken care of, and receptive (oral) trends, is less readily explained. These traits, unlike the six just described, are not found to vary in incidence among the body types of the non-delinquents despite their dominant criminogenic impact on the mesomorphs.

Expectedly, a defect of intellect (reflected in low verbal intelligence) is more likely to embroil in delinquency youngsters of the energetic, outlet-seeking body type than other boys.

As for the feeling of not being taken care of, this seems to have a more profound effect on delinquency among mesomorphs than on any other body type. This trait reflects a lack of active interest on the part of others (especially of parents) in situations in which the child feels himself entitled to such interest. It should be pointed out that this feeling plays far less of a role in the delinquency of all the other body types. Why it operates so heavily on mesomorphs we can only surmise. It seems reasonable to assume, however, that mesomorphs, who are normally energetic and dynamic, tend to seek active outlets for the tensions and frustrations that are engendered in them by the feeling of parental neglect.

Finally, as to receptive (oral) trends, the greater role of this trait in the delinquency of mesomorphs (as contrasted with boys of balanced physique) may be clarified if we remember that the expression of receptive trends as a typical mode of satisfaction reflects a more or less unconscious expectation that one will somehow be taken care of by others and therefore need not make any effort to assume responsibilities. This tendency, according to Schachtel (*Unraveling,* p. 235) may take a passive form or it may take a more active form leading to outwardly expressed greed or to attempts to secure the desired object without effort (stealing) or without assuming any obligations. It could reasonably be postulated that because of the great need of mesomorphs for energy outlets they are less likely to be passive than other boys not so endowed, and that receptive trends in this physique habitus are more likely to seek an *active* expression.

In connection with such speculative explanations of the impact of certain traits on the delinquency of a particular physique type, it must of course be borne in mind that persistent delinquency cannot be attributed to any single trait, be it one of ideation, attitude, feeling, or emotional mechanism. There is always an interplay of numerous influences in the misconduct of both the individual delinquent and of groups of delinquents. It is the piling up of such pressures to a degree where they over-balance the internal and external monitors and inhibitors of antisocial conduct which results in prohibited action. It must not be forgotten, further, that those traits which have not been found, by statistical computation, to exert a significantly diverse influence among the body types but which do significantly distinguish delinquents from non-delinquents as a

Exhibit 3.   DISTRIBUTION OF NINE TRAITS HAVING GREATER
DELINQUENCY INDUCING IMPACT ON MESOMORPHS

Number of Delinquency Inducing Traits Present	139 Delinquent Mesomorphs			70 Non-Delinquent Mesomorphs		
	Number	% of Total		Number	% of Total	
		Actual	Cumulative		Actual	Cumulative
9	0	0.00%	0.00%	0	0.00%	0.00%
8	3	2.16	2.16	0	0.00	0.00
7	11	7.91	10.07	0	0.00	0.00
6	27	19.42	29.49	1	1.43	1.43
5	40	28.78	58.27	4	5.71	7.14
4	23	16.55	74.82	8	11.43	18.57
3	18	12.95	87.77	13	18.57	37.14
2	7	5.04	92.81	17	24.29	61.43
1	8	5.75	98.56	11	15.71	77.14
0	2	1.44	100.00	16	22.86	100.00

whole, are also involved in the total dynamic interplay of organism and environment that results in delinquency.

It should be noted (Exhibit 3) that of the nine traits found to exert a significantly heavier criminogenic impact on mesomorphs than on one or another of the remaining physique types, four or more were found to be present in 75% of the delinquent mesomorphs in contrast with only 19% of the non-delinquent mesomorphs; and three or more of the traits characterize 88% of the delinquent mesomorphs as compared with 37% of the non-delinquent mesomorphs. Evidently, therefore, the greater effect of the traits in question on the delinquency of mesomorphs depends, ordinarily, on the cumulative impact of at least three traits.

Sociocultural Factors Contributing Selectively to Delinquency of Mesomorphs

Exhibit 4 again reveals the phenomenon previously noted of a sharp contrast between mesomorphs and ectomorphs, this time in respect to differences in the sociocultural forces that affect their behavior. Yet there is a striking difference; for while certain traits have an excessive influence on the delinquency of mesomorphs, the

Exhibit 4. SOCIOCULTURAL FACTORS CONTRIBUTING SELECTIVELY TO DELINQUENCY OF MESOMORPHS

Table	Highest (H) or Lowest (L) as Compared with		
	Endo-morphs	Ecto-morphs	Balanced Type
71. Emotional Disturbance in Father		L	
79. Gainful Employment of Mother		L	
82. Careless Household Routine	H		
83. Lack of Cultural Refinement in Home		L	
84. Broken Home		L	
85. Rearing by Parent Substitute		L	
90. Low Conduct Standards of Family		L	
91. Incompatibility of Parents		L	
92. Family Group Recreations Lacking	H		
94. Meager Recreational Facilities in Home	H		
95. Lack of Family Cohesiveness		L	
98. Mother Not Attached to Boy		L	
99. Siblings Not Attached to Boy		L	
103. Careless Supervision by Mother		L	

factors of home and family life have more of an effect on the antisocial behavior of ectomorphs than of mesomorphs.

Of the 42 sociocultural factors included in the present work, only three are found to have a greater influence on the delinquency of mesomorphs (in contrast to endomorphs only): careless household routine, lack of family group recreations, and meagerness of recreational facilities in the home. It seems reasonable to attribute this outcome to the fact that mesomorphs, who are usually of healthy, vigorous body build, and are dynamic and outgoing in their impulses, are more likely than other boys (especially endomorphs) to overreact to a lack of recreational facilities in disordered homes and, because of their greater vigor and energy, to seek adventure and recreation elsewhere.

It should be noted (Exhibit 5) that of the three sociocultural factors found to exert a significantly heavier criminogenic impact on mesomorphs than on one or another body type, at least two were present in 74% of the delinquent mesomorphs as contrasted with 39% of the non-delinquent mesomorphs.

But certain aspects of their home environment have *less* of an effect on the delinquency of mesomorphs than on that of ectomorphs (the fragile, sensitive body type): emotional disturbance in the father, working mothers, careless supervision of boy by mother, indifference or hostility of mothers and/or of brothers and sisters

Exhibit 5. DISTRIBUTION OF THREE SOCIOCULTURAL FACTORS HAVING GREATER IMPACT ON DELINQUENCY OF MESOMORPHS

Number of Delinquency Inducing Factors Present	289 Delinquent Mesomorphs			146 Non-Delinquent Mesomorphs		
	Number	% of Total		Number	% of Total	
		Actual	Cumulative		Actual	Cumulative
3	121	41.87%	41.87%	28	19.18%	19.18%
2	92	31.83	73.70	29	19.86	39.04
1	49	16.96	90.66	48	32.88	71.92
0	27	9.34	100.00	41	28.08	100.00

to the boy, lack of cultural refinement in the home, broken homes, rearing by substitute parents, low conduct standards in the family, quarrelsome parents, disharmony in the family group.

Clearly, these provocations to childhood anxiety and insecurity, with their resultant deprivation of affection and their building up of a feeling of isolation, do not exert nearly as potent an influence on mesomorphs as on ectomorphs. The more rugged constitution of mesomorphs and their generally hardier temperamental makeup are evidently powerful enough to withstand many of the assaults on emotional life which exert a more damaging influence on the fragile, sensitive overreactive ectomorphs.

MESOMORPHIC CONSTITUTION AND DELINQUENCY

In considering the evidence regarding the role of body structure in the delinquency of the predominantly mesomorphic physique, there is a permeative difficulty that must be kept in mind. Apart from the fact that the inquiry covers only a relatively modest number of traits and factors that are more or less involved in the totality of criminogenic influences, it should be pointed out that there is probably no exact point-to-point "stimulus-response" nexus between any particular criminogenic trait, or even small group of traits, and any specific sociocultural element or group of elements. It is the *total organism* in its morphologic, temperamental, and characterial aspects that is involved in the antisocial reaction of any physique type to a battery of external influences. Hence, not only the relatively few traits which have been found to have a *greater* association with the delinquency of mesomorphs than of one or more of the remaining physique types, but also the ones that are quite *uniformly* causal, and even the traits found to characterize the *"normal"* (i.e., the non-delinquent) mesomorphs must be taken into account in assessing the behavioral response of the predominantly mesomorphic type to the threats, tensions, and unwholesome provocations of home and family life.

It remains true, nevertheless, that our data permit of at least tentative answers to two questions: (a) How account for the finding in *Unraveling* that there is a 60 per cent incidence of mesomorphs among the delinquents in comparison with only 12-14 per cent of each of the other body types? (b) Why do some mesomorphs become delinquent, others not?

(a) Regarding the reason for the excess of mesomorphs among our delinquents, the current inquiry has revealed that this physique type is more highly characterized by traits particularly suitable to the commission of acts of aggression (physical strength, energy, insensitivity, the tendency to express tensions and frustrations in action), together with a relative freedom from such inhibitions to antisocial adventures as feelings of inadequacy, marked submissiveness to authority, emotional instability, and the like.

It must further be kept in mind that although recognizing the greater delinquency potential of mesomorphs, the admixture of the *uniformly* criminogenic ("common ground") traits with those affecting the physique types variously, may result in more widespread delinquency among mesomorphs than in other body types. For example, a trait such as adventurousness, when it occurs in boys of the strong, energetic, and uncontrolled mesomorphic physique, may well have more of a bearing on their behavior than when occurring in the less dynamic endomorph; emotional conflict may well have a different destiny in the dynamic mesomorph than in the sensitive but inhibited ectomorph.

(b) As for the question of which boys among mesomorphs actually become delinquent, the striking finding is that most of the traits that have a special impact on the delinquency of mesomorphs are *not usually typical of that physique*. It would seem reasonable to postulate that those mesomorphs in whom traits alien to the constitutional host are present are the ones more likely to be selected for delinquency. But in large measure, the uniformly criminogenic ("common ground") traits of course also exert an influence in selecting from among all mesomorphs those who will become delinquent, as they do in the case of the other physique types.

NOTES

1. W. H. Sheldon, *The Varieties of Human Physique* (New York: Harper & Brothers, 1940), p. 5.

2. The discussion in the text involves a clustering of more or less associated traits and hence does not follow the order of traits in the exhibit.

XII

Endomorphs and Delinquency

INTRODUCTORY

In the prior chapter we brought into focus the traits that distinguish the non-delinquent mesomorphs from one or another body type and also the traits and sociocultural factors that contribute selectively to the delinquency of the mesomorphs. As the mesomorphs have proven to be the "core type" among the delinquents, it is of major interest to determine how the other physique types compare with them.

TRAITS DISTINGUISHING ENDOMORPHS FROM OTHER PHYSIQUE TYPES

Unlike mesomorphy, in which there is an emphasis on bone and muscle, "*Endomorphy* means relative predominance of soft roundness throughout the various regions of the body. When endomorphy is dominant the digestive viscera are massive and tend relatively to dominate the bodily economy. The digestive viscera are derived principally from the *endodermal* embryonic layer."[1]

First of all, what evidence is there of difference between the "norm" of this body type and the mesomorphic?

As regards physical endowment, Exhibit 6 shows that genital underdevelopment is more characteristic of endomorphs than of mesomorphs; and that endomorphs do not have as much strength of hand as do mesomorphs.

As regards traits of temperament, endomorphs are found to be less socially assertive and more submissive to authority than mesomorphs. Further, they are more inhibited in motor responses to stimuli, that is, less likely than mesomorphs to resolve their tensions in action. Although endomorphs are more sensuous than mesomorphs (and than all the other body types) they are also more conventional in their ideas and behavior.

These distinguishing characteristics appear consistent with the soft, round endomorphic physique as opposed to the muscular, outgoing mesomorphic type and would seem to provide a lower delinquency *potential* among the endomorphs as contrasted with the mesomorphs.

Exhibit 6. TRAITS DISTINGUISHING NON-DELINQUENT ENDOMORPHS FROM OTHER PHYSIQUE TYPES

Table	Highest (H) or Lowest (L) as Compared with		
	Meso-morphs	Ecto-morphs	Balanced Type
2. Susceptibility to Contagion		L	
6. Cyanosis		L	
8. Tremors		L	
9. Genital Under-development	H		H
10. Strength of Hand Grip	L		
21. Social Assertiveness	L	L	L
23. Marked Submissiveness	H	H	
31. Fear of Failure and Defeat			H
36. Destructiveness		L	
39. Marked Dependence on Others			H
43. Masochistic Trends			H
44. Destructive-Sadistic Trends		L	
47. Vivacity		L	L
51. Sensitivity		L	L
56. Uninhibited Motor Responses to Stimuli	L		
57. Emotional Instability		L	
58. Aestheticism		L	
59. Sensuousness	H	H	H
60. Acquisitiveness		L	
61. Conventionality	H	H	H

The contrast in respect to some of these traits of the endomorphic norm is not only with mesomorphs but with other physique types. Thus they are, as a group, not only less well developed genitally than mesomorphs, but also than boys of balanced physique. Not only are they more markedly submissive to authority, more sensuous, and more conventional than mesomorphs, but, in these respects, they are likewise more so than ectomorphs. And it is to be especially noted that endomorphs are more sensuous and more conventional than boys of *all* the other body types.

It seems clear then that lesser energy, greater inhibition, greater submissiveness to authority, and a greater tendency to conventional modes of thinking and acting, are characteristics providing, at the outset, a lower *delinquency potential* among endomorphs than among mesomorphs.

Which traits are, however, in fact found to exert a special criminogenic impact on endomorphs in contrast with mesomorphs?

Traits Contributing Selectively to Delinquency of Endomorphs

Examination of Exhibit 7 reveals a significant difference in the impact of six characteristics on the delinquency of endomorphs as contrasted with mesomorphs: cyanosis, high performance intelligence, ambivalence to authority, feeling of being able to manage

Exhibit 7.   TRAITS CONTRIBUTING SELECTIVELY TO DELINQUENCY OF ENDOMORPHS

Table	Highest (H) or Lowest (L) as Compared with		
	Mesomorphs	Ectomorphs	Balanced Type
6. Cyanosis	H		
12. High Performance Intelligence	H		
24. Ambivalence to Authority	H		
27. Feeling of Not Being Taken Care of	L		
31. Fear of Failure and Defeat			L
33. Good Surface Contact with Others	H	H	
39. Marked Dependence on Others			L
40. Feeling of Being Able to Manage Own Life	H		

own life, good surface contact with others, feeling of not being taken care of.

In respect to cyanosis (impaired oxygenization of the blood probably reflecting some neurological imbalance), this condition occurring in endomorphs appears to constitute more of a danger signal of delinquency than when it exists in mesomorphs, despite the fact that endomorphs are not found to be normally (i.e., among non-delinquents) more cyanotic as a group than mesomorphs.

Regarding the ability to manipulate concrete things (high performance intelligence), this too has more of a bearing on the delinquency of endomorphs than of mesomorphs. It will be recalled from Chapter XI that, on the contrary, low verbal intelligence rather than high performance intelligence is more likely to embroil *mesomorphs* in delinquency.

As to temperamental and emotional traits, ambivalence to authority in endomorphs plays more of a role in their delinquent behavior than when it occurs in mesomorphs. This is true also of the feeling of being able to manage one's own affairs.

There is one other trait which exerts a greater influence on the

Exhibit 8. DISTRIBUTION OF FIVE TRAITS HAVING GREATER DELINQUENCY INDUCING IMPACT ON ENDOMORPHS

Number of Delinquency Inducing Traits Present	31 Delinquent Endomorphs			35 Non-Delinquent Endomorphs		
	Number	% of Total		Number	% of Total	
		Actual	Cumulative		Actual	Cumulative
5	4	12.90%	12.90%	0	0.00%	0.00%
4	11	35.48	48.38	4	11.43	11.43
3	6	19.35	67.73	10	28.57	40.00
2	8	25.81	93.54	13	37.14	77.14
1	1	3.23	96.77	7	20.00	97.14
0	1	3.23	100.00	1	2.86	100.00

delinquency of endomorphs than of mesomorphs—good surface contact with others.

However, the feeling of not being taken care of, has *less* of an influence on the delinquency of endomorphs than of mesomorphs.

Thus there are five traits which are found to exert an excessive influence on the delinquency of endomorphs as contrasted with mesomorphs. Of these (Exhibit 8), four or five are present in 48% of the *delinquent* endomorphs and 11% of the *non-delinquent* endomorphs; at least three in 68% of the delinquent endomorphs as compared with their presence in 40% of the non-delinquent endomorphs. Evidently, therefore, the criminogenic influence of the traits in question does not depend on the presence of any one trait but rather on the cumulative impact of at least three traits.

With one exception (cyanosis), the traits that have a distinctive bearing on the delinquency of endomorphs as contrasted with mesomorphs are not found to differ significantly in incidence among *non-delinquent* endomorphs and mesomorphs.

It is to be noted from Exhibits 2 and 7 that the traits which contribute selectively to the delinquency of the endomorphs are not the same as those which exert a special criminogenic influence on mesomorphs. Also, Exhibit 6 reveals that what might be called *temperamental disharmony* is less related to the delinquency of endomorphs than of mesomorphs.

SOCIOCULTURAL FACTORS CONTRIBUTING SELECTIVELY TO DELINQUENCY OF ENDOMORPHS AS CONTRASTED WITH MESOMORPHS

Consultation of Exhibit 9 strikingly reveals that, in contrast to the mesomorphs, on whom three factors of home and family exert a greater delinquency-inducing influence than they do on the endomorphs, not one of the sociocultural factors studied is found

Exhibit 9. SOCIOCULTURAL FACTORS CONTRIBUTING SELECTIVELY TO DELINQUENCY OF ENDOMORPHS

Table	Highest (H) or Lowest (L) as Compared with		
	Meso-morphs	Ecto-morphs	Balanced Type
79. Gainful Employment of Mother		L	
82. Careless Household Routine	L		
91. Incompatibility of Parents		L	
92. Family Group Recreations Lacking	L		
94. Meager Recreational Facilities in Home	L		
95. Lack of Family Cohesiveness		L	
99. Siblings Not Attached to Boy			H
104. Unsuitable Discipline by Father		L	

to have more influence on the delinquency of endomorphs than of mesomorphs. On the contrary, the fat, soft endomorphs *under-react* to certain unwholesome conditions in their home life which have a special influence on the delinquency of the mesomorphs: namely, a hit-or-miss routine in the household, absence of family group recreations, and insufficient provision of recreational opportunities in the home.

However, lack of attachment of brothers and sisters to them is more involved in the delinquency of endomorphs than of boys of balanced type. The reason for this is obscure. It may be speculated that the endomorphs are excessively in need of affection; and in seeking companionship to substitute for that denied by brothers and sisters, they are likely to get into trouble.

Endomorphic Constitution and Delinquency

What conclusions can be drawn from the foregoing analysis of traits and sociocultural factors having a special influence on the delinquency of endomorphs in contrast (largely) with mesomorphs?

As in the case of mesomorphs, it is not possible to arrive at definitive answers solely on the basis of the small number of traits found within the limitations of this inquiry to exert a special influence on the delinquency of endomorphs. The distinctive traits of the endomorphic *non-delinquents* must be taken into account, for these enter as *potentials* in the total dynamic system that ultimately determines the much lower incidence of delinquency among endomorphs than among mesomorphs. These endomorphic traits, as opposed to those present in the mesomorphic norm, would not appear to be useful in delinquent activity.

For example, the more marked tendency of endomorphs to submit to authority is inconsistent with the enterprise and daring required for so much of delinquent activity. Their greater tendency to conventional modes of thinking and behaving are bulwarks against antisocial activity. Their lesser assertiveness and lesser tendency to work off their emotional tensions in action would also account for the far lower participation of endomorphs than of mesomorphs in delinquent activity. While endomorphs are the most sensuous (self-indulgent) of all the physique types, this might at times impel them to theft for the satisfaction of appetites but is not consistent with the more dangerous delinquent escapades.

These traits are, in a nutshell, *not conducive to a career of criminalistic aggression*. They are better suited to one of law-abidingness. Endomorphs, in other words, have a *lower delinquency potential* than mesomorphs, who are typically energetic and outgoing.

It should be emphasized that this explanation is more in the nature of a reasonable hypothesis than a definitive conclusion, based as it necessarily is on incomplete evidence. There is enough probative value in it, however, to make it well worth pursuing further on a much larger sample of cases.

As for the traits that are found to have a distinctive bearing on the delinquency of endomorphs, they are not numerous—five in all; and they all play more of a role in the delinquency of endomorphs than of mesomorphs. But not one of the factors of home and family which exert a special impact on delinquency in other body types is especially involved in impelling endomorphs to delinquency as compared with mesomorphs. On the contrary, the three factors of home and family life which are influential in the delinquency of mesomorphs exert a distinctly *lesser* influence on the endomorphs.

In brief, the relatively low incidence of endomorphic delinquents in contrast with mesomorphic delinquents is attributable essentially to the characteristics that are typical of the soft, round, easy-going endomorphic norm and which by their very nature preclude excessive delinquency. It is rather to the traits and factors that furnish the "common ground" of delinquency-inducing influences described in Chapter X to which we must look for explanation of such delinquency as does exist among endomorphs.

NOTE

1. W. H. Sheldon, *The Varieties of Human Physique* (New York: Harper & Brothers, 1940), p. 5.

XIII

Ectomorphs and Delinquency

INTRODUCTORY

We turn now to the ectomorphs, whom we have already noted as contrasting most sharply with mesomorphs not only in their general characteristics, but in the traits and sociocultural factors that have a bearing on their delinquency. We are interested to throw light on why they constitute only 14.4% of the delinquent group as contrasted with 60.1% of mesomorphic delinquents.

TRAITS DISTINGUISHING ECTOMORPHS FROM OTHER PHYSIQUE TYPES

Ectomorphy has been defined as involving "relative predominance of linearity and fragility . . . In proportion to his mass, the ecto-morph has the greatest surface area and hence relatively the greatest sensory exposure to the outside world. Relative to his mass he also has the largest brain and central nervous system. In a sense, there-fore, his bodily economy is relatively dominated by tissues derived from the *ectodermal* embryonic layer."[1]

Such a fragile constitutional type would hardly be likely to have many traits shown to distinguish mesomorphs from other body types, but would on the contrary be likely to possess traits not generally associated with the robust, energetic mesomorphic type.

What picture of the normal (i.e., *non-delinquent*) ectomorphic body type emerges from the analysis of the tables?

In Exhibit 10 will be found not only significant contrasts in the characteristics of ectomorphs and mesomorphs but also between the ectomorphs and endomorphs and, to a far lesser extent, the balanced physique.

First, in regard to clinical findings, ectomorphs are as a group more likely to be subject to tremors than mesomorphs. They are more susceptible to the contagious diseases of childhood than all other body types. Their genitalia (like those of the endomorphs) are

Exhibit 10. TRAITS DISTINGUISHING NON-DELINQUENT ECTOMORPHS
FROM OTHER PHYSIQUE TYPES

Table	Highest (H) or Lowest (L) as Compared with		
	Meso-morphs	Endo-morphs	Balanced Type
2. Susceptibility to Contagion	H	H	H
6. Cyanosis		H	
8. Tremors	H	H	
9. Genital Under-development	H		
10. Strength of Hand Grip	L		
17. Tendency to Phantasy	H		
21. Social Assertiveness		H	
23. Marked Submissiveness		L	
31. Fear of Failure and Defeat			H
36. Destructiveness	H	H	
44. Destructive-Sadistic Trends	H	H	
47. Vivacity		H	
51. Sensitivity	H	H	
53. Inadequacy	H		
56. Uninhibited Motor Responses to Stimuli	L		
57. Emotional Instability	H	H	H
58. Aestheticism	H	H	
59. Sensuousness		L	H
60. Acquisitiveness		H	H
61. Conventionality	L	L	
64. Practicality	L		
65. Emotional Conflicts	H		H

less fully developed than those of mesomorphs. And (like the endomorphs) they do not as a group have as great strength of hand grip as mesomorphs.

So far, then, the picture suggests less physical sturdiness than in the mesomorphs.

The temperamental traits of the ectomorphic norm suggest a more delicately organized innate system than in mesomorphs. Thus, ectomorphs are more inclined to phantasy than mesomorphs; they are more sensitive and more aesthetic and have a greater tendency to feel inadequate than mesomorphs. They are less stable emotionally, not only than mesomorphs but than the other two physique types; and a greater proportion of them than of mesomorphs are prone to emotional conflict. Ectomorphs are, further, more inhibited in motor responses to stimuli, tending to "bottle up" their impulses instead of resolving their tensions in action as do the mesomorphs. Ectomorphs are less conventional in ideas and conduct than mesomorphs. As a group, ectomorphs are also more destructive and sadistic than mesomorphs. Finally, ectomorphs are not as practical as mesomorphs.

While the basic contrast is between ectomorphs and mesomorphs, secondary contrasts exist differentiating ectomorphs from endomorphs and from the balanced type.

As distinguished from *endomorphs*, ectomorphs are more susceptible to contagion, more cyanotic, and more prone to conditions of which tremors are symptomatic. Apart from these clinical signs, ectomorphs are psychologically different from endomorphs in that they are more sensitive and aesthetic and less sensuous. They are more destructive and sadistic. They are less stable emotionally. They are less conventional in their ideas and behavior than endomorphs and more acquisitive. Ectomorphs are more socially assertive and more vivacious than endomorphs and not as markedly submissive.

In contrast with the *balanced* type, ectomorphs are more susceptible to childhood contagions, more sensuous (albeit less so than endomorphs), more acquisitive, more unstable emotionally, more fearful of failure and defeat, and more prone to emotional conflicts.

The sketch of the non-delinquent ectomorphs reflects characteristics that contrast largely with those of mesomorphs and endomorphs. In the ectomorphic body type there appears to be less vitality, greater sensitivity and aestheticism; a greater tendency to emotional disturbance; greater acquisitiveness; less conventionality in ideas and behavior particularly in contrast with the mesomorphs. The general impression is gained of a *less smooth functioning and less well-integrated organism, one more susceptible to "the slings and arrows of outrageous fortune" and finding outlets for frustrations not in action but in internal emotional tension with resultant neurotic symptoms.* While there are only six traits that distinguish meso-morphs from one or another of the physique types, there are 17 which distinguish the ectomorphs from the others.

Certainly, *the traits that are more characteristic of the ectomorphic norm (non-delinquents) than of the mesomorphic are, by and large, not of a kind involving the vigor, daring, enterprise, and "acting out" of impulse necessary for adventures in delin-quency.* It may be concluded, therefore, that the *delinquency poten-tial* of the ectomorphic physique type is much lower than that of mesomorphs. This probably explains, in part, not only the lesser incidence of delinquency in this body type than in the mesomorphic, but also the finding in *Unraveling* that the ectomorphic is the only body type in which the proportion of delinquents was substantially *lower* than among the non-delinquent controls.

In the light of these findings we are ready to consider the syn-drome of traits that have in fact been found to exert a greater influence on the delinquency of ectomorphs than on that of other body types.

TRAITS CONTRIBUTING SELECTIVELY TO DELINQUENCY OF ECTOMORPHS

From Exhibit 11 it becomes evident that extreme restlessness in early childhood, when occurring in boys of ectomorphic physique, is more likely to be a forerunner of delinquency than when it occurs in mesomorphs. The same is true of the clinical sign of skin sensitivity (dermographia). These are the only two traits which contribute significantly more to the delinquency of ectomorphs than of mesomorphs. The physical conditions reflected in these two traits, together with the overly sensitive temperament of ectomorphs, ren-der them somehow especially vulnerable.

On the other hand, it is to be noted that, by and large, the traits that have a greater bearing on the delinquency of mesomorphs than on one or more of the other body types, have *less* to do with the delinquency of ectomorphs: namely, susceptibility to contagious diseases, low verbal intelligence, the feeling of not being taken care of, destructiveness, destructive-sadistic trends, feelings of inadequacy, emotional instability, emotional conflicts. With only two

Exhibit 11. TRAITS CONTRIBUTING SELECTIVELY TO DELINQUENCY OF ECTOMORPHS

Table	Highest (H) or Lowest (L) as Compared with		
	Meso-morphs	Endo-morphs	Balanced Type
2. Susceptibility to Contagion	L		L
3. Extreme Restlessness in Early Childhood	H		
7. Dermographia	H		
11. Low Verbal Intelligence	L		
27. Feeling of Not Being Taken Care of	L		
33. Good Surface Contact with Others		L	
36. Destructiveness	L		
42. Receptive Trends			H
44. Destructive-Sadistic Trends	L		
53. Inadequacy	L		
57. Emotional Instability	L		
59. Sensuousness			L
65. Emotional Conflicts	L		

exceptions (low verbal intelligence and feeling of not being taken care of) *ectomorphs as a group normally are more often than mesomorphs characterized by the very traits that contribute so heavily to the delinquency of mesomorphs.*

Turning now to a comparison of ectomorphs with endomorphs and boys of balanced type, despite the fact that ectomorphs differ as markedly from endomorphs (the soft, round physique) as from mesomorphs (the physique heavily endowed with bone and muscle), not one trait among the 67 studied is found to contribute significantly more to the delinquency of ectomorphs than of endomorphs. But receptive (oral) trends (a tendency often expressed in a more or less unconscious expectation that others—people, society, God—will take care of one) seem to have more of a part in the delinquency of ectomorphs than in that of boys of balanced type.

Of the three traits found to exert a greater criminogenic impact

on ectomorphs than on one or another body type (Exhibit 12)—
extreme restlessness in early childhood, dermographia, receptive
trends—two or three were present in 61% of the delinquent ectomorphs in contrast with 24% of the non-delinquent ectomorphs.

Exhibit 12. DISTRIBUTION OF THREE TRAITS HAVING GREATER
DELINQUENCY INDUCING IMPACT ON ECTOMORPHS

Number of Delinquency Inducing Traits Present	64 Delinquent Ectomorphs			168 Non-Delinquent Ectomorphs		
	Number	% of Total		Number	% of Total	
		Actual	Cumula-tive		Actual	Cumula-tive
3	9	14.06%	14.06%	4	2.38%	2.38%
2	30	46.88	60.94	37	22.02	24.40
1	20	31.25	92.19	89	52.98	77.38
0	5	7.81	100.00	38	22.62	100.00

SOCIOCULTURAL FACTORS CONTRIBUTING SELECTIVELY TO DELINQUENCY OF ECTOMORPHS

Turning to the criminogenic influence on ectomorphs of what
must be regarded as unfavorable environmental conditions (largely
in home and family life), it becomes strikingly clear from Exhibit
13 that *overreactivity* is the keynote to the antisocial response of
this more fragile and sensitive physique type to unfavorable family
conditions, in contrast, largely, with the lesser effect of these same
circumstances and conditions on the delinquency of mesomorphs.

Exhibit 13. SOCIOCULTURAL FACTORS CONTRIBUTING SELECTIVELY
TO DELINQUENCY OF ECTOMORPHS

Table	Highest (H) or Lowest (L) as Compared with		
	Meso-morphs	Endo-morphs	Balanced Type
71. Emotional Disturbance in Father	H		
79. Gainful Employment of Mother	H	H	
83. Lack of Cultural Refinement in Home	H		
84. Broken Home	H		
85. Rearing by Parent Substitute	H		
90. Low Conduct Standards of Family	H		H
91. Incompatability of Parents	H	H	H
95. Lack of Family Cohesiveness	H	H	
98. Mother Not Attached to Boy	H		
99. Siblings Not Attached to Boy	H		H
103. Careless Supervision by Mother	H		
104. Unsuitable Discipline by Father		H	

All but three of the fifteen factors that have been found to have a varied influence on the delinquency of boys of the four body types exert a selective criminogenic impact on ectomorphs largely in contrast with their significantly *lesser* involvement in the delinquency of mesomorphs.

Thus, ectomorphs are more likely than mesomorphs to become delinquent if they are the sons of emotionally disturbed fathers and/or working mothers, of mothers who give them little personal supervision; if they are reared in homes lacking cultural refinement and in which the conduct standards are low; if they have grossly incompatible parents; if they belong to families not unified in deed and spirit; if they are deprived of warm affection from their mothers and brothers and sisters; if their homes are broken by death, separation, or desertion of parents; if they are reared by parent substitutes.

All such unwholesome influences of hearth and home are more likely to be conducive to delinquency in the more delicately structured ectomorphs than in the sturdier mesomorphs.

Apart from this major contrast, the ectomorphs were also found to respond differently than the endomorphs to certain potentially injurious home influences. Ectomorphs are evidently more likely to become delinquents than are endomorphs if subjected to paternal discipline which is not firm and kindly; and they have a greater tendency to misbehavior than endomorphs (and mesomorphs) if their mothers work, if they are reared in discordant homes, and if they are reared by parents who are not well mated.

Ectomorphs are also more prone to delinquency than boys of balanced physique if reared in families of low conduct standards, by parents who are incompatible, and when surrounded by sisters and brothers who are not attached to them.

Of the twelve sociocultural factors exerting a greater influence on the delinquency of ectomorphs than on one or another body type (Exhibit 14), it is to be noted that at least seven were present among 83% of the delinquents as contrasted with 15% of the non-delinquents.

Exhibit 14. DISTRIBUTION OF TWELVE SOCIOCULTURAL FACTORS HAVING
GREATER IMPACT ON DELINQUENCY OF ECTOMORPHS

Number of Delinquency Inducing Factors Present	58 Delinquent Ectomorphs			141 Non-Delinquent Ectomorphs		
	Number	% of Total		Number	% of Total	
		Actual	Cumulative		Actual	Cumulative
12	2	3.45%	3.45%	0	0.00%	0.00%
11	6	10.34	13.79	0	0.00	0.00
10	7	12.07	25.86	1	0.71	0.71
9	17	29.31	55.17	2	1.42	2.13
8	6	10.34	65.51	8	5.67	7.80
7	10	17.24	82.75	10	7.09	14.89
6	5	8.62	91.37	15	10.64	25.53
5	3	5.17	96.54	16	11.35	36.88
4	1	1.73	98.27	7	4.96	41.84
3	1	1.73	100.00	19	13.47	55.31
2				30	21.28	76.59
1				28	19.86	96.45
0				5	3.55	100.00

ECTOMORPHIC CONSTITUTION AND DELINQUENCY

Despite the heavier impact on their delinquency of unwholesome influences of home and family life, only 14% of the delinquents were of ectomorphic physique as contrasted with 60% of the mesomorphic body type. A reasonable explanation of this is *a greater deficiency among ectomorphs generally of energy, drive, and outflowing motor tendency, coupled with an excess of such curbing traits as a tendency to phantasy, emotional instability, emotional conflict, and feelings of inadequacy.* The basic finding appears to be that the traits of the ectomorph naturally tend to a bottling up of aggressive impulse, while the traits of the mesomorph naturally tend to an acting out of impulse. However, the *overreactivity in terms of delinquent behavior of the ectomorphic physique type to the pressures and tensions of family life is a major finding of the analysis, made intelligible by the basic constitutional makeup, especially the sensitivity, of this body type which renders it especially vulnerable to environmental influences.*

NOTE

1. W. H. Sheldon, *The Varieties of Human Physique* (New York: Harper & Brothers, 1940), pp. 5-6.

XIV

Balanced Type and Delinquency

INTRODUCTORY

We have completed a description of the mesomorphs, endomorphs, and ectomorphs and turn now to the balanced physique which comprises about equal elements of all three body structures. Delinquents of this body type encompass 13.5% of our delinquent group.

TRAITS DISTINGUISHING BALANCED TYPE FROM OTHER PHYSIQUE TYPES

The balanced physique type is assessed by anthropologists as having a "mid-range physical endowment in which none of the three traits assumes dominance over the other two in any marked degree."[1] Because of this we shall depart from our usual practice of first comparing the "norm" of each body type with the mesomorphs, but will rather compare the balanced physique with all the other body types.

Exhibit 15 shows that in respect to indicia of physical health, boys of the balanced type do not have as strong a hand grip as mesomorphs; they are less susceptible to contagion than ectomorphs; they have better genital development than endomorphs.

As regards traits of temperament, boys of balanced type have a greater tendency to phantasy than mesomorphs; they are more sensitive than both mesomorphs and endomorphs, and feel less adequate than do mesomorphs. They are less likely to seek outlets for their tensions in action than are mesomorphs. Boys of balanced type are more assertive socially than endomorphs, less dependent on others and less self-punishing (masochistic). They are also more vivacious (lively) than endomorphs. Boys of balanced type are less conventional in their attitudes and behavior than endomorphs.

In contrast with ectomorphs, boys of balanced type are more stable emotionally and tend less than ectomorphs to have emotional conflicts. They are not as sensuous as either ectomorphs or endomorphs, and they are not as acquisitive as ectomorphs.

Exhibit 15.   TRAITS DISTINGUISHING NON-DELINQUENTS OF THE BALANCED TYPE FROM OTHER PHYSIQUE TYPES

Table	Highest (H) or Lowest (L) as Compared with		
	Meso-morphs	Endo-morphs	Ecto-morphs
2. Susceptibility to Contagion			L
9. Genital Under-development		L	
10. Strength of Hand Grip	L		
17. Tendency to Phantasy	H		
21. Social Assertiveness		H	
31. Fear of Failure and Defeat	L	L	L
39. Marked Dependence on Others		L	
43. Masochistic Trends		L	
47. Vivacity		H	
51. Sensitivity	H	H	
53. Inadequacy	H		
56. Uninhibited Motor Responses to Stimuli	L		
57. Emotional Instability			L
59. Sensuousness		L	L
60. Acquisitiveness			L
61. Conventionality		L	
65. Emotional Conflicts			L

It is to be especially noted, however, that they are less fearful of failure and defeat than all the other physique types, this being the only trait in which the balanced physique contrasts with all the others.

We certainly do not get as clear a picture of the balanced type or of its delinquency potential as in the case of the other body types. This is probably attributable to the nature of this physique which is poised, as it were, in the middle of three more or less conflicting constitutional tendencies.

TRAITS CONTRIBUTING SELECTIVELY TO DELINQUENCY
OF BALANCED PHYSIQUE

There are six traits in all (see Exhibit 16) that have a significantly *greater* impact on the delinquency of boys of balanced physique than on that of one or another body type: susceptibility to contagion, strong hand grip, high performance intelligence, fear of failure and defeat, marked dependence on others, and sensuousness. There are two traits that are *less* influential in the delinquency of boys of

Exhibit 16. TRAITS CONTRIBUTING SELECTIVELY TO DELINQUENCY
OF THE BALANCED TYPE

Table	Highest (H) or Lowest (L) as Compared with		
	Meso-morphs	Endo-morphs	Ecto-morphs
2. Susceptibility to Contagion			H
10. Strength of Hand Grip	H		
12. High Performance Intelligence	H		
27. Feeling of Not Being Taken Care of	L		
31. Fear of Failure and Defeat		H	
39. Marked Dependence on Others		H	
42. Receptive Trends	L		L
59. Sensuousness			H

balanced physique than among one or more of the other body types: feeling of not being taken care of and receptive trends.

In contrast with *mesomorphs*, only four traits among the 20 that were found to exert a varied influence on the delinquency of one or another body type contribute selectively (excessively or in lesser degree) to the delinquency of boys of balanced type.

Strength of hand grip is more markedly involved in the delinquency of boys of balanced physique than in that of mesomorphs (who, normally, i.e., among non-delinquents, have a stronger hand grip than boys of all other body types). High performance intelligence when existing in boys of balanced type has more of a bearing on their delinquency than when it occurs in mesomorphs (in this regard they are like the endomorphs).

The feeling of not being taken care of has *less* of an influence on the delinquency of boys of balanced type than when it occurs in boys of predominantly mesomorphic physique (in this regard they are also like the endomorphs and the ectomorphs). Receptive (oral) trends in boys of this body type have *less* to do with their being delinquent than when they occur in mesomorphs.

As contrasted with *endomorphs,* only two traits have more of a bearing on the delinquency of boys of balanced type—fear of failure and defeat and marked dependence on others.

Exhibit 17. DISTRIBUTION OF SIX TRAITS HAVING GREATER DELINQUENCY INDUCING IMPACT ON BOYS OF BALANCED TYPE

Number of Delinquency Inducing Traits Present	53 Delinquents of Balanced Type			58 Non-Delinquents of Balanced Type		
	Number	% of Total		Number	% of Total	
		Actual	Cumula-tive		Actual	Cumula-tive
6	0	0.00%	0.00%	0	0.00%	0.00%
5	0	0.00	0.00	0	0.00	0.00
4	6	11.32	11.32	1	1.73	1.73
3	17	32.08	43.40	14	24.14	25.87
2	18	33.96	77.36	22	37.93	63.80
1	8	15.09	92.45	15	25.86	89.66
0	4	7.55	100.00	6	10.34	100.00

As contrasted with *ectomorphs,* susceptibility to contagion and sensuousness have more to do with the delinquency of boys of balanced physique, while receptive (oral) trends have *less* of a bearing on their delinquency.

At least three of the six traits which impel the balanced type to delinquency (Exhibit 17) were present in 43% of the delinquents as contrasted with 26% of the non-delinquents. One or two such traits in a boy of balanced physique do not exert a sufficient delinquency-inducing pressure, since 64% of boys of balanced type who remained non-delinquent had one or two such traits as contrasted with 77% of those who became delinquent.

SOCIOCULTURAL FACTORS CONTRIBUTING SELECTIVELY TO DELINQUENCY OF BALANCED TYPE

It will immediately be noted from Exhibit 18 that not one factor was found to exert a greater influence on the delinquency of the balanced type as contrasted with the mesomorphs. In the few differentiative factors involved, their special impact on the delinquency of boys of balanced type is rather in contrast with endomorphs and ectomorphs.

Indifference or hostility of brothers and sisters to boys of balanced type has less to do with their delinquency than it does with that of endomorphs. And boys of balanced type are less likely than ecto-

Exhibit 18. SOCIOCULTURAL FACTORS CONTRIBUTING SELECTIVELY TO DELINQUENCY OF THE BALANCED TYPE

Table	Highest (H) or Lowest (L) as Compared with		
	Meso-morphs	Endo-morphs	Ecto-morphs
90. Low Conduct Standards of Family			L
91. Incompatibility of Parents			L
99. Siblings Not Attached to Boy		L	L

morphs to become delinquent if reared in homes in which the conduct standards are low, the parents constantly bickering, and brothers and sisters are not attached to the boy.

BALANCED CONSTITUTION AND DELINQUENCY

It is impossible to discern any consistent pattern of special criminogenic involvement either in the traits or in the sociocultural influences involving the balanced type.

The considerably lower incidence of delinquents of the balanced constitution than of mesomorphic delinquents may be attributable to the relative scarcity of this physique type in the general population from which our samples were drawn and/or to their lower criminalistic potential, as indicated, for example, by such traits as their greater sensitivity, greater feeling of inadequacy, and lesser tendency to seek outlets for emotional tension in action than is characteristic of mesomorphs.

We have now indicated the main features of each of the body types as they relate to delinquency. What is the relevancy of these differentiative characteristics to the prevention and treatment of delinquent conduct?

Some hints on this score are given in the next chapter.

NOTE

1. *Unraveling*, p. 342.

XV

Physique and the Management of Juvenile Delinquency

INTRODUCTORY

What do our findings suggest regarding the more effective management of juvenile delinquency? Incomplete as are the data of this analysis, there is certainly evidence that differences in bodily morphology are not only implicated in the genesis of delinquency, but must also be taken into account in its management. Although it is quite apparent that physique alone does not adequately explain delinquent behavior, it is nevertheless clear that, in conjunction with other forces, it does bear a relationship to delinquency.

The current inquiry has led us to three major conclusions:

(1) The basic morphologic differentiation of the physique types is accompanied by differences in the incidence among them of certain traits, some of which are actually associated with delinquency, others potentially so.

(2) Differences in the physical and temperamental structure of body types bring about some variation in their response to environmental pressures.

(3) Differences in the incidence of certain traits among the physique types, as well as divergences in their reactions to the environment, are reflected in certain differences in the etiology of delinquency among the body types.

Thus, even if other researchers should confirm our finding that

60 per cent of delinquents (at least in disorganized urban areas) are of the mesomorphic body type, thereby suggesting a focus in prophylactic and therapeutic endeavors on the mesomorphs in the child population, the special characteristics of the other physique types point to the need of some *diversity* of approach to the prevention and treatment of antisocial behavior in boys of different body structures. There is enough evidence of differences in clusters of traits and sociocultural factors that have a selective influence on the delinquency of the body types to warrant taking into account variations in bodily structure in the planning of general programs of prevention and control and in applying therapeutic measures for the individualized treatment of delinquents.

Need for New Approaches

There are no nostrums or "pink pills" that will "cure" delinquency; nor, from the fact of the multiplicity and complexity of the influences that have been shown to be involved, can there be any general prophylactic agent which will prevent delinquency, as the stamping out of mosquito-breeding swamps will prevent malaria. The task of coping with antisocial behavior not only has many ramifications but is dependent on fields of science in which knowledge is as yet very imperfect, and involves almost all our social institutions.

We must move forward, however, because there is no assurance that the methods now employed in coping with delinquency either curb or "cure" it in substantial measure. Individual counseling, supportive psychotherapy, psychoanalysis, hypnoanalysis, chemotherapy, group therapy, play therapy, psychodrama, and family case work have not been adequately tested to evaluate their effectiveness; but there is already evidence to suggest that, by and large, many of the measures in use have not as yet produced sufficiently encouraging results in the very difficult task of rebuilding character.[1] A crying need is for carefully designed experiments directed toward improving existing practices and toward the discovery of new methods of prophylaxis and therapy; and in this connection certain ideas arising out of the current inquiry may be helpful.

There are four major areas in which efforts in the direction of better management of delinquency are suggested by the present work: (a) *Family Life,* (b) *Schooling,* (c) *Use of Leisure,* and (d) *Clinical Practices.*

Before offering a few suggestions (intended merely as illustrative of how application of the knowledge gleaned in this inquiry might be relevant to the prevention and treatment of juvenile delinquency), it will help if we keep in mind a condensed formulation of the most distinguishing features of each body type as determined in this inquiry:

Mesomorphs (the bone-and-muscle physique) present a portrait of an essentially sturdy physical and nervous and emotional structure, with a tendency to express impulse in action.

Endomorphs (the soft, round physique) are less sturdy, less energetic, and less dynamic than the mesomorphs, and are more inhibited and conventional in their ideas and behavior.

Ectomorphs (linear, fragile body type) have less sturdiness and are more delicately organized than mesomorphs and present a more sensitive and aesthetic exterior to the world. They are more tense, inhibited, and conflict-ridden, bottling up their impulses and their destructive-sadistic trends.

Balanced physique. The only trait found to distinguish boys of this body type from all the others is that they are less fearful of failure and defeat. Otherwise, a clear picture does not emerge. They appear to have some characteristics of each physique.

It is the personality as a whole that is involved in behavior, not independent and dissociated fragments. Therefore suggestions regarding the management of delinquency should take account of bodily morphology with special reference to those traits found in the present work to yield a varied delinquency *potential* to each of the physique types, those traits and sociocultural factors demonstrated to exert an *excessive* criminogenic impact on one or another of the body types, and those traits and sociocultural influences which, although not shown to vary in impact on the physique types, are nevertheless criminogenic (see Chapters XI, XII, XIII, XIV).

Family ·Life

A striking finding from the current inquiry is the considerable association to the delinquency of *ectomorphs* of such adverse conditions as absence of the mother from the home, careless personal oversight of the boy by the mother, indifference or hostility of mother and siblings to boy, emotional illness of father, unsuitable discipline of boy by father, incompatibility of parents, disunited families, families having low standards of behavior, homes lacking in cultural refinement, broken homes, rearing by parent substitutes.

On the basis of this knowledge, preventive and rehabilitative efforts can be improved, for example, by a recognition of the excessive effect on *ectomorphs* of deprivation of a confidence-inspiring father figure, so necessary for the achievement of integration and a balanced attitude toward authority. Although this is a serious handicap to any boy, it is even more crucial to ectomorphic youngsters, probably because this sensitive physique type requires more reassurance of love and security than, say, the mesomorphs. In handling ectomorphs who are potential delinquents or already frankly delinquent, it may, for example, be even more necessary than in the case of other body types to include their parents in psychotherapy, teaching them what is involved from a mental hygiene point of view in their attitudes and practices, and, if necessary, even to provide parental adjuncts whom nature has endowed with therapeutic personalities.[2]

In respect to the delinquency of *mesomorphs,* on the other hand, we have found that growing up in disorderly households where family group recreations are lacking and play facilities are meager has a greater bearing on the delinquency of mesomorphs than on other body types. In dealing with mesomorphic boys, therefore, stress has to be placed on means of making their homes less expulsive and of providing vigorous, exciting, but socially acceptable, avenues of recreation for them in order to forfend antisocial escapades to which boys of this body build might otherwise be attracted in seeking outlets for their natural vigor and dynamism.

As regards *endomorphs,* the *lesser* influence on their delinquency than on that of the other body types of such conditions as careless household routine, working mother, incompatibility of parents, lack of family group recreations, meager recreational facilities in the home, might well be kept in mind in order to avoid a stress on conditions and influences that do not have too great a bearing on the delinquency of endomorphs. The only aspect of the family life of endomorphs (within the compass of the present inquiry) that appears to have a *greater* association with their delinquency (in contrast with boys of balanced type) is a lack of a close attachment to them of the other children in the family. This would seem to suggest that they are in particular need of warmth and affection from their peers. On the whole, in dealing with pre-delinquent or delinquent *endomorphs*, those sociocultural factors that were found to be *generally* criminogenic (see Chapter X, "Common Ground of Criminogenesis") are the ones to which attention must be largely directed.

As is true of endomorphs, so of boys of *balanced type*, the sociocultural factors that are generally criminogenic must be taken into account in dealing with them, since there is evidence that some of the factors that have a special bearing on the delinquency of one or more of the other physique types exert *less* of an influence on the delinquency of boys of balanced type (low conduct standards in the family, incompatibility of parents, and lack of attachment of brothers and sisters).

These few suggestions are meant only as illustrations of the need for sharpening preventive and therapeutic efforts in the light of the special needs of each physique type.

However, in keeping in mind the special needs of boys of the different physiques, we must not overlook the pervasive criminogenic influences that have a similar impact on all the body types and the general preventive measures which they suggest. Many crucial differences were found in *Unraveling* between the family life of the delinquents and non-delinquents which call for constructive efforts to improve family life. Since, in *Unraveling Juvenile Delinquency*[3] and *Delinquents in the Making*[4], we have already discussed their implications for the management of juvenile delinquency, there is no need to repeat them here, except to re-emphasize that little progress can be expected in the prevention of delinquency until family life is strengthened and enriched by a large-scale, continuous, and pervasive program designed to bring to bear all the resources of mental hygiene, social work, education, and religious and ethical instruction upon the cradle of character, the home. Experimentation must be directed to the discovery of means to break the vicious circle of character-damaging influences on children exerted by parents who are themselves the distorted personality products of pathogenic parental influences. A tremendous multiplication of psychiatric, social, pastoral, and educational resources to improve the basic equipment of present and prospective parents for assumption of a wholesome parental role is indispensable to the control of delinquency.

SCHOOLING

What do the findings of the current inquiry suggest as regards the need for reorienting school programs to meet the special needs of boys of the different body types? The facts derived from *Unraveling Juvenile Delinquency*[5] suggest that emotional disturbance rather than intellectual deficiency is the fundamental root of maladaptation to school life, expressing itself in a disharmony of relationship between the boy and the small society of the school which often continues into the larger society whose code is the law. Because of the early age of onset of delinquency, it becomes clear that the school stands in the front line of a community-wide attack on antisocial behavior, especially in the opportunity for its early recognition.

Our current findings suggest a need for (a) some re-emphasis in teacher training programs; (b) adaptation of school curricula to meet the special needs of youngsters of the different body types; and (c) experimentation with screening devices that take into account the variations in the influence of certain traits and sociocultural factors on the development of antisocial behavior in the different body types.

Training of Teachers. It would seem of value to create an aware-ness in teachers and school counselors of fundamental divergencies in the temperamental equipment of children of the various body types. For example, because of the excessive sensitivity of *ectomorphs,* teachers and counselors might unwittingly cause particular damage to them unless alerted to the special needs of children of this phy-sique and temperament. Because of the pathologic parent-child re-lationships prevailing in most families of delinquents, such young-sters have difficulty in finding in their own fathers an affectionate, sympathetic, and understanding adult around whom to weave the ideals, values, and standards of behavior that are incorporated in them through identification with and emulation of parents—a proc-ess that is at the core of character and of respect for authority.

We have elsewhere suggested that perhaps young adult male teachers are needed in greater numbers, even in the kindergarten and early grades; perhaps husband-wife teams of teachers would provide a more natural and warm emotional climate in the classroom.[6]

Adaptation of Curricula. In the light of differences in the charac-teristics of boys of the various body types and of their selective re-sponse to certain delinquency-inducing sociocultural influences, it becomes evident that forcing all types of children into a single academic mold is likely to result in increased tension, frustration, and revolt. To cite but a few of the traits in which each of the body types differs from one or more of the others (see Chapters XI, XII, XIII, XIV), the need for diversification of school activity is sug-gested by the strength and uninhibited motor response to stimuli of mesomorphs; the greater submissiveness, sensuousness, and con-ventionality of endomorphs; the greater aestheticism, feeling of in-adequacy, and emotional instability of ectomorphs. If the school is to function in the network of crime preventive agencies, obviously a broader range of curricula must be devised to enlist the interest and take into account the distinctive needs of boys of the various body types.

As regards the management of boys already delinquent, the flexibility of school programs is also important. For example (see Exhibit 19), although delinquents in general are far more behind grade for their age than non-delinquents, *mesomorphic* delinquents are found to be clearly more so than delinquents of balanced type and probably than endomorphs; and although many delinquents want to leave school as early as possible, *mesomorphs* are found to be much more eager to do so than endomorphs or ectomorphs.

Exhibit 19. SCHOOL HISTORY OF DELINQUENTS

Percentages of the Respective Physique Type Totals

	Wants to Leave School		Two or More Years Retarded	
	Number	%	Number	%
Total	206	43.2%	202	. 40.8%
Mesomorphs	144	50.0	135	45.1
Endomorphs	16	28.1	18	30.5
Ectomorphs	19	27.9	30	42.2
Balanced	27	42.2	19	28.8
Significance of Differences between Physique Types				
Meso-Endo	.05		–	
Meso-Ecto	.02		–	
Meso-Balanced	–		.05	
Endo-Ecto	–		–	
Endo-Balanced	–		–	
Ecto-Balanced	–		–	

More intensive study of other aspects of school activities would no doubt disclose other distinctive inclinations and needs of the different physique types.

Screening of Delinquents. The importance of identifying predelinquents before they are fully embarked on delinquent careers is gaining recognition. In the application of screening devices the school is in the "front line," because, by and large, it is in a position to reach all children before maladapted behavior expresses itself overtly or, if already in evidence, before it becomes too deeply rooted. A prime need therefore is to distinguish at school entrance between those children who are headed for delinquency and those who are not likely to embark on criminal careers; and also to distinguish true forerunners of delinquency from merely transient phenomena of healthy experimentation with reality. Bits of maladapted behavior during the first few years of life are not necessarily symptomatic of future delinquency.

Our pioneer effort in the construction of three screening devices[7] and several validations of one of them[8] encourages us to recommend experimentation with such instrumentalities as a basis for a wide and comprehensive prophylactic attack on the growing scourge of juvenile delinquency. It therefore becomes pertinent to raise the question as to whether, and how, the newly established dimension of physique type in the patterning of delinquency modifies and/or enhances the development and usefulness of screening devices.

How does the knowledge gained in the current inquiry regarding the role of physique in delinquency assist, if at all, in identifying pre-delinquents? Examination of the traits found in *Unraveling Juvenile Delinquency* to be highly associated with delinquency reveals that by and large these do not vary significantly in their impact on the delinquency of the body types. In the screening device based on the five traits of character structure derived from the *Rorschach Test*—social assertiveness, defiance, suspiciousness, destructiveness, and emotional lability—only *destructiveness* varies in association with the delinquency of the physique types, being much more criminogenic when occurring in mesomorphs than in ectomorphs. Of the five traits of temperament based on *psychiatric findings*—adventurousness, extroversiveness, suggestibility, stubbornness, and emotional instability—only *emotional instability* varies in its influence on the delinquency of the physique types, it also being more likely to result in delinquency when occurring in mesomorphs than in ectomorphs.

In contrast to these findings, however, of the five *sociocultural* factors in *Unraveling* which comprise a screening device for distinguishing pre-delinquents from non-delinquents—discipline of boy by father, supervision of boy by mother, affection of father for boy, affection of mother for boy, and family cohesiveness—only one, *lack of affection of father for boy,* was *not* found in the present inquiry to be more largely associated with the delinquency of one body type than of the others. It is to be noted that all four of the sociocultural factors which do play a selective role in the delinquency of the body types have more to do with impelling *ectomorphs* to delinquency than mesomorphs and/or endomorphs (see Tables 95, 98, 103, and 104).

Thus it will be seen that the efficacy of the first two of the three screening devices developed in connection with *Unraveling* is largely independent of body build, but that the third table would appear to have an even *greater* prognostic power in the case of ectomorphic boys than when applied to boys irrespective of body build.

Although the above findings point to the likelihood of enhancing even further the usefulness of the screening instrumentality as regards boys of ectomorphic physique beyond its already quite satisfactory power, there would appear to be no particular urgency for this,[9] especially in view of the fact that the added problem of somatotyping children as a preliminary to screening them for their delinquency potential might discourage its use. However, once a predelinquent has been identified, the additional knowledge that certain sociocultural factors exert an even more harmful influence on ectomorphs than on other body types should serve to diversify prophylactic and therapeutic efforts in accordance with the special vulnerabilities of each body type.

Were it to appear desirable, however, there are some additional findings in the current inquiry that might serve as a basis for developing separate screening devices for boys of each physique type, designed to establish their vulnerability to delinquency even more accurately than do the prediction tables in *Unraveling Juvenile Delinquency.* For example, in the case of mesomorphs, we have found a cluster of three traits (feeling of inadequacy, emotional instability, and emotional conflicts) which, more markedly than any other pattern of traits within the compass of the current inquiry, distinguish delinquent from non-delinquent mesomorphs (90.5%:9.5%). In addition to this are two aspects of the home environment (careless household routine and lack of family group recreations) which in combination most sharply differentiate delinquent from non-delinquent mesomorphs (78.1%:21.9%). (See Appendix E.)

As regards ectomorphs, there appears to be a combination of two traits more sharply distinguishing delinquent from non-delinquent ectomorphs—extreme restlessness in early childhood and receptive trends (85.7%:14.3%); and a cluster of four sociocultural factors—rearing in homes of low conduct standards, in homes lacking cultural refinement, in families lacking cohesiveness, and by fathers whose discipline of the boy is other than firm and kindly—that in combination more sharply distinguish delinquent from non-delinquent ectomorphs than any other cluster of sociocultural factors within the compass of the present inquiry (91%:9%). (See Appendix E.)

As regards endomorphs and boys of balanced type, there is *no specific* cluster of traits that significantly differentiate endomorphic delinquents from non-delinquents; and no pattern of sociocultural factors that significantly distinguishes delinquent from non-delinquent endomorphs. (See Appendix E.)

Although it does not appear to be too necessary to organize the findings concerning the mesomorphs and ectomorphs into formal screening instrumentalities, school personnel and others should find the trait and factor clusters suggestive in designing preventive and therapeutic services.

Use of Leisure

In *Unraveling Juvenile Delinquency* differences in the use of leisure among delinquents as compared with non-delinquents were revealed. The recreational preferences of delinquents are for risky and adventurous energy outlets, reflected not only in excessive truck-hopping, keeping late hours, bunking out, but also in seeking play places at a considerable distance from their homes, and hunting for exciting locales of risk and adventure such as railroad yards and waterfronts. These tendencies are also reflected in the greater extent to which the delinquents have serious street accidents and, vicariously, in their much more frequent movie attendance. Most of the delinquents run around in gangs or crowds, and many prefer companions older than themselves. There is also strong evidence that delinquents dislike the confinement of playgrounds, supervised recreations, or attendance at boys' clubs or community centers, which they rarely join of their own volition.

Apart from this, what do our current findings suggest about the special recreational needs of the different physique types? A few ex-

Exhibit 20.   LEISURE TIME ACTIVITIES OF NON-DELINQUENTS

Percentages of the Respective Physique Type Totals

	Total		Mesomorphs		Endomorphs		Ectomorphs		Balanced	
	No.	%	No.	%	No.	%	No.	%	No.	%
Runs Around with a Crowd	215	44.4%	76	51.0%	23	31.9%	76	39.8%	40	55.6%
Enjoys Competitive Sports	130	28.4	56	38.6	12	17.9	37	21.3	25	35.2
Dislike of Supervised Recreations	178	62.7	52	61.9	30	61.2	74	69.2	22	50.0
Prefers Adventuresome Activities	45	9.8	20	13.8	3	4.5	17	9.8	5	7.0
Steals Rides/Hops Trucks	116	24.0	42	28.2	10	13.9	44	23.0	20	27.8
Seeks Recreations in Distant Neighborhoods	69	14.3	27	18.1	5	6.9	30	15.7	7	9.7
Plays on Waterfronts	76	15.8	28	18.8	6	8.3	25	13.1	17	23.6

Significance of Differences between Physique Types						
	Meso-Endo	Meso-Ecto	Meso-Balanced	Endo-Ecto	Endo-Balanced	Ecto-Balanced
Runs Around with a Crowd	.05	-	-	-	.05	-
Enjoys Competitive Sports	.05	.05	-	-	.10	-
Dislike of Supervised Recreations	-	-	-	-	-	-
Prefers Adventuresome Activities	.10	-	-	-	-	-
Steals Rides/Hops Trucks	.05	-	-	-	-	-
Seeks Recreations in Distant Neighborhoods	.10	-	-	-	-	-
Plays on Waterfronts	-	-	-	-	.05	-

amples will illustrate the point (see Exhibit 20): Although delinquents in general tend to have more companions than non-delinquents, a breakdown by physique type reveals that *mesomorphs* and boys of *balanced* physique are more likely than endomorphs and ectomorphs to have many playmates. Such constitutional preferences need to be taken into account in the planning of recreational programs. To push ectomorphs and endomorphs into group activities would obviously "go against the grain." Although delinquents have somewhat *less* interest in competitive sports than non-delinquents, boys of *mesomorphic* and *balanced* physique are found in general to have greater preference for such activities than do ectomorphs and endomorphs. This is also illustrative of the need for tailoring recreational activities to meet the special needs of the different body types.

Youngsters in today's culture have ample leisure; and unless channels of legitimate energy-outlet are provided it is natural that uninhibited drive-tendencies may result in delinquency. Especially in the case of *mesomorphs,* opportunities need to be created not only in the home or in school, but in the community, for adventuresome yet socially harmless physical activity in the company of other boys, as diversions from antisocial expression of the strong drives of this body type, keeping in mind that mesomorphic boys typically "live by action."[10] A basic need in preventing antisocial aggression in mesomorphs is the provision of "moral equivalents" for the acts of aggressive energy which are especially easy, congenial, satisfying, and even *necessary* to boys of this vigorous physique.

Some boys prefer quieter and less aggressive recreational outlets. For example, *endomorphs* have less need for adventuresome activities than mesomorphs. This is evidenced by the lower proportion who have the urge to steal rides and hop trucks, by their less frequent seeking of recreations in neighborhoods distant from their homes, and by less playing on waterfronts. And *ectomorphs* have more dislike of *supervised* recreations than do boys of balanced physique.

In planning their programs, boys' clubs, camps, settlement houses, and other recreational agencies obviously need to take into account divergencies of preference related to differences in basic constitutional nature; and to educate the boys themselves to appreciate that there are varieties of recreational preferences related to temperamental needs and physical and mental abilities.

CLINICAL PRACTICES

Psychotherapists also might well incorporate into their treatment of pre-delinquents and delinquents some of the findings of this and similar research.

It has been shown that the delinquency potential of *mesomorphs* is especially high in that (compared to one or more of the other physique types) they possess some traits (e.g., physical strength, social assertiveness, uninhibited motor response to stimuli) which if improperly channeled might lead to delinquency and criminalism. This has to be taken into account not only by all those engaged in broad preventive efforts, but by therapists dealing with individual pre-delinquents and delinquents.

Clinically, in the treatment of *mesomorphs* already delinquent, it should be helpful, together with other data relevant to the understanding and treatment of socially maladapted children, to consider the characteristics especially impelling mesomorphs to delinquency. That susceptibility to contagion, low verbal intelligence, feelings of not being taken care of, destructiveness, destructive-sadistic trends, feelings of inadequacy, emotional instability, and emotional conflicts play a special criminogenic role *in a physique habitus where they do not usually occur in excess* is an important source of insight that should help clinicians to understand what they and their associates must take into account in the treatment of mesomorphic delinquents in order to provide satisfying emotional support and physical outlets for them.

Endomorphs, also, present some special problems for the clinician. Because of lower vitality than that possessed by mesomorphs, a lesser tendency to resolve their tensions in action, greater conventionality, and greater submissiveness to authority, their delinquency potential is not nearly as great as that of mesomorphs. But certain traits found in fact to have an excessive criminogenic impact on endomorphs need to be taken into account by those called upon to treat them for distortions of personality, character, or conduct. Among the influences especially related to the delinquency of endomorphs are cyanosis, ambivalence to authority, feeling of not being able to manage one's own life. The first of these is a reflection of some neurologic disturbance and is therefore a medical concern; of the other two traits, the first may require psychiatric attention, and both need constructive channeling.

Ectomorphs, too, require specialized clinical attention. Their sensitiveness, their excessive inclination to emotional conflicts, their tendency to keep their affective tensions bottled up, and the relative deficiency among ectomorphs generally of an outflowing motor tendency, gives them a far lower delinquency potential than mesomorphs. To lessen the chances of this potential becoming actual may often require intensive psychotherapy and special instruction to the parents and teachers of ectomorphs. Clinically, a history of extreme restlessness in early childhood, dermographia (skin sensitivity), and receptive (oral) trends must be noted as particularly related to delinquency in this body type. On the other hand, the delinquency of ectomorphs is not especially associated with those traits that operate with excessive force on mesomorphs.

Boys of *balanced type* possess some of the characteristics of each of the other physiques, the only trait found to differentiate them from *all* the other body types being a lesser fear of failure and defeat. Since they are less acquisitive, more stable emotionally, and have less tendency to emotional conflicts than ectomorphs, and are less likely to seek outlets for tensions in action than are mesomorphs, they too present a relatively low delinquency potential. Clinically, it is well to take into account the traits having an especial impact on the delinquency of this body type: e.g., susceptibility to contagion, strong hand grip, high performance intelligence, lack of fear of failure and defeat, marked dependence on others, and sensuousness. Some or all such traits, operating with the generally etiologic ones, exert a sufficient pressure to impel boys of the balanced type in the direction of delinquency.

CONCLUSION

We wish it were possible to speak with as much confidence regarding the prevention and "cure" of delinquency as we do regarding the traits and reactions of delinquents, incomplete as our findings are as to these. In the management of emotional and behavioral disorders, it is a far cry from diagnosis to therapy. A basic difficulty is, of course, the relative imperfection of the psychiatric and behavioral disciplines. Another difficulty (established in *Unraveling Juvenile Delinquency*) is that the tendency to maladaptation originates very early in life. A striking finding in that work was that half the delinquents showed persistent evidence of antisocial behavior when still under the age of eight, and nine-tenths when under the age of eleven. Therefore, it is clear that a major focus must be on the early years.

The foregoing discussion indicates that although many preventive and therapeutic indications flow from differences in the personality and temperamental makeup of boys of the different body types and require consideration in the effective management of delinquency, we must not lose sight of the *permeative* criminogenic influences that must needs be dealt with. It is particularly necessary to be realistic about the fact that there are limits to effective prophylactic action laid down by the general sociocultural situation. Our mores and wide-spread social influences are slow to change. In the meantime, children have to live in the world as it is; nor can they be made good by removing evil out of their experience. Character is not built that way and strength of character comes out of coping with evils, temptations, and problems to the best of one's ability. There is no doubt of the need of direct, repressive action against obvious evils, such as the peddling of drugs to children. But there are general cultural pressures and disharmonies and contradictions in our civilization involved in the broad and deep background of antisocial behavior that are difficult to change and can only be modified by an over-all social policy framed and projected over a long period of time by civic, political, and religious leaders.

As in *Unraveling Juvenile Delinquency,* and in *Delinquents in the Making* based thereon, we have not attempted to go into detail about techniques to be employed in coping with the antisocial conduct of children. Our aim has been simply to give some illustrations of the relevancy of physique type and constitutional psychology to the problem. We must leave to social practitioners the task of more fully implementing the indications of this inquiry if they find them challenging.

The evidence of the present research, added to that of *Unraveling,* does not lead us to the pessimistic conclusion that persistent delinquency springs largely from the germ plasm and is inevitable. We repeat what we have previously said:[11] *In delinquency we are dealing not with predestination but with destination.* We believe that imaginative and intensive experimentation with prophylactic and therapeutic measures, providing it is timely and thorough, should produce evidence that the destination of children toward delinquency is capable of change in a substantial proportion of instances. At the same time, we cannot escape the conclusion that differences in body structure can no longer be ignored in assessing the causal involvements of delinquency, and in shaping measures to cope with it.

In the final chapter we present a few etiologic hypotheses or theories in the confidence that they are worthy of further exploration.

NOTES

1. See S. and E. T. Glueck, *One Thousand Juvenile Delinquents* (Cambridge: Harvard University Press, 1934); E. Powers and H. Witmer, *An Experiment in the Prevention of Delinquency* (New York: Columbia University Press, 1951); and H. L. Witmer and E. Tufts, *The Effectiveness of Delinquency Prevention Programs,* Children's Bureau Publication, Number 350 (Washington, D. C.: U. S. Department of Health, Education and Welfare, Social Security Administration, 1954).

2. We have long believed that there is a great deal of natural talent in dealing with human beings that is going to waste. It is well known that certain persons are so endowed with "personal magnetism" or warmth, or strength of character, as to be able to exert an influence on children without necessarily being equipped with technical knowledge of child psychology. It has been found that certain social workers

and probation and parole officers have a better success rate than others, without necessarily having a better technical education. In police departments, in school systems, and in other fields, perhaps 5-10 per cent of the personnel have this precious "X" quality. Because of the great shortage of psychiatrists and psychiatric social workers, systematic effort should be made to discover such persons and guide them into work with pre-delinquent and delinquent children. Perhaps it will be possible to evolve a series of projective and other tests through which the basic constituents can be defined and which could then be used by civil service agencies to help select and place persons naturally qualified to guide youth. Many a young police officer, for example, is better endowed to influence youth than to guide traffic. Upon selection of the men and women possessing the *therapeutic personality,* they could be given in-service training in the elements of mental hygiene and other disciplines that might make them understand their work better without dampening their natural abilities.

3. Chap. XXII.

4. Chap. XVI.

5. Chap. XII.

6. *Delinquents in the Making* (New York: Harper & Brothers, 1952), pp. 200-201.

7. *Unraveling,* Chapter XX.

8. Sidney Axelrad and Selma J. Glick, "Application of the Glueck Social Prediction Table to 100 Jewish Delinquent Boys," *The Jewish Social Quarterly,* Vol. 30, No. 2 (1953), pp. 127-136; Richard E. Thompson, "A Validation of the Glueck Social Prediction Scale for Proneness to Delinquency," *The Journal of Criminal Law, Criminology and Police Science,* Vol. 43, No. 4 (Nov.-Dec., 1952), pp. 451-470.

9. At least, until the experiment now going on in New York City under the auspices of the New York City Youth Board has been completed. See article by Ralph Whelan, *Journal of Criminal Law and Criminology,* Vol. 45, No. 4 (Nov.-Dec., 1954), pp. 432-441, describing this experiment.

10. Sheldon's striking expression for "the energetic characteristic" of "Somatotonia." See W. H. Sheldon with the collaboration of S. S. Stevens, *The Varieties of Temperament* (New York and London: Harper & Brothers, 1942), p. 51.

11. *Unraveling,* p. 289; *Delinquents in the Making,* p. 210.

XVI

Hypotheses Regarding Physique in the Etiology of Delinquency

Before closing, it may be helpful to point to some hypotheses or theories regarding the etiologic involvement of physique types, traits, and sociocultural factors in the processes that make for delinquency. These we believe to be worthy of further exploration and testing on larger and more varied samples than those embraced in the present study.

IMPROBABILITY OF UNITARY "CAUSE" OR THEORY OF DELINQUENCY

Although the current inquiry on the role of body structure in delinquency has thrown some new light on causal "mechanisms" and broadened our knowledge of "causation," it should be even more evident than ever that there is no unit cause of delinquency. There is a natural urge for a simple explanation of the multiplicity of factors and forces involved in delinquent behavior. Such an abstraction of causal involvements is exceedingly difficult to arrive at. It would have to span the gap between heredity and environment; between the individual and his family; between the individual, the family, and the community; between the individual, the family, the community, and society in general. It would have to take account of conscious and subconscious motivations. Theories of crime causation are not notable for the extent to which they meet these specifications; and a major reason is that human personality, character, and motivation are far from simple. It is moreover doubtful whether a search for the very highest abstraction in a hierarchy of causal forces—the attempt to explain everything by one thing—will produce much of value in the study of delinquency. Considering the great variation in the kind of behavior patterns the law condemns as delinquent and criminal, it would be strange indeed to discover one underlying and all-pervasive "cause" or theory.

The nearest approximation to a theory that will cover the facts is a rather broad generalization that may be useful to bear in mind both in planning preventive programs and in dealing with the individual case:

At any time, the person is poised between a natural tendency to egoistic antisocial behavior and a habit-disciplined tendency to conform to the sociolegal taboos. Biosocial pressures of one combination or another tend to turn the scales in one direction or another. (Of course, the relationship between energy pressure and inhibitory tendency is not usually simple or direct; there are, as a rule, complex intermediary processes.) Consequently, it is not bodily structure, or strong instinctual impulse, or an hereditary aggressive tendency, or a weak inhibitory mechanism, or low intelligence, or excessive emotional lability, or marked suggestibility, or residence in a poverty-stricken "delinquency area" or in a region with a tradition of delinquency, or broken homes, or "differential association" with those already criminal, or any other biologic or sociocultural factor that either *exclusively or inevitably* conduces to delinquent behavior. Any of these factors alone or in various combinations may or may not bring about delinquency, depending on the balance of energy-and-inhibitory tendencies of the particular individual at the particular time. In other words, the cause of delinquency, like the cause of any effect, is the totality of conditions sufficient to produce it. Thus many boys may be very close to delinquency, yet not experience sufficient internal and external pressure to be thrust across the line of customary and legal prohibitions. This, incidentally, indicates how enormously important it is to develop instruments for the detection of potential delinquents early enough in life, in order so to accommodate the internal and external situation of a child as to counterpoise an almost dominant tendency to commit crime.

As was shown in *Unraveling Juvenile Delinquency*, certain factors in combination are found to occur so frequently in the constitution and developmental history of delinquents and so seldom among non-delinquents that we may legitimately conclude that the weight they contribute to the causal scales is excessive, in comparison to other forces.

This is a realistic conception of causation; for by isolating the biosocial syndromes most *usually operative* in the lives of delinquents and most *usually absent* in those of non-delinquents, it not only adds to understanding of cause and effect but it highlights the traits, factors, and areas *most relevant* both to therapeutic effort in the individual case and to prophylactic effort in general.

ETIOLOGIC PATTERNS

From the evidence in this inquiry and in *Unraveling Juvenile Delinquency,* we cannot conclude that there is a "delinquent personality," either among the majority of our delinquents—the mesomorphs—or in any other body type, in the sense of a relatively constant and stable combination of physique, character, and temperament which always, or even usually, determines that the individual possessing such traits will become delinquent.

In *Unraveling Juvenile Delinquency* when summarizing criminogenic influences we expressed the opinion that although, by and large, the dynamic interplay of certain traits and factors from all levels of the inquiry—physical constitution, intelligence, character structure, temperament, sociocultural stresses—results in a high probability that certain boys in disorganized urban regions will become delinquent, there are *sub-patterns* in the composite totality of delinquents. In the present work, certain influences, although found in *Unraveling* to distinguish delinquents from non-delinquents, are now seen to be constituents of varying etiologic syndromes stemming from differences in traits and factors that have a selective impact on the delinquency of the physique types. Thus, while the complex of forces that results in antisocial behavior in a particular physique has many elements in common with that which is etiologically involved in the delinquency of another physique, there are also *distinctive* etiologic elements. Also, some influences are more permeative etiologically than others, affecting a large group of delinquents; others, a smaller number.

Just as there are sub-categories of causal patterning in the total group of delinquents, so are there probably also sub-clusters of etiologic influence *within each body type,* the total of delinquents in each type being therefore a composite of boys who have become persistently antisocial because of the sufficient pressure of one or another causal syndrome. In other words, in each body type there are very probably several bisocial sequences that lead to a "breaking point" resulting in persistent delinquency.

DELINQUENCY POTENTIAL

In summarizing the findings by body type (Chapters XI-XIV), we have considered as the *norm* of each physique those traits among *non-delinquents* that significantly differentiate a particular body type from the other body types; and we have suggested that some of the traits having an excessive affinity for a particular physique may contribute to delinquency when combined with certain other criminogenic traits and sociocultural conditions.

Thus, for example, the basic reason for the excess of mesomorphs among delinquents as compared with other body types may well be that boys of predominantly mesomorphic physique are endowed with traits that equip them well for a delinquent role under the pressure of unfavorable sociocultural conditions; while endomorphs, being less energetic and less likely to act out their "drives," have a lower *delinquency potential* than mesomorphs. True, many of the traits we have studied—aggressiveness, adventurousness, acquisitiveness, for example—do not significantly vary in incidence among body types although they are etiologically involved in the end-product of delinquency. Nevertheless, boys who possess certain other characteristics, such as excessive energy and a tendency to act out tensions, frustrations, feelings of aggression, thirst for adventure, acquisitive impulses, and the like, are especially prone to delinquency, particularly if they live in the exciting and culturally disorganized regions of underprivileged urban areas.

Direct and Indirect Criminogenic Impulses

It would seem that actions which the legal order frowns upon may be either largely *direct* and uncomplicated expressions of "original nature" in the form of excessive instinctual energy and weak or erratic inhibitory apparatus, or largely *indirect* (reactive, defensive, or compensatory) in the sense that their roots lie in an underdeveloped or unconventional conscience (superego) attributable essentially to early distortions in parent-child relationships. Such striking forerunners, accompaniments, and sequelae of delinquency as marked aggressiveness, for example, may well be relatively straightforward manifestations of the physical and temperamental equipment of the naturally energetic and outgoing mesomorphic constitution, but largely indirect, reactive, or compensatory phenomena when they occur in the naturally sensitive (ectomorphic) and obese (endomorphic) body types. It is also probable that the tolerance for frustrating experiences is at a much lower level in the naturally extroversive mesomorphs than in the naturally sensitive ectomorphs, the former having a strong innate tendency to "go into action" and the latter to bottle up their frustrations or turn them against themselves. Here is an area in which physical anthropology can combine with dynamic psychology and psychiatry in testing out some fundamental hypotheses that might bring more illumination to all three disciplines.

Delinquency Involving Internal Disharmony

There are some traits which seemingly create an internal disharmony in a particular body type to which they are normally alien, and which necessitate a struggle to restore a temperamental balance. Given the other predisposing conditions, this trait-disharmony tends to find an outlet in delinquency. It will be recalled, for example, that feelings of inadequacy, emotional instability, emotional conflict, destructiveness, and destructive-sadistic trends, are all *less* characteristic of *mesomorphs* than of one or more of the other physique types; yet when they do occur among mesomorphs they are found to exert an excessive impact on their delinquency as compared with that of one or more of the other body types.

SELECTIVE INFLUENCE OF ENVIRONMENT

The emphasis in American criminology and in psychoanalysis since the turn of the century regarding the formation of personality and character has been on the "conditioned," the acquired. The stress placed on the construction of the ego and superego through the emotion-laden experiences of the growing child in relation to the adults close to him during his earliest formative years, and on regional cultural influences in later years, has tended to obscure the fact that there are also differences in original nature. The processes of ego and superego differentiation and crystallization and the sociocultural stresses of the disorganized family and community have varying original constitutional materials to work upon. It has been established, for example, that the predominantly mesomorphic constitution has greater strength and a different rhythm of energy discharge and control of impulse than the obese endormorphic or the fragile ectomorphic types. It has also been shown that the delinquency of ectomorphs would seem to stem largely from their oversensitiveness and over-responsiveness to the unwholesome influences of home and family life. Consequently, though an essentially genetic explanation of varying behavioral inclinations may be criticized as onesided, essentially psychoanalytic or sociocultural explanations are open to like criticism.[1]

The foregoing observations are more than mere speculation; they are hypotheses suggested upon reflection on the materials of the present inquiry and of *Unraveling Juvenile Delinquency*. We believe they are leads to further fruitful research of a basic nature.

NOTE

1. Freud long ago recognized the role of heredity in respect to the etiology of the *neuroses*: "Experience shows, as might have been anticipated, that among the problems of aetiology that of the quantitative relationship of the aetiological factors to one another should not be neglected. But one would not have guessed the fact which seems to follow from my observations, that heredity and the specific causes may replace one another quantitatively, that the same pathological effect will be produced by the co-existence of a very grave specific aetiology and a moderate degree of predisposition as by that of a severe neuropathic heredity with a slight specific factor." S. Freud, "Heredity and the Aetiology of the Neuroses," 1896, in Vol. I of *Collected Papers* (tr. by Riviere), (New York, London, Vienna: The International Psychoanalytical Library, No. 7, 1924), p. 143.

APPENDIX A

EXPLANATION OF STATISTICAL METHOD

by JANE WORCESTER

Harvard University School of Public Health

In the preparation of their monograph, *Unraveling Juvenile Delinquency,* the authors found themselves faced with a relatively simple statistical problem. Most of the comparisons they wished to make could be reduced to simple fourfold tables which showed the presence and absence of a specified trait in the delinquent and non-delinquent groups. It was possible in each of these tables to compute Chi-square (X^2) and to assign to each a probability (P) which measured the chance that sampling variation had produced the difference between the percentages of delinquents and non-delinquents who showed the specified trait. When $P \leq .01$ it was concluded that sampling variation did not account for the difference and that the trait was in fact associated with delinquency.

The present situation is more complex. Difficulties arise because the delinquent and non-delinquent groups have now been broken down into four physique types and the authors wish to make comparative statements about the behavior of a trait in four physique groups. Reference to a particular trait will make things clearer. The table below gives the breakdown for the trait *feeling of not being taken care of* (this is an expansion of Table 27 in the text).

In the initial study, the Gluecks were interested only in the information in Line 1 of the above table which shows that 29.2% of the delinquents (96/329) and 24.7% of the non-delinquents (75/304) had the trait. The difference between the two percentages, 4.5, was tested by X^2 which gave a value of P between .25 and .30. This indicates that approximately 25% of the differences which would result from taking random samples of similar size from a single universe would be 4.5% or larger; it was concluded that this difference was not significant.

In the present volume, however, interest is centered not so much in

FEELING OF NOT BEING TAKEN CARE OF

Physique Type	Delinquents				Non-Delinquents				Difference in Percentages between Delinquents and Non-Delinquents
	TOTAL	No. with Trait	No. without Trait	% with Trait	TOTAL	No. with Trait	No. without Trait	% with Trait	
1 Total	329	96	233	29.2	304	75	229	24.7	4.5
2 Meso.	203	74	129	36.5	96	18	78	18.8	17.7
3 Endo.	39	7	32	17.9	35	11	24	31.4	−13.5
4 Ecto.	43	9	34	20.9	127	32	95	25.2	− 4.3
5 Balanced	44	6	38	13.6	46	14	32	30.4	−16.8
Columns	a=	b	c	d=	e=	f	g	h=	i=
	b+c			b/a	f+g			f/e	d−h

the variation shown in the lines of the table but in the columns. The authors wish to discuss the variation in the percentages of individuals with the trait in the four physique types of the delinquent group (Column d), of the non-delinquent group (Column h), and in the differences in the percentages between the delinquents and non-delinquents (Column i). Preliminary analyses consisted of the computations of X^2 for the delinquent and for the non-delinquent groups and of experimentation with a variety of procedures for analysis of variance on the differences. It was found in this table that the percentages showing the trait varied significantly from physique type to physique type in the delinquent group (P from $X^2 < .01$). The non-delinquent group did not show significant variation in the incidence of the trait in the physique types (P from X^2 between .4 and .5); the differences also appeared to vary significantly. The difficulty with these methods is that they tell only that there is significant variation (at a certain

ILLUSTRATIVE TABLE

Comparison	Difference in Percentages*	Probability
Mesomorph with Endomorph	$36.5 - 17.9 = 18.6$	$.02 < P < .05$
Mesomorph with Ectomorph	$36.5 - 20.9 = 15.6$	$.10 < P < .15$
Mesomorph with Balanced	$36.5 - 13.6 = 22.9$	$.01 < P < .02$
Endomorph with Ectomorph	$17.9 - 20.9 = -3.0$	$P > .30$
Endomorph with Balanced	$17.9 - 13.6 = 4.3$	$P > .30$
Ectomorph with Balanced	$20.9 - 13.6 = 7.3$	$P > .30$

* The comparisons were made in the percentage scale rather than in the scale $0 - \arcsin \sqrt{p}$ since standard deviations of the percentages had already been computed for other purposes and since the percentage scale was believed to be more meaningful.

probability level). They do not permit statements as to which of the physique types are responsible for the significance.

At this point, Frederick Mosteller, Professor of Mathematical Statistics in the Department of Social Relations, Harvard University, suggested a method of allowances for multiple comparisons which is discussed in an as yet unpublished monograph, "The Problem of Multiple Comparison," prepared by John W. Tukey of Princeton University. By means of this method it is possible to make a statistical statement at a fixed level of probability about the family of six comparisons between the four physique types. For example, from the illustrative table the following family of comparisons may be made among the delinquents. The column "Difference in Percentages" lists the six contrasts between the four physique types. If interest had centered *only* on the second difference, 15.6% between the mesomorphs and the ectomorphs, it would have been possible to test its significance by a Chi-square test with one degree of freedom which would have given a probability of .05 that random sampling could account for the difference. However, this is not the case; this difference is one of a family of six, and when considered in this context, $P = .05$ no longer applies; instead a value of P (the error rate family-wise) between .10 and .15 is obtained, showing that as one of a family of six comparisons this difference would occur rather more frequently than was indicated by $P = .05$.

This probability was obtained as follows. The variance of each of the percentages was computed from the formula (percentage) $(100 -$ percentage$)/n$ and s; the standard deviation of the difference between the two percentages involved in the comparisons was obtained as the square root of the sum of the two variances. In the example given the standard deviation of the difference, $36.5 - 20.9 = 15.6$, is

$$\sqrt{\frac{(36.5)\ (63.5)}{203} + \frac{(20.9)\ (79.1)}{43}} = 7.06.$$ The difference was then divided by its standard deviation, $\frac{15.6}{7.06} = 2.21$.

In order to find the probability to be associated with this ratio, which is the "wholly significant difference divided by its standard deviation" (WSD/s), the following procedures were followed: reference to Tukey's Table 1 shows that LSD/s (least significant difference divided by the estimated standard deviation) is 2.77, since the denominator degrees of freedom are large for the comparisons involved here; also in Table 1, WSD/LSD is found to be 1.32 for four determinations (the four physique types); hence WSD/s is $(2.77)\ (1.32) = 3.66$ and the allowance is 3.66 $s/\sqrt{2} = 2.59s$. (These methods are discussed in Tukey's monograph.) This allowance refers to the level $P = .05$. In order to shift to other levels of WSD and P, let

$$.05h = P \text{ (specified)}$$
$$u = -\log_{10} h$$
$$c = .138 + .0124h \text{ (from Tukey's Table 9)}$$
$$\log_{10} WSD_P = \log_{10} WSD_{.05} + uc$$
$$\log_{10} WSD_P = \log_{10} 2.59 + uc$$

Substitution of different values of P in this equation results in the following values:

P	WSDs
.01	5.07
.02	3.54
.05	2.59
.10	2.31
.15	2.14
.20	1.99
.25	1.87
.30	1.77

The value of P for WSD/s $= 2.21$ is found to lie between .10 and .15.

Probabilities were computed in this manner for each of the six contrasts for the 68 traits in the delinquent and in the non-delinquent groups. (One of these traits was ultimately discarded in the final manuscript.) Probabilities were also computed for the six contrasts involving the differences between the four differences in percentages between the delinquents and non-delinquents (Column i of the table). In this case the standard deviation, s, was set equal to the square root of the sum of the variances of the four percentages involved. The calculations were the same in other respects. Thus, probabilities are available for three families of six comparisons for each of 68 traits. The probabilities were computed in this way so that the significance level (error rate) could be determined by comparing the observed distributions of the probabilities with the expected distribution. In order to decide what significance level to set, the least of the six probabilities was tabulated for each of the three families of comparisons. The following distributions resulted from the 68 traits:

Probability	Delinquents	Non-Delinquents	Differences	Expected in Random Samples
< .01	2	7	0	.68
.01—.02	5	7	1	.68
.02—.05	11	7	11	2.04
.05—.10	8	4	6	3.40
.10—.20	7	5	8	6.80
.20—.30	6	5	6	6.80
.30 and over	29	33	36	47.60
	68	68	68	68.00

The expected distribution is the one which would arise if each family of comparisons involved only sampling variability. The hypothesis underlying the expected distribution for the delinquents is that the physique types constitute four random samples from a single universe of a particular trait. The same statement can be made for the non-delinquents. In the case of the differences the expected distribution arises under the hypothesis of constant difference for a specified trait in the percentages between the delinquents and non-delinquents in the four physique types.

Comparison of the three observed distributions with the expected shows that the small probabilities are occurring more frequently in the observed than can be accounted for by a random sampling hypothesis. Sixty-nine probabilities $<.10$ were observed when only 20.4 were expected. On the basis of this evidence, the significance level was set at $P < .10$. Apparently 48.6/69 or about 70% of all extreme comparisons with $P \geqq .10$ did not arise by chance. Comparisons giving $P > .10$ are not stated to be significant; comparisons giving $P < .10$ are stated to be significant. In the final table the probabilities $< .10$ have been written in abbreviated form.

Probability	Probability as it appears in the tables
$<.01$	.01
.01—.02	.02
.02—.05	.05
.05—.10	.10
.10 and over	—

It should be remembered that $P=.10$ is greater than the significance level, $P=.01$, which was used in *Unraveling Juvenile Delinquency.*

The tables as presented in the text are less detailed than the one used here as illustration. Table 27 in its final form is shown on page 87.

This form of presentation is common to the 68 traits. Three families of statements can be made from the bottom part of the table.

1) The delinquents: The mesomorphs show a higher percentage with the trait than do the endomorphs or balanced type. The other comparisons are not significant.

2) The non-delinquents: There are no comparisons which are significant.

3) The differences: The difference in the percentages between the delinquents and non-delinquents who possess the trait is greater for the mesomorphs than for any of the other three types. The differences for the endomorphs, ectomorphs, and balanced type do not depart significantly one from the other.

It should be noted that these three families of comparisons are not independent. The three have been included in the trait analysis because they lend themselves to somewhat different interpretations in terms of the presumed constitutional origin of the traits.

The tables for the 42 sociocultural factors include only the comparisons within the delinquent group since these factors are not constitutionally oriented. However, in the analysis the three families of comparisons were carried out. It is of some interest to compare the observed and expected probability distributions in this situation.

Probability	Delinquents	Non-Delinquents	Differences	Expected in Random Samples
<.01	0	0	0	.42
.01—.02	3	1	0	.42
.02—.05	7	1	4	1.26
.05—.10	5	2	5	2.10
.10—.20	3	4	4	4.20
.20—.30	5	5	3	4.20
.30 and over	19	29	26	29.40
	42	42	42	42.00

The delinquent group has 15 families of comparisons below the .10 level where only 4.20 are expected. This is a significant departure from expectation, showing that 10.8/15 or 72% of these comparisons did not arise by chance. This presumably indicates that these factors have different impacts toward delinquency in the physique types. The observed and expected distributions for the non-delinquents are almost identical. The departure from expectation for the differences (9 below the .10 level against an expected value of 4.20) arises because of the delinquent group. The physique types of the delinquent group only are thus shown to depart from expectation in the analysis of the 42 sociocultural factors, whereas the physique type of both the delinquent and non-delinquent groups were found to depart from expectation in the analysis of the 68 traits.

It should be remembered that the departures from expectation have been calculated under the assumption that the various characteristics which are being investigated (the 68 traits and the 42 sociocultural factors) are independent. Such is not the case since the same individuals are reported on many items. This complication means that there will be correlation between the traits and factors, and consequently that the successive tables are not independent. There is at present no satisfactory way of dealing with this situation.

Tukey, writing in the *Journal of the American Statistical Association*,

December 1954, in an article called, "Unsolved Problems of Experimental Statistics," asks "How soon are we going to develop a well-informed and consistent body of opinion on the multiple comparison problem? Can we start soon with the immediate end of adding to knowledge? And even agree on the place of short cuts?" Because of the newness of the method used here and the volume of the material, there is good reason to show how the probability levels determined here compare with those determined from X^2 (Chi-square). The illustrative table in its final form includes a probability based on the X^2 test for the comparison of the percentage of all delinquents showing the trait with that of all non-delinquents. In the situation where only two determinations are involved in the comparison, the two methods are equivalent and, of course, give the same probabilities. The following table shows the relationship between the probability determined from the X^2 based on three degrees of freedom and the probability (the least in each set of six comparisons) determined from the method of multiple comparisons in the 68 traits in the four physique types of the delinquent group.

PROBABILITIES

From X^2	.01	.01—.05	.05—.10	.10—.20	.20—.30	.30 and over	Total
		From Multiple Comparison					
.01	7	8					15
.01—.05		3	1	2			6
.05—.10		3	2	1			6
.10—.20			1	2	2	1	6
.20—.30					2	4	6
.30 and over					1	28	29
Total	7	14	4	5	5	33	68

The table shows, not unexpectedly, the close relationship between the two methods. If $P = .10$ had been used as the dividing line, X^2 would have picked out 27 traits as showing significant variability over the physique types, whereas the method of multiple comparisons picks out 25. However, 24 traits are common to both groups. The advantage of the method of multiple comparisons is that it has allowed more definite statements as to how the physique types differ one from another.

APPENDIX B

METHOD OF SOMATOTYPING

Extract from *Unraveling Juvenile Delinquency*
(Appendix C, pp. 340-347, by Carl C. Seltzer, Ph.D.)

The analysis of the delinquent and non-delinquent series for somatotypes of the individual subjects presented a difficult problem owing to the absence of established norms for this age group. The nearest comparable norms were established for 18-year-old male college students by Sheldon and his colleagues . . . In connection with the present study, it was decided not to adopt Sheldon's technique of assigning ratings to the juveniles by estimating what their somatotypes would most likely be when they reach early adulthood. This method was discarded for the following reasons: (1) Ratings made in this manner are too highly subjective to inspire confidence in their accuracy. (2) There are no established norms. (3) Proof is lacking of Sheldon's postulate with respect to the permanency and immutability of the somatotype. (4) It is necessary to deal with the morphological constitution of the subjects in their juvenile state, since the behavioral correlates refer to the present and not to what they may be in the future as adults.

The somatotype analysis, therefore, was handled in these two complementary ways: (1) an inspectional, over-all somatotype rating of the subjects "as is," and (2) a matched-pair comparison between the delinquent and non-delinquent series for component differences.

Over-All Inspectional Somatotype Ratings

Since the two methods are quite different in their approach, they have the distinct advantage of serving as independent checks against each other . . . The procedure adopted in making over-all inspectional somatotype ratings of the series of delinquent and non-delinquent adolescents was based on the assignment of ratings to the subjects as they appeared in the photographs at that time. The two series were not considered separately but were combined into one and thoroughly mingled in order to obliterate their group identification. No outside arbitrary somatotype

286

standards were used, for each subject was considered in relation to the combined series as a whole.

The photographs were examined and a judgment made with respect to which component of physique was predominant: endomorphy, mesomorphy, or ectomorphy. In this manner each photograph was placed into one of three categories. The photographs of each of these groups were examined a second time with an ultimate selection of those photographs which appeared to represent the *extreme* presence of the particular physical component in question. The three groups of extremes were designated respectively: extreme endomorphs, extreme mesomorphs, and extreme ectomorphs.

The remaining photographs of the original sorting were examined for a third time and arrayed in groups of threes for each component of physique. In the group considered to be primarily endomorphic, the groupings were: mesomorphic endomorphs, endomorphs, and ectomorphic endomorphs. In the group judged to be primarily mesomorphic, the categories were: endomorphic mesomorphs, mesomorphs, and ectomorphic mesomorphs. In the group regarded as primarily ectomorphic, the sortings were: mesomorphic ectomorphs, ectomorphs, and endomorphic ectomorphs. Photographs considered to represent a balance of physical component endowment formed a separate grouping.

From this procedure there resulted a triangular distribution or sorting of subjects, with assignment of each photograph to one of thirteen categories. In making judgments and assigning somatotype ratings, reference was made to the description of physical differences as described by Sheldon.

Extreme endomorphs. This rating is indicated by roundness, softness, and impression of extreme obesity of the physique, with minimum expression of either heavy bone-muscle structure or general hardness of the body, at the same time presenting little evidence of linearity or fragility of physical structure. This group contains 30 individuals, or 3.1 per cent of the combined series.

Endomorphs. This rating is indicated by roundness and softness of the body as the dominant characteristic, but at the same time presenting a balance between bone-muscle structure on the one hand, and linearity-fragility of physique on the other. This grouping possesses 37 individuals, or 3.8 per cent of the combined series.

Mesomorphic endomorphs. In this group the subjects are predominantly soft and round, but not extremely so, with evidence of some strength of bone-muscle structure as a secondary consideration, and without manifest fragility of physique. This group consists of 23 individuals, or 2.3 per cent of the combined series.

Ectomorphic endomorphs. This designation is on the basis of predominance of the endomorph configuration, less than the extreme, but at the same time displaying a thinness and brittleness of structure lacking evident bone-muscle support. In this group there are 41 individuals, or 4.2 per cent of the combined series.

Extreme mesomorphs. The subjects included in this rating are of particularly heavy bone and large muscle structure, displaying little or no softness or fragility of physical make-up. This group consists of 149 subjects, or 15.2 per cent of the combined series.

Mesomorphs. This category includes those predominantly of heavy bone-muscle structure short of the degree of endowment apparent in the extreme mesomorph. There is secondarily a balance between the traits of the endomorph and the ectomorph. This grouping contains 143 subjects, or 14.6 per cent of the combined series.

Endomorphic mesomorphs. This group retains the heavy bone-muscle characteristic, though not as pronounced as the one previously mentioned, and with strong support of traits of physique possessed by the endomorphic group, with linearity and fragility at a minimum. In this group there are 81 individuals, or 8.3 per cent of the combined series.

Ectomorphic mesomorphs. This rating includes those who are of moderately heavy bone-muscle structure, lacking softening aspects, but displaying considerable evidence of physical traits of the thin, fragile ectomorph. In this category are 73 individuals, or 7.5 per cent of the combined series.

Extreme ectomorphs. This group is represented by subjects who are extremely thin and display a delicate, light bodily frame. There is minimal presence of either the softness of the endomorph or the hard massiveness of the mesomorph. There are 79 extreme ectomorphs, or 8.1 per cent of the combined series.

Ectomorphs. Assignment of this rating is indicated by definite but not excessive physical fragility, combined with a balance and moderate expression of physical traits displayed by the endomorph and mesomorph. Here there are 96 subjects, or 9.8 per cent of the combined series.

Endomorphic ectomorphs. This group includes those who are primarily thin and elongated but secondarily give evidence of the roundness and softness of the endomorph, noticeably lacking bone-muscle support. There are 36 endomorphic ectomorphs, or 3.7 per cent of the combined series.

Mesomorphic ectomorphs. Placement in this group is on the basis of predominance of a thin, fragile physical make-up short of the extreme, with some display of bone-muscle strength, but with no significant presence of traits describing the endomorph. This category contains 52 individuals, or 5.3 per cent of the combined series.

Balanced. Subjects included in this designation are regarded as displaying mid-range physical endowment in which none of the three traits assumes dominance over the other two in any marked degree. This group consists of 138 individuals, or 14.1 per cent of the combined series.

Table C-68 [reproduced in Chap. I, p. 9 of the present work] compares the frequency of the somatotype categories among the delinquents and non-delinquents. It is readily apparent from a study of this table that there is marked differentiation between the two juvenile series in somatotype frequencies. Among the delinquents the dominant component is mesomorphy in contrast to the non-delinquent series where the dominant component is ectomorphy. Approximately 60 per cent of the delinquent group is classified as having one form or another of mesomorphic dominance, the rest of the series being almost equally divided between dominant ectomorphs (14.5 per cent), balanced type (13.5 per cent), and dominant endomorphs (11.9 per cent). There is no such ascendancy of any single component in the non-delinquent series. In this group although the dominant ectomorphs are found to be the most frequent, amounting to 39.6 per cent of the series, the dominant mesomorphs are not very far behind with 30.7 per cent in this classification. The dominant endomorphs and balanced type show almost identical frequencies among the non-delinquents with 14.9 and 14.7 per cent, respectively. What is striking here is not the distribution of somatotypes among the non-delinquents, but the outstanding strength of the mesomorphic component among the delinquents and the accompanying relative weakness of the ectomorphic and endomorphic elements.

Investigation into the detailed somatotype categories accentuates the contrasts between the two juvenile series. If we consider first those somatotypes in which the endomorphic component predominates, we find that the extreme endomorphs are more than four times as frequent in the non-delinquent series as in the delinquent group. The percentile difference between them is statistically significant with a C.R. of 3.4 standard errors. Endomorphs are almost twice as frequent in the non-delinquents as in the delinquents but in this case the percentile difference does not reach the critical level of statistical significance. Mesomorphic endomorphs, on the other hand, are more than twice as frequent in the delinquents as in the non-delinquents, but again the difference is not statistically significant although it approaches it closely. There is no essential difference between the two groups in their frequency of ectomorphic endomorphs. Taking all the endomorphic dominants as a whole, there is a small but insignificant excess of these individuals in the non-delinquent series, 14.9 per cent, as compared with 11.9 per cent for the delinquent group.

With regard to those categories in which the mesomorphic component predominates, the extreme mesomorphs are more than three times as frequent among the delinquents as among the non-delinquents, the mesomorphs 1.4 times as frequent, and the endomorphic mesomorphs more than four times as frequent in the delinquent group. In all three instances the percentile differences are statistically significant. Ectomorphic mesomorphs are very slightly in excess among the non-delinquents but the difference is not statistically significant.

Ectomorphic dominance is clearly an outstanding feature of the non-delinquent series. It occurs in 39.6 per cent of the non-delinquents, compared with only 14.5 per cent of the delinquents. Extreme ectomorphs are more than eight times as frequent in the non-delinquent group, ectomorphs almost three times as frequent, and mesomorphic ectomorphs more than twice as frequent. The differences are all statistically significant.

The balanced type, in which there is no single component dominance, is about equally represented in the two series.

Matched-Pair Comparisons for Somatotype Component Differences

A radically different approach was adopted for this somatotype analysis. Instead of contrasting the delinquent and non-delinquent series as a group, all the subjects were arranged according to matched pairs —each delinquent with his companion non-delinquent. Then a direct comparison was made between each pair for somatotype component differences. The comparison was on a relative basis and not on an absolute basis as in the previous analysis. Accordingly, after careful study of each set of paired photographs, a judgment was made for each component separately as to its strength in the delinquent relative to his matched non-delinquent. These relative differences were recorded on a fourfold scale: *same, slight, moderate, marked*. For example, in the case of a comparison between a delinquent mesomorph and a non-delinquent ectomorph, the judgments might be recorded as follows:

Endomorphy: Delinquent *slightly stronger* than non-delinquent
Mesomorphy: Delinquent *markedly stronger* than non-delinquent
Ectomorphy: Delinquent *markedly weaker* than non-delinquent

Differences were recorded only when they were clear-cut and readily observable; otherwise the component was designated as being in the *same* strength in both subjects. It should be remembered that since the comparisons are on a relative basis, a designation of *markedly stronger* or *weaker* does not necessarily signify that the component in question is present in outstanding strength in one of the matched pairs. If in one individual the component is in minimal strength and in the other in average strength, the difference between them may well be *marked*. In other words, the recorded differences between the matched pairs are not necessarily indicative of the absolute strength of the components.

This method of somatotype analysis is an important complementary verification of the procedure and results presented in the previous section. Not only were the two methods worked out by different observers, but it becomes readily apparent that the accuracy and reliability of the over-all ratings are surprisingly high. (The matched-pair comparison is the work of Dr. Carl C. Seltzer, while the over-all inspectional somatotype ratings were made by Ashton M. Tenney.)

The results of the matched-pair comparisons are presented here, each somatotype component being analyzed separately.

Endomorphic component. From the figures in Table C-69 it may be seen that endomorphy is on the whole in greater strength among the delinquents than among their matched non-delinquents. More endo-morphy is found in the delinquents in 53.2 per cent of the matched cases, compared with 27.4 per cent of the matched pairs wherein the non-delinquents are greater in endomorphic strength. In 19.3 per cent of matched cases the *same* degree of endomorphy occurs in the de-linquent and non-delinquent pair. With respect to the grades of differ-ences, instances of markedly stronger endomorphy are somewhat more frequent in the non-delinquents (5.6 per cent) than in the delinquents (4.1 per cent). This is undoubtedly a reflection of the greater occurrence of extreme endomorphy previously indicated for the non-delinquents. However, instances of slightly stronger and moderately stronger endo-morphy are more than twice as frequent in the delinquent pair as in the non-delinquents.

Mesomorphic component. A study of Table C-69 shows clearly the mesomorphic strength of the delinquents over the matched non-delin-quents. This is evident in all the grades of differences. Instances of markedly stronger mesomorphy occur in the delinquents in the ratio of about 12 to 1 over the non-delinquents; cases of moderately stronger mesomorphy in the ratio of about 4 to 1, and slightly stronger meso-morphy in the ratio of somewhat under 2 to 1. All told, greater strength of all types of the mesomorphic component is found in 62 per cent of the delinquent boys and in only 23.8 per cent of the non-delinquent boys.

	Matched Pairs	
Endomorphic Component	No.	%
Delinquent *markedly stronger* than non-delinquent	20	4.1
Delinquent *moderately stronger* than non-delinquent	70	14.5
Delinquent *slightly stronger* than non-delinquent	167	34.6
Delinquent *same* as non-delinquent	93	19.3
Non-delinquent *slightly stronger* than delinquent	70	14.5
Non-delinquent *moderately stronger* than delinquent	35	7.3
Non-delinquent *markedly stronger* than delinquent	27	5.6
Total	482	99.9
Mesomorphic Component		
Delinquent *markedly stronger* than non-delinquent	68	14.1
Delinquent *moderately stronger* than non-delinquent	96	19.9
Delinquent *slightly stronger* than non-delinquent	135	28.0
Delinquent *same* as non-delinquent	68	14.1
Non-delinquent *slightly stronger* than delinquent	85	17.6
Non-delinquent *moderately stronger* than delinquent	24	5.0
Non-delinquent *markedly stronger* than delinquent	6	1.2
Total	482	99.9
Ectomorphic Component		
Delinquent *markedly stronger* than non-delinquent	24	5.0
Delinquent *moderately stronger* than non-delinquent	42	8.7
Delinquent *slightly stronger* than non-delinquent	83	17.2
Delinquent *same* as non-delinquent	79	16.4
Non-delinquent *slightly stronger* than delinquent	114	23.7
Non-delinquent *moderately stronger* than delinquent	76	15.8
Non-delinquent *markedly stronger* than delinquent	64	13.3
Total	64	100.1

Ectomorphic component. According to the data in Table C-69, the non-delinquents exhibit greater ectomorphy than the delinquents. This condition exists in the case of 52.8 per cent of the matched pairs, while the delinquents have greater ectomorphic strength over the non-delinquents in 30.9 per cent of cases. No difference in ectomorphy between the matched pairs is found in 79 out of 482 matched cases, or 16.4 per cent. The largest disparity between the two groups is to be seen in the markedly stronger ectomorphic category: The non-delinquents are markedly stronger ectomorphs than the delinquents in 13.3 per cent of the matched pairs, compared with only 5 per cent of marked delinquent superiority.

Influence of age differential. The somatotype differences between the matched pairs of delinquents and non-delinquents are substantial. However, the question may arise as to the extent of influence in these comparisons of the age differential between the matched pairs. Even though in the matching process similarity in age was an important factor, there still remained age differentials which in a few instances ranged up to 12 months. In order to investigate any possible modification of the somatotype differences due to age, a special analysis was made, the results of which are presented in Table C-70. In this table the delinquents who are older than their matched non-delinquents have been compared with those delinquents who are younger than their matched non-delinquents for somatotype component differences.

A study of the figures in Table C-70 clearly establishes the fact that the somatotype differences found above are unaffected by the age disparities existing between the matched pairs. The delinquents exhibit more of the endomorphic component than the non-delinquents in 53.1 per cent of cases wherein the delinquents are older, compared with 53.5 per cent where the delinquents are younger. The delinquents exhibit the same degree of endomorphy as the non-delinquents in 18.7 per cent of cases where the delinquents are older, compared with 19.2 per cent where the delinquents are younger. The delinquents exhibit less endomorphy than the non-delinquents in 28.2 per cent of the matched pairs where the delinquents are older, and in 27.2 per cent of cases where the delinquents are younger. Similar results are found for mesomorphy and ectomorphy. In each instance the comparison of matched cases where the delinquents are older than the non-delinquents with those in which the delinquents are younger produces almost identical percentages of mesomorphic and endomorphic strength and weakness. The conclusion is obvious that we may ignore the question of age differentials in the somatotype comparisons.

SUMMARY OF SOMATOTYPES

Analysis of the somatotype photographs of the delinquents and non-delinquents was made by two quite different methods.

In the first instance an over-all inspectional rating was given the subjects "as is" and assignment made to one of thirteen somatotype categories. Comparison of the delinquent group with the non-delinquent group reveals marked and significant differences between them. *Among the delinquents, mesomorphy is far and away the most dominant component, with ectomorphic, endomorphic, and balanced types about equally represented but in relatively minor strength.* Among the non-delinquents, there is no single component in such clear-cut predominance as the mesomorphy of the delinquents. *The outstanding feature of the control series is the predominance of individuals with ectomorphy, this body build type occurring more frequently than the mesomorphic.* The endomorphs and balanced type are about equally represented but follow well behind the ectomorphs and mesomorphs in incidence.

These detailed comparisons reveal seven statistically significant differences between the delinquents and non-delinquents, which are describable as follows for the delinquents:

A deficiency of extreme endomorphs
An excess of extreme mesomorphs
An excess of mesomorphs
An excess of endomorphic mesomorphs
A deficiency of extreme ectomorphs
A deficiency of ectomorphs
A deficiency of mesomorphic ectomorphs

It should be noted that any statistically reliable endomorphic difference between the two series is limited to the extreme endomorphs only.

The second method of somatotype analysis by its very nature is a more sensitive barometer of component differences between the two juvenile groups. Each delinquent was compared with his matched non-delinquent for relative differences in the three somatotype components. *As a result of this analysis, it was found that mesomorphic strength is consistently greater and ectomorphy consistently weaker among the delinquent members of the matched pairs.* With respect to the endomorphic component, instances of markedly stronger endomorphy are somewhat more frequent among the non-delinquent members of the matched pairs, while slightly stronger and moderately stronger endomorphic differentiation is more in favor of the delinquent members.

Further study shows that the somatotype differences indicated by this comparison are unaffected by the age disparities existing between the matched pairs.

Throughout this section, the magnitude of the differences between the delinquents and non-delinquents and the uniformity of the results achieved by the two methods of analysis are very impressive. They serve most sharply to consolidate the findings derived previously from the measurements and indices.

TABLE C-70. SOMATOTYPE DIFFERENCES BETWEEN MATCHED DELINQUENTS AND NON-DELINQUENTS IN ACCORDANCE WITH AGE DIFFERENTIALS

	Delinquents Older Than Matched Non-Delinquents		Delinquents Younger Than Matched Non-Delinquents	
	No.	%	No.	%
Endomorphy				
Delinquents *markedly stronger* than non-delinquents	6	3.1 ⎫	14	4.9 ⎫
Delinquents *moderately stronger* than non-delinquents	19	9.9 ⎬ 53.1	49	17.1 ⎬ 53.5
Delinquents *slightly stronger* than non-delinquents	77	40.1 ⎭	90	31.5 ⎭
Delinquents *same* as non-delinquents	36	18.7	55	19.2
Delinquents *slightly weaker* than non-delinquents	32	16.7 ⎫	38	13.3 ⎫
Delinquents *moderately weaker* than non-delinquents	8	4.2 ⎬ 28.2	27	9.4 ⎬ 27.2
Delinquents *markedly weaker* than non-delinquents	14	7.3 ⎭	13	4.5 ⎭
TOTAL	192	100.0	286	99.9
Mesomorphy				
Delinquents *markedly stronger* than non-delinquents	21	10.9 ⎫	45	15.7 ⎫
Delinquents *moderately stronger* than non-delinquents	37	19.3 ⎬ 57.8	57	19.9 ⎬ 62.2
Delinquents *slightly stronger* than non-delinquents	53	27.6 ⎭	76	26.6 ⎭
Delinquents *same* as non-delinquents	29	15.1	39	13.6
Delinquents *slightly weaker* than non-delinquents	38	19.8 ⎫	47	16.4 ⎫
Delinquents *moderately weaker* than non-delinquents	9	4.7 ⎬ 27.1	18	6.3 ⎬ 24.1
Delinquents *markedly weaker* than non-delinquents	5	2.6 ⎭	4	1.4 ⎭
TOTAL	192	100.0	286	99.9
Ectomorphy				
Delinquents *markedly stronger* than non-delinquents	13	6.8 ⎫	10	3.5 ⎫
Delinquents *moderately stronger* than non-delinquents	13	6.8 ⎬ 31.8	29	10.1 ⎬ 30.0
Delinquents *slightly stronger* than non-delinquents	35	18.2 ⎭	47	16.4 ⎭
Delinquents *same* as non-delinquents	29	15.1	48	16.8
Delinquents *slightly weaker* than non-delinquents	49	25.5 ⎫	65	22.7 ⎫
Delinquents *moderately weaker* than non-delinquents	30	15.6 ⎬ 53.1	45	15.7 ⎬ 53.1
Delinquents *markedly weaker* than non-delinquents	23	12.0 ⎭	42	14.7 ⎭
TOTAL	192	100.0	286	99.9

APPENDIX C

APPENDIX C-1

SUMMARY OF INCIDENCE OF 67 TRAITS AMONG DELINQUENT AND NON-DELINQUENT PHYSIQUE TYPES

(Percentages of the Respective Physique Type Totals)

	Delinquent					Non-Delinquent				
	Total	Meso-morph	Endo-morph	Ecto-morph	Bal-anced	Total	Meso-morph	Endo-morph	Ecto-morph	Bal-anced
DEVELOPMENTAL HEALTH HISTORY										
1. (XIV-1) Poor Health in Infancy	14.7%	13.7%	13.5%	19.7%	15.1%	9.3%	8.1%	12.5%	8.3%	11.1%
2. (XIV-3) Susceptibility to Contagion	27.0	30.0	13.6	21.4	31.8	20.0	15.0	8.3	32.4	9.7
3. (XIV-2) Extreme Restlessness in Early Childhood	59.6	52.2	59.3	83.1	68.2	30.4	26.8	31.9	34.0	26.4
4. (XIV-2) Enuresis in Early Childhood	28.5	23.1	28.8	43.7	36.4	13.8	10.1	18.1	15.7	12.5
NEUROLOGIC FINDINGS										
5. (XIV-6) Irregular Reflexes	34.2%	35.9%	23.7%	38.0%	31.8%	38.3%	38.9%	36.1%	38.9%	37.5%
6. (XIV-13) Cyanosis	41.5	36.6	52.6	50.7	43.9	43.1	39.6	30.5	49.5	45.9
7. (XIV-13) Dermographia	45.2	38.0	55.9	62.0	50.0	58.0	59.1	59.8	60.0	48.6
8. (XIV-13) Tremors	18.8	16.9	11.9	25.3	25.8	21.1	15.4	9.7	30.6	19.4
OTHER PHYSICAL FINDINGS										
9. (XIV-9) Genital Under-development	11.5%	6.7%	18.6%	25.3%	10.6%	13.5%	4.7%	27.7%	16.5%	9.7%
10. (XIV-4) Strength of Hand Grip	51.4	63.3	43.1	17.1	42.4	43.9	73.6	38.1	23.9	30.3
SOME ASPECTS OF INTELLIGENCE										
11. (App. D-11) Low Verbal Intelligence	27.5%	31.5%	17.0%	18.2%	28.8%	16.2%	12.8%	11.1%	18.3%	22.2%
12. (App. D-12) High Performance Intelligence	39.3	32.1	42.5	42.2	66.6	42.0	45.0	30.5	43.4	44.0
13. (XVII-1) Originality	27.7	29.9	22.4	28.2	21.9	25.9	23.7	21.4	28.9	26.8
14. (XVII-3) Banality	26.1	26.6	27.6	22.0	27.0	30.9	37.5	25.8	29.8	25.0

298

		Delinquent					Non-Delinquent				
		Total	Meso-morph	Endo-morph	Ecto-morph	Bal-anced	Total	Meso-morph	Endo-morph	Ecto-morph	Bal-anced
SOME ASPECTS OF INTELLIGENCE (Cont.)											
15. (XVII-4)	Marked Power of Observation	63.9%	61.2%	67.8%	70.0%	65.6%	70.3%	68.1%	65.3%	72.9%	73.2%
16. (XVII-7)	Intuition	16.3	17.6	11.9	20.3	10.8	15.7	12.8	11.5	17.5	21.5
17. (XVII-8)	Tendency to Phantasy	39.1	38.4	30.5	43.7	45.2	32.5	24.4	28.6	36.8	42.0
18. (XVII-6)	Common Sense	75.2	77.5	68.4	64.6	81.2	80.7	84.7	74.3	78.7	84.1
19. (XVII-10)	Unmethodical Approach to Problems	78.8	74.8	84.2	82.7	88.9	65.0	65.0	60.0	64.8	70.0
20. (XVII-11)	Potential Capacity for Objective Interests	44.5	46.6	32.5	49.0	40.0	54.3	48.5	54.7	56.6	61.9
BASIC ATTITUDES TO AUTHORITY AND SOCIETY											
21. (XVIII-2)	Social Assertiveness	45.3%	51.3%	40.5%	33.9%	35.3%	20.2%	21.1%	8.0%	22.0%	26.9%
22. (XVIII-3)	Defiance	50.4	47.2	50.9	50.8	63.3	11.5	12.3	7.5	11.6	13.6
23. (XVIII-4)	Marked Submissiveness	26.8	27.0	22.4	26.5	30.8	80.0	77.4	90.0	78.4	79.1
24. (XVIII-5)	Ambivalence to Authority	40.6	32.9	52.9	45.3	57.4	19.6	19.1	11.9	20.8	26.6
FEELINGS OF RESENTMENT, ANXIETY, INFERIORITY, AND FRUSTRATION											
25. (XVIII-7)	Enhanced Feelings of Insecurity	18.5%	18.8%	12.7%	25.0%	16.1%	28.8%	26.6%	33.3%	31.5%	21.0%
26. (XVIII-8)	Marked Feeling of Not Being Wanted or Loved	84.1	80.8	89.4	89.8	87.7	88.0	88.2	83.9	89.6	87.3
27. (XVIII-9)	Feeling of Not Being Taken Care of	29.2	36.5	17.9	20.9	13.6	24.7	18.8	31.4	25.2	30.4
28. (XVIII-10)	Marked Feeling of Not Being Taken Seriously	44.1	43.7	45.8	36.0	53.1	52.3	47.2	64.4	51.8	50.0
29. (XVIII-12)	Feeling of Helplessness	42.1	46.4	33.3	40.9	32.2	55.2	53.7	65.5	54.6	49.1
30. (XVIII-11)	Feeling of Not Being Appreciated	35.9	40.0	28.6	32.7	27.8	24.8	19.3	25.0	27.1	30.6

| | Delinquent | | | | | Non-Delinquent | | | | |
---	Total	Meso-morph	Endo-morph	Ecto-morph	Bal-anced	Total	Meso-morph	Endo-morph	Ecto-morph	Bal-anced
FEELINGS OF RESENTMENT, ANXIETY, INFERIORITY, AND FRUSTRATION (cont.)										
31. (XVIII-13) Fear of Failure and Defeat	44.3%	44.7%	45.3%	41.9%	43.8%	63.6%	67.7%	75.8%	62.7%	45.0%
32. (XVIII-14) Feeling of Resentment	74.2	76.0	72.0	65.3	75.9	51.6	50.5	52.3	52.5	50.0
FEELING OF KINDLINESS AND HOSTILITY										
33. (XVIII-17) Good Surface Contact with Others	91.6%	92.0%	96.6%	82.6%	95.3%	96.6%	98.6%	91.2%	96.8%	97.1%
34. (XVIII-22) Hostility	79.6	79.3	76.9	82.8	80.0	56.0	50.5	57.7	61.6	50.0
35. (XVIII-23) Marked Suspiciousness	51.4	51.3	47.9	53.1	52.7	26.8	24.6	35.1	28.8	17.5
36. (XVIII-24) Destructiveness	48.4	51.9	38.7	39.6	50.0	15.7	11.1	7.8	21.8	17.2
37. (XVIII-25) Feeling of Isolation	45.5	46.2	38.2	46.1	46.5	36.9	32.7	41.6	40.1	31.4
38. (XVIII-26) Defensive Attitude	56.0	56.2	56.9	58.3	51.8	45.0	47.6	50.0	44.5	35.5
DEPENDENCE AND INDEPENDENCE										
39. (XVIII-27) Marked Dependence on Others	68.8%	67.9%	68.4%	64.9%	77.0%	86.4%	85.8%	92.8%	87.5%	77.6%
40. (XVIII-32) Feeling of Being Able to Manage Own Life	73.1	70.7	81.6	64.9	85.4	63.3	67.0	51.1	62.5	70.0
GOALS OF STRIVINGS										
41. (XVIII-33) Narcissistic Trends	23.3%	25.7%	22.4%	21.2%	15.0%	14.3%	12.7%	13.8%	15.2%	16.4%
42. (XVIII-35) Receptive Trends	29.6	35.0	24.5	25.0	15.8	13.8	16.3	12.6	9.4	21.9
43. (XVIII-34) Masochistic Trends	15.4	18.4	13.0	8.2	11.9	37.5	38.9	45.9	38.6	22.8
44. (XVIII-36) Destructive-Sadistic Trends	48.7	51.9	38.8	41.7	50.0	16.2	11.9	7.8	22.4	17.2

		Delinquent					Non-Delinquent				
SOME GENERAL QUALITIES OF PERSONALITY		Total	Meso-morph	Endo-morph	Ecto-morph	Bal-anced	Total	Meso-morph	Endo-morph	Ecto-morph	Bal-anced
45. (XVIII-37)	Emotional Lability	43.1%	47.7%	41.8%	33.4%	34.0%	19.1%	17.9%	16.7%	20.0%	21.6%
46. (XVIII-38)	Self-Control	38.9	42.3	37.2	36.9	27.7	66.0	64.6	69.7	64.6	68.7
47. (XVIII-39)	Vivacity	50.2	51.3	50.0	50.0	42.1	23.6	20.4	9.1	29.0	34.6
48. (XVIII-40)	Compulsory Trends	20.7	20.2	26.3	21.5	16.4	30.7	29.1	31.2	33.0	27.2
49. (XVIII-41)	Preponderance of Extroversive Trends	54.3	58.2	48.8	43.5	51.2	35.7	33.3	33.8	36.8	38.9
50. (XVIII-42)	Preponderance of Introversive Trends	27.6	28.7	14.3	33.4	28.6	24.3	23.6	19.7	23.9	32.1
DEEP-ROOTED EMOTIONAL DYNAMICS											
51. (XIX-1)	Sensitivity	31.9%	26.2%	28.1%	52.1%	39.4%	36.2%	20.8%	22.2%	50.5%	44.4%
52. (XIX-1)	Suggestibility	60.0	61.1	66.7	52.1	57.6	26.3	22.1	36.1	22.1	36.1
53. (XIX-1)	Inadequacy	85.2	80.9	93.0	90.1	92.4	69.4	54.4	66.7	80.0	75.0
54. (XIX-1)	Stubbornness	41.5	44.6	36.8	38.0	34.8	7.9	8.7	8.3	8.4	4.2
55. (XIX-1)	Adventurousness	55.3	58.1	52.6	45.1	56.1	18.2	22.1	11.1	16.3	22.2
56. (XIX-1)	Uninhibited Motor Responses to Stimuli	56.5	61.7	52.6	39.4	54.5	28.8	45.0	19.4	20.5	26.4
57. (XIX-1)	Emotional Instability	81.7	79.5	82.5	88.7	83.3	49.9	35.6	45.8	63.7	47.2
APPETITIVE-AESTHETIC TENDENCIES											
58. (XIX-2)	Aestheticism	17.1%	13.1%	12.3%	32.4%	22.7%	37.7%	27.5%	29.2%	48.9%	37.5%
59. (XIX-2)	Sensuousness	20.1	18.1	40.4	9.9	22.7	5.6	2.7	20.8	4.2	0.0
60. (XIX-2)	Acquisitiveness	20.5	18.5	15.8	32.4	21.2	13.9	14.1	5.6	20.0	5.6

		Delinquent					Non-Delinquent				
PERSONALITY ORIENTATION		Total	Meso-morph	Endo-morph	Ecto-morph	Bal-anced	Total	Meso-morph	Endo-morph	Ecto-morph	Bal-anced
61. (XIX-3)	Conventionality	25.0%	27.9%	33.3%	12.7%	18.2%	48.4%	51.7%	75.0%	36.3%	47.7%
62. (XIX-3)	Lack of Self-Criticism	29.1	28.5	35.1	26.8	28.8	10.8	12.8	13.9	6.8	13.9
63. (XIX-3)	Conscientiousness	8.7	9.1	8.8	7.0	9.1	54.0	49.0	56.9	55.3	58.3
64. (XIX-3)	Practicality	18.7	21.8	7.0	14.1	19.7	34.8	43.0	33.3	29.5	33.3
SOME ASPECTS OF MENTAL PATHOLOGY											
65. (XIX-4)	Emotional Conflicts	75.0%	71.1%	84.9%	80.9%	77.2%	37.7%	22.7%	36.8%	52.5%	31.7%
66. (XVIII-43)	Neuroticism	25.1	23.7	28.8	28.7	24.3	37.0	36.0	37.9	37.1	37.7
67. (XVIII-43)	Psychopathy	24.7	27.5	20.3	19.7	21.2	6.5	8.2	6.1	4.8	8.7

APPENDIX C-2

SUMMARY OF INCIDENCE OF 42 SOCIOCULTURAL FACTORS AMONG DELINQUENT AND NON-DELINQUENT PHYSIQUE TYPES

(Percentages of the Respective Physique Type Totals)

		Delinquent					Non-Delinquent				
		Total	Meso-morph	Endo-morph	Ecto-morph	Bal-anced	Total	Meso-morph	Endo-morph	Ecto-morph	Bal-anced
NATIVITY OF PARENTS											
68. (IX-2)	Nativity of Parents	57.9%	61.9%	51.8%	54.5%	49.3%	61.3%	68.5%	54.9%	60.3%	55.6%
PATHOLOGY OF PARENTS											
69. (IX-10)	Delinquency of Father	66.3%	66.2%	61.0%	71.8%	65.2%	32.0%	33.6%	26.4%	33.0%	31.9%
70. (IX-10)	Alcoholism of Father	62.4	59.5	62.7	70.4	66.7	38.6	36.2	34.7	39.8	44.4
71. (IX-10)	Emotional Disturbance in Father	44.2	39.5	45.8	56.3	51.5	18.2	14.1	23.6	19.9	16.7
72. (IX-10)	Serious Physical Ailment in Father	39.8	40.5	44.1	33.8	39.4	28.7	33.6	22.2	29.3	23.6
73. (IX-10)	Delinquency of Mother	44.6	45.5	35.6	53.5	39.4	15.5	20.1	12.5	12.0	18.1
74. (IX-10)	Alcoholism of Mother	23.0	22.7	20.3	29.6	19.7	7.2	6.7	4.2	8.9	6.9
75. (IX-10)	Emotional Disturbance in Mother	40.6	38.8	44.1	45.1	40.9	17.6	14.8	19.4	19.4	16.7
76. (IX-10)	Serious Physical Ailment in Mother	48.3	46.8	55.9	50.7	45.5	33.1	38.3	31.9	34.0	20.8
ECONOMIC CONDITIONS											
77. (IX-14)	Financial Dependence of Family	36.6%	37.5%	39.0%	32.4%	34.9%	15.1%	18.1%	9.7%	15.7%	12.5%
78. (X-1)	Poor Management of Family Income	66.0	66.2	57.6	71.4	66.7	44.1	44.5	37.5	46.6	43.7
79. (X-9)	Gainful Employment of Mother	46.9	43.0	42.1	62.8	51.5	33.1	34.9	37.5	30.3	31.8

| | | Delinquent | | | | | Non-Delinquent | | | | |
		Total	Meso-morph	Endo-morph	Ecto-morph	Bal-anced	Total	Meso-morph	Endo-morph	Ecto-morph	Bal-anced
PHYSICAL ASPECTS OF HOME											
80. (VIII-7)	Crowded Home	33.0%	35.0%	34.5%	31.4%	24.2%	25.3%	28.2%	13.9%	26.7%	26.8%
81. (VIII-8)	Unclean and Disorderly Home	51.6	53.5	44.1	47.1	54.5	34.7	33.6	38.9	34.4	33.8
82. (X-2)	Careless Household Routine	75.6	80.6	59.3	71.4	72.3	51.2	53.7	44.4	52.2	50.0
83. (X-3)	Lack of Cultural Refinement in Home	91.6	88.9	94.8	97.1	95.5	81.3	85.1	81.7	81.7	71.8
INSTABILITY OF HOME AND NEIGHBORHOOD											
84. (XI-8)	Broken Home	60.4%	54.8%	64.4%	73.2%	68.2%	34.3%	35.6%	33.3%	32.5%	37.5%
85. (XI-12)	Rearing by Parent Substitute	45.9	42.1	44.1	59.2	50.0	12.2	9.4	19.4	9.4	18.1
86. (XIII-2)	Frequency of Moving	53.7	50.5	52.5	62.0	60.6	18.8	16.1	19.5	18.9	23.6
ATMOSPHERE OF FAMILY LIFE											
87. (X-8)	Dominance of Mother in Family Affairs	50.4%	48.7%	54.7%	49.3%	55.6%	51.9%	48.6%	56.9%	51.4%	55.1%
88. (X-4)	Self-Respect of Parents Lacking	43.2	44.8	32.2	47.9	40.9	10.2	12.2	5.6	10.9	8.5
89. (X-5)	Ambition of Parents Lacking	89.5	90.3	79.7	93.0	90.8	70.1	72.6	67.6	72.0	62.5
90. (X-6)	Low Conduct Standards of Family	90.3	88.6	93.2	98.6	86.3	54.1	55.7	41.7	56.1	58.4
EVIDENCE OF FAMILY DISUNITY											
91. (X-7)	Incompatibility of Parents	63.2%	60.4%	56.9%	81.4%	61.5%	34.8%	29.5%	32.4%	38.8%	38.0%
92. (X-11)	Family Group Recreations Lacking	67.2	70.4	54.2	68.6	63.7	38.5	41.9	34.3	35.8	43.1
93. (X-12)	Parents Uninterested in Children's Friends	79.8	82.0	72.4	80.6	75.8	61.9	55.0	70.8	63.8	62.0
94. (X-13)	Meager Recreational Facilities in Home	53.2	55.2	39.0	54.4	56.1	36.6	33.6	34.7	40.5	34.7
95. (X-14)	Lack of Family Cohesiveness	81.8	80.5	76.4	94.4	84.8	38.2	33.5	33.3	42.4	41.7

		Delinquent					Non-Delinquent				
		Total	Meso-morph	Endo-morph	Ecto-morph	Bal-anced	Total	Meso-morph	Endo-morph	Ecto-morph	Bal-anced
AFFECTION OF FAMILY FOR BOY											
96. (XI-5)	Rank of Boy Among Siblings	39.6%	36.4%	40.7%	46.5%	45.4%	52.5%	40.2%	66.7%	58.6%	47.1%
97. (XI-13)	Father Not Attached to Boy	59.5	57.5	58.6	63.4	65.2	19.3	17.7	21.1	20.3	18.6
98. (XI-14)	Mother Not Attached to Boy	27.7	24.2	32.8	39.1	27.7	4.3	4.8	2.8	3.8	6.9
99. (XI-18)	Siblings Not Attached to Boy	28.4	24.9	39.3	41.2	19.3	7.2	5.9	6.9	7.8	8.8
FEELING OF BOY FOR PARENTS											
100. (XI-15)	Boy Not Attached to Father	67.5%	67.4%	63.1%	66.2%	72.8%	35.2%	34.9%	30.6%	35.2%	40.4%
101. (XI-16)	Father Unacceptable to Boy for Emulation	30.8	30.7	34.0	26.3	32.7	7.3	5.6	12.1	6.5	7.9
102. (XI-17)	Boy Not Attached to Mother	34.7	34.6	31.7	39.4	33.3	10.4	10.8	5.6	13.2	6.9
SUPERVISION AND DISCIPLINE OF BOY											
103. (X-10)	Unsuitable Supervision by Mother	63.9%	60.3%	61.0%	76.1%	69.7%	13.3%	11.6%	13.9%	13.4%	15.7%
104. (XI-22)	Unsuitable Discipline by Father	94.5	94.9	87.5	98.4	95.2	45.2	47.8	44.8	43.7	44.6
105. (XI-23)	Physical Punishment by Father	67.7	67.8	76.4	70.9	57.1	35.3	38.2	25.8	36.6	35.9
106. (XI-23)	Scolding or Threatening by Father	32.0	31.1	38.2	36.4	27.0	30.9	35.1	27.3	30.8	26.6
107. (XI-22)	Unsuitable Discipline by Mother	95.7	95.3	96.6	97.1	95.5	35.3	29.2	38.9	42.1	26.4
108. (XI-23)	Physical Punishment by Mother	55.3	55.7	58.6	50.8	55.4	34.9	37.5	31.0	33.3	37.5
109. (XI-23)	Scolding or Threatening by Mother	46.8	46.7	43.1	52.3	44.6	37.4	41.0	25.4	37.6	41.7

APPENDIX D

APPENDIX D-1

SUMMARY OF SIGNIFICANT VARIATIONS IN TRAIT INCIDENCE BY PHYSIQUE TYPES

Table	MESOMORPHS — Delinquents Compared with: Endo	Ecto	Bal.	Non-Delinquents Compared with: Endo	Ecto	Bal.	Difference between Delinquents and Non-Delinquents Compared with: Endo	Ecto	Bal.	ENDOMORPHS — Delinquents Compared with: Meso	Ecto	Bal.	Non-Delinquents Compared with: Meso	Ecto	Bal.	Difference between Delinquents and Non-Delinquents Compared with: Meso	Ecto	Bal.
2. Susceptibility to Contagion	H				L			H		L		L		L				
3. Extreme Restlessness in Early Childhood		L	L					L			L							
4. Emuresis in Early Childhood		L																
6. Cyanosis							L							L		H		
7. Dermographia	L	L						L		H								
8. Tremors					L									L				
9. Genital Under-development		L		L	L								H				H	
10. Strength of Hand Grip	H	H	H	H	H	H			L	L	H		L					
11. Low Verbal Intelligence	H	H						H		L								
12. High Performance Intelligence			L				L		L			L					H	
17. Tendency to Fantasy					L	L												
19. Unmethodical Approach to Problems			L															
21. Social Assertiveness		H		H									L	L	L			
22. Defiance			L															
23. Marked Submissiveness		L											H	H				
24. Ambivalence to Authority	L	L					L			H							H	
27. Feeling of Not Being Taken Care of	H				H		H	H	H	L							L	
31. Fear of Failure and Defeat						H											H	L
33. Good Surface Contact with Others							L				H					H	H	
36. Destructiveness					L			H						L				
39. Marked Dependence on Others														H				L
40. Feeling of Being Able to Manage Own Life		L					L							H				
42. Receptive Trends		H							H									
43. Masochistic Trends		H												H				
44. Destructive-Sadistic Trends					L		H							L				
46. Self-Control			H															
47. Vivacity													L	L				
50. Preponderance of Introversive Trends	H									L								
51. Sensitivity		L			L	L					L			L	L			
53. Inadequacy	L		L		L	L	H			H								
56. Uninhibited Motor Responses to Stimuli		H		H	H	H							L					
57. Emotional Instability					L			H						L				
58. Aestheticism		L			L						L			L				
59. Sensuousness	L			L						H	H		H	H	H			
60. Acquisitiveness		L												L				
61. Conventionality		H		L	H						H		H	H	H			
64. Practicality	H				H					L								
65. Emotional Conflicts	L				L			H		H								

Note: H = Highest; L = Lowest

	ECTOMORPHS									BALANCED TYPE								
	Delinquents Compared with			Non-Delinquents Compared with			Difference between Delinquents and Non-Delinquents Compared with			Delinquents Compared with			Non-Delinquents Compared with			Difference between Delinquents and Non-Delinquents Compared with		
	Meso	Endo	Bal.	Meso	Endo	Bal.	Meso	Endo	Bal.	Meso	Endo	Ecto	Meso	Endo	Ecto	Meso	Endo	Ecto
2.				H	H	H	L		L		H			L				H
3.	H	H					H			H								
4.	H																	
6.					H													
7.	H						H											
8.				H	H													
9.	H			H										L				
10.	L	L	L	L						L		H	L				H	
11.	L						L											
12.			L							H	H	H					H	
17.				H									H					
19.										H								
21.	L				H									H				
22.										H								
23.						L												
24.										H								
27.							L			L						L		
31.						H							L	L	L		H	
33.		L	L					L				H						
36.				H	H		L											
39.														L			H	
40.										H								
42.									H	L				L				L
43.	L													L				
44.				H	H		L											
46.										L								
47.					H									H				
50.																		
51.	H	H		H	H								H	H				
53.				H			L			H			H					
56.	L			L									L					
57.				H	H	H	L								L			
58.	H	H		H	H													
59.		L			L	H		L						L	L			H
60.	H				H	H								L				
61.	L	L		L	L									L				
64.				L														
65.				H		H	L							L				

SUMMARY OF SIGNIFICANT VARIATIONS IN INCIDENCE OF SOCIOCULTURAL FACTORS BY PHYSIQUE TYPES

Table	Mesomorphic Delinquents Compared with			Endomorphic Delinquents Compared with			Ectomorphic Delinquents Compared with			Balanced Type Delinquents Compared with		
	Endo	Ecto	Bal.	Meso	Ecto	Bal.	Meso	Endo	Bal.	Meso	Endo	Ecto
71. Emotional Disturbance in Father		L					H					
79. Gainful Employment of Mother		L				L	H	H				
82. Careless Household Routine	H			L								
83. Lack of Cultural Refinement in Home		L					H					
84. Broken Home		L					H					
85. Rearing by Parent Substitute		L					H					
90. Low Conduct Standards of Family		L					H		H			L
91. Incompatibility of Parents		L				L	H	H	H			L
92. Family Group Recreations Lacking	H			L	L							
94. Meager Recreational Facilities in Home	H				L							
95. Lack of Family Cohesiveness		L				L	H	H				
98. Mother Not Attached to Boy		L					H	H				
99. Siblings Not Attached to Boy		L				H	H	H	H		L	L
103. Unsuitable Supervision by Mother		L					H					
104. Unsuitable Discipline by Father						L	H					

Note: H = Highest; L = Lowest

APPENDIX E

CLUSTERS OF DELINQUENCY INDUCING TRAITS FOR PHYSIQUE TYPES

MESOMORPHS

Code

Trait 1. Susceptibility to Contagion
2. Low Verbal Intelligence
3. Feeling of Not Being Taken Care of   A = Absent
4. Destructiveness   P = Present
5. Receptive Trends
6. Destructive-Sadistic Trends
7. Inadequacy
8. Emotional Instability
9. Emotional Conflicts

Traits: 1	2	3	4	5	6	7	8	9	Number of Delinquents	Number of Non-Delinquents
8 Traits										
A	P	P	P	P	P	P	P	P	3	
7 Traits										
A	A	P	P	P	P	P	P	P	3	
A	P	A	P	P	P	P	P	P	2	
P	A	A	P	P	P	P	P	P	2	
A	P	P	P	A	P	P	P	P	2	
P	P	A	P	P	P	A	P	P	1	
P	P	P	P	A	P	P	A	P	1	
6 Traits										
A	A	P	P	A	P	P	P	P	6	
A	P	P	A	P	A	P	P	P	5	
A	A	A	P	P	P	P	P	P	4	
P	A	A	P	A	P	P	P	P	3	1
A	P	A	P	A	P	P	P	P	2	
A	A	P	P	P	P	P	P	A	2	
A	P	A	P	P	P	A	P	P	1	
A	A	P	P	P	P	A	P	P	1	
P	P	A	P	A	P	P	P	A	1	
P	A	P	A	P	P	P	A	1	
P	P	A	A	P	A	P	P	P	1	

Traits: 1	2	3	4	5	6	7	8	9	Number of Delinquents	Number of Non-Delinquents
5 Traits										
A	A	A	P	A	P	P	P	P	12	
A	A	P	P	A	P	P	P	A	5	
A	P	A	P	A	P	P	P	A	4	
A	A	P	A	P	A	P	P	P	3	
A	P	P	A	A	A	P	P	P	2	1
A	P	A	A	P	A	P	P	P	2	
A	P	P	A	P	A	P	P	A	2	
A	A	P	P	P	P	A	P	A	2	
P	P	A	A	A	A	P	P	P	1	
A	A	A	P	P	P	A	P	P	1	
P	A	A	A	P	A	P	P	P	1	2
P	A	A	P	P	P	A	A	P	1	
A	A	A	P	P	P	P	P	A	1	
A	P	P	A	P	A	P	A	P	1	
A	A	P	P	P	P	A	A	P	1	
A	A	P	P	A	P	A	P	P	1	
A	A	P	A	P	A	P	P	P		1
4 Traits										
P	A	A	A	A	A	P	P	P	8	
A	A	A	A	P	A	P	P	P	5	
A	P	A	A	A	A	P	P	P	2	1
A	P	A	A	P	A	A	P	P	1	
A	A	P	A	P	A	P	P	A	1	1
A	A	P	P	A	P	P	A	A	1	
A	A	P	P	P	P	A	A	A	1	
A	P	P	A	A	A	P	A	P	1	
A	A	A	P	A	P	P	P	A	1	1
A	P	P	A	A	A	P	P	A	1	
A	A	A	P	A	P	A	P	P	1	
A	A	A	P	P	P	A	A	P		1
P	P	A	A	A	A	A	P	P		1
A	A	P	A	P	A	P	A	P		2
A	A	A	P	P	P	P	A	A		1
3 Traits										
A	A	A	A	A	A	P	P	P	7	2
A	P	A	A	A	A	P	P	A	3	
A	P	A	A	P	A	A	A	P	1	
A	P	A	A	A	A	P	A	P	1	
A	A	A	P	A	P	A	A	P	1	
A	A	A	A	P	A	P	A	P	1	
A	A	P	A	A	A	P	P	A	1	
A	A	P	P	A	P	A	A	A	1	2
A	P	P	A	P	A	A	A	A	1	
A	A	P	A	P	A	A	A	P	1	
P	A	A	A	A	A	P	P	A		3
A	A	P	A	P	A	A	P	A		1
P	P	A	A	A	A	P	A	A		2
A	A	P	A	P	A	P	A	A		2
A	A	A	A	P	A	P	P	A		1

Traits: 1	2	3	4	5	6	7	8	9	Number of Delinquents	Number of Non-Delinquents
2 Traits										
A	A	A	A	A	A	P	A	P	3	3
P	A	A	A	A	A	A	P	A	1	
A	A	P	A	A	A	A	P	A	1	
A	A	A	P	A	P	A	A	A	1	
P	P	A	A	A	A	A	A	A	1	
P	A	A	A	P	A	A	A	A		1
A	P	P	A	A	A	A	A	A		1
A	A	A	A	P	A	P	A	A		1
A	A	P	A	P	A	A	A	A		1
A	P	A	A	A	A	P	A	A		2
P	A	A	A	A	A	P	A	A		3
A	A	A	A	A	A	A	P	P		1
A	A	P	A	A	A	P	A	A		1
A	A	A	A	A	A	P	P	A		3
1 Trait										
A	A	A	A	P	A	A	A	A	4	2
A	A	A	A	A	A	P	A	A	2	4
A	A	A	A	A	A	A	A	P	1	2
A	A	P	A	A	A	A	A	A	1	1
A	A	A	A	A	A	A	P	A		1
A	P	A	A	A	A	A	A	A		1

Code

Trait 1. Cyanosis
    2. High Performance Intelligence   A = Absent
    3. Ambivalence to Authority   P = Present
    4. Good Surface Contact with Others
    5. Feeling of Being Able to Manage Own Life

Traits: 1 2 3 4 5	Number Delinquents	Number of Non-Delinquents
4 Traits		
A P P P P	6	1
P A P P P	4	2
P P A P P	1	1
3 Traits		
A P A P P	3	
P A A P P	2	5
A A P P P	1	1
P P A P A		2
P P P A A		1
A P P P A		1
2 Traits		
P A A P A	3	3
A A A P P	3	6
A A P P A	1	
P P A A A	1	
A P A P A		4
1 Trait		
A A A P A	1	5
P A A A A		1
A P A A A		1

ECTOMORPHS

Code

Trait 1. Extreme Restlessness in
       Early Childhood   A = Absent
   2. Dermographia   P = Present
   3. Receptive Trends

Traits: 1	2	3	Number of Delinquents	Number of Non-Delinquents
2 Traits				
P	P	A	24	30
P	A	P	6	1
A	P	P		6
1 Trait				
P	A	A	14	25
A	P	A	5	60
A	A	P	1	4

BALANCED TYPE

Code

Trait 1. Susceptibility to Contagion
    2. Strength of Hand Grip   A = Absent
    3. High Performance Intelligence   P = Present
    4. Fear of Failure and Defeat
    5. Marked Dependence on Others
    6. Sensuousness

Traits: 1	2	3	4	5	6	Number of Delinquents	Number of Non-Delinquents
4 Traits							
P	A	P	P	P	A	4	1
P	A	P	A	P	P	1	
P	A	A	P	P	P	1	
3 Traits							
A	A	P	P	P	A	8	12
A	A	P	A	P	P	2	
P	A	P	A	P	A	2	1
A	A	A	P	P	P	2	
P	A	A	P	A	P	1	
P	A	A	A	P	P	1	
P	A	A	P	P	A	1	1
2 Traits							
A	A	A	P	P	A	5	12
A	A	P	A	P	A	3	8
P	A	A	A	P	A	3	1
A	A	P	P	A	A	2	
A	A	A	A	P	P	2	
A	A	P	A	A	P	2	
A	A	A	P	A	P	1	
P	A	P	A	A	A		1
1 Trait							
A	A	A	A	P	A	5	10
A	A	A	A	A	P	1	
A	A	P	A	A	A	1	3
P	A	A	A	A	A	1	1
A	A	A	P	A	A		1

CLUSTERS OF SOCIOCULTURAL FACTORS HAVING
SELECTIVE INFLUENCE ON THE DELINQUENCY OF THE PHYSIQUE TYPES

MESOMORPHS

Code

Factor 1. Careless Household Routine   A = Absent
      2. Family Group Recreations Lacking   P = Present
      3. Meager Recreational Facilities in Home

Factors: 1 2 3	Number of Delinquents	Number of Non-Delinquents
2 Factors		
P P A	57	16
P A P	25	6
A P P	10	7
1 Factor		
P A A	31	28
A A P	4	9
A P A	14	11

ECTOMORPHS

Code

Factor
1. Gainful Employment of Mother
2. Unsuitable Supervision by Mother
3. Low Conduct Standards of Family
4. Unsuitable Discipline by Father   A = Absent
5. Incompatability of Parents   P = Present
6. Mother Not Attached to Boy
7. Siblings Not Attached to Boy
8. Lack of Cultural Refinement in Home
9. Lack of Family Cohesiveness
10. Emotional Disturbance in Father
11. Broken Home
12. Rearing by Parent Substitute

Factors: 1	2	3	4	5	6	7	8	9	10	11	12	Number of Delinquents	Number of Non-Delinquents
11 Factors													
P	P	P	P	P	P	P	P	P	A	P	P	3	
P	P	P	P	P	P	A	P	P	P	P	P	2	
P	P	P	P	P	P	P	P	P	P	P	A	1	
10 Factors													
P	P	P	P	P	P	A	P	P	A	P	P	3	
A	P	P	P	P	P	P	P	P	A	P	P	1	
A	P	P	P	P	P	P	P	P	P	P	A	1	
P	P	P	P	P	A	P	P	P	A	P	P	1	
P	P	P	P	P	P	P	P	P	A	P	A	1	
P	P	P	P	P	P	A	P	P	P	P	A		1
9 Factors													
P	P	P	P	P	A	A	P	P	A	P	P	3	
P	P	P	P	P	A	A	P	P	P	P	A	2	
P	P	P	P	P	P	P	P	P	A	A	A	2	
A	P	P	P	P	A	P	P	P	A	P	P	1	
A	P	P	P	P	P	P	P	P	A	A	P	1	
P	P	P	P	P	A	A	P	P	P	A	P	1	
A	P	P	P	P	P	P	P	P	A	P	A	1	
P	P	P	P	P	A	P	P	P	A	P	A	1	
A	P	P	P	P	A	A	P	P	P	P	P	1	
P	P	P	P	P	P	A	P	P	A	P	A	1	
A	A	P	P	P	A	P	P	P	P	P	P	1	
A	A	P	P	P	P	A	P	P	P	P	P	1	
P	A	P	P	P	A	P	P	A	P	P	P	1	
P	P	P	P	P	A	P	P	P	P	A	A		1
P	A	P	P	P	P	A	P	P	A	P	P		1

Factors: 1	2	3	4	5	6	7	8	9	10	11	12	Number of Delinquents	Number of Non-Delinquents
8 Factors													
A	P	P	P	A	A	P	P	P	A	P	P	1	
P	A	P	P	A	P	P	P	P	P	A	A	1	
A	P	P	A	P	P	A	P	P	A	P	P	1	
P	P	P	P	P	A	P	P	P	A	A	A	1	
P	P	P	P	P	A	A	P	P	P	A	A	1	
A	P	P	P	P	A	A	P	P	A	P	P	1	
P	A	P	P	P	A	A	P	P	A	P	P		1
P	P	P	P	P	A	A	P	P	A	P	A		1
P	A	P	P	P	A	A	P	P	P	P	A		2
P	P	P	P	P	A	A	P	P	P	A	A		1
A	P	P	A	P	A	P	A	P	P	P	A		1
P	A	P	P	P	P	P	P	P	A	A	A		1
A	A	P	P	P	A	A	P	P	P	P	P		1
7 Factors													
P	A	P	P	P	A	A	P	P	A	P	A	3	2
P	P	P	P	A	A	A	P	P	A	P	A	1	
A	A	P	P	P	A	A	P	P	A	P	P	1	
P	P	P	P	P	A	A	P	P	A	A	A	1	2
P	P	P	P	A	A	A	P	P	A	A	P	1	
A	P	P	P	A	A	A	P	P	P	P	A	1	
A	P	P	P	A	P	A	P	P	A	A	P	1	
A	A	P	P	P	A	A	A	P	P	P	P	1	
A	P	P	P	P	A	A	P	P	P	A	A		1
P	A	P	P	P	A	A	P	P	P	A	A		1
A	A	P	P	P	A	A	P	P	P	P	A		1
P	A	P	A	P	A	P	A	P	A	P	P		1
A	P	P	P	P	A	P	P	P	P	A	A		1
A	P	P	A	P	P	A	P	P	A	P	A		1
6 Factors													
A	A	P	P	P	A	P	P	P	A	A	A	1	2
A	A	P	P	P	A	A	A	P	A	P	P	1	
A	P	P	P	A	P	A	P	P	A	A	A	1	
A	P	P	P	A	A	P	P	P	A	A	A	1	
P	P	P	P	A	A	A	P	A	A	A	P	1	
P	A	P	P	P	A	A	P	P	A	A	A		1
A	P	P	P	P	A	A	P	P	A	A	A		3
A	P	P	A	A	A	A	P	P	A	P	P		2
P	A	P	A	P	A	A	P	P	A	P	A		1
A	A	P	P	P	A	A	P	P	A	P	A		1
P	P	A	P	P	A	A	A	A	P	P	A		1
A	A	P	P	P	A	A	P	P	A	P	A		2
A	P	A	A	P	A	A	P	P	P	P	A		1

Factors: 1	2	3	4	5	6	7	8	9	10	11	12	Number of Delinquents	Number of Non-Delinquents

5 Factors

1	2	3	4	5	6	7	8	9	10	11	12	Number of Delinquents	Number of Non-Delinquents
A	A	P	P	P	A	A	P	P	A	A	A	2	3
A	P	P	P	A	A	A	P	A	A	A	P	1	
A	A	P	A	A	A	A	P	P	A	P	P		1
A	A	P	P	P	A	A	A	P	A	P	A		2
A	A	P	A	A	A	P	P	P	P	A	A		1
A	A	P	A	P	A	A	P	A	P	P	A		1
P	A	A	P	P	A	P	A	P	A	A	A		1
A	A	P	A	P	A	A	P	P	A	P	A		1
A	A	A	A	P	A	A	P	P	P	P	A		1
P	A	P	A	A	A	A	P	A	P	A	A		2
P	A	P	P	P	A	A	P	A	A	A	A		1
P	P	P	P	A	A	A	P	A	A	A	A		1

4 Factors

1	2	3	4	5	6	7	8	9	10	11	12	Number of Delinquents	Number of Non-Delinquents
A	A	P	P	A	A	A	P	A	A	A	P	1	
A	A	P	A	A	A	A	P	P	A	P	A		1
A	A	P	P	A	A	A	P	P	A	A	A		2
A	A	P	A	P	A	A	P	P	A	A	A		1
A	P	P	P	A	A	A	P	A	A	A	A		1
A	P	A	P	A	A	A	P	P	A	A	A		1
A	A	P	A	P	A	A	A	A	A	P	P		1

3 Factors

1	2	3	4	5	6	7	8	9	10	11	12	Number of Delinquents	Number of Non-Delinquents
A	A	A	P	A	A	A	P	A	A	A	P	1	
A	A	P	P	A	A	A	P	A	A	A	A		5
A	P	P	A	A	A	A	P	A	A	A	A		1
A	A	A	A	P	A	A	P	A	P	A	A		1
A	A	P	A	A	A	A	P	A	P	A	A		2
A	A	P	A	A	A	P	P	A	A	A	A		1
P	A	A	A	A	A	A	P	A	P	A	A		1
A	A	P	P	A	A	P	A	A	A	A	A		1
P	A	P	A	A	A	A	P	A	A	A	A		1
A	A	P	A	P	A	A	A	P	A	A	A		1
A	A	P	A	A	A	A	P	A	A	P	A		1
A	A	P	A	A	A	A	P	P	A	A	A		1
A	A	A	P	A	A	P	A	P	A	A	A		1
A	A	A	A	A	A	A	P	A	A	P	P		1

ECTOMORPHS (Concluded)

Factors: 1	2	3	4	5	6	7	8	9	10	11	12	Number of Delinquents	Number of Non-Delinquents

2 Factors

1	2	3	4	5	6	7	8	9	10	11	12	Delinquents	Non-Delinquents
P	A	A	A	A	A	A	P	A	A	A	A		7
A	A	P	A	A	A	A	P	A	A	A	A		7
A	A	A	P	A	A	A	P	A	A	A	A		5
A	A	A	A	A	A	P	P	A	A	A	A		2
P	A	A	P	A	A	A	A	A	A	A	A		2
A	A	A	A	P	A	A	A	P	A	A	A		1
A	A	A	A	A	A	A	P	P	A	A	A		1
P	A	A	A	A	A	A	A	A	P	A	A		1
A	A	A	A	A	A	A	P	A	A	P	A		1
A	A	A	A	P	A	A	P	A	A	A	A		1
P	A	P	A	A	A	A	A	A	A	A	A		2

1 Factor

1	2	3	4	5	6	7	8	9	10	11	12	Delinquents	Non-Delinquents
A	A	A	A	A	A	A	P	A	A	A	A		25
P	A	A	A	A	A	A	A	A	A	A	A		1
A	A	A	P	A	A	A	A	A	A	A	A		1
A	A	P	A	A	A	A	A	A	A	A	A		1

322

APPENDIX F

THE RORSCHACH TEST AND ITS RELATION TO THE PSYCHIATRIC FINDINGS

RORSCHACH TEST

The Rorschach Tests were given in Boston by Henry C. Patey, Edward A. Lincoln, and Libbie B. Bower, and interpreted in New York (without indication of which protocols came from delinquents and which from non-delinquents) by Ernest G. Schachtel and Anna Hartoch Schachtel.

Dr. Schachtel's detailed description of how the complete list was established is as follows:

"Since delinquency as defined in this study is not a psychological category and since the motivations for delinquency may vary widely, an attempt had to be made to get at the significant motivational dynamisms in the character structure of the individual in order to find out whether some of these were more typically found in delinquents or in certain groups of delinquents than in non-delinquents and vice versa. Because the more enduring motivational dynamisms that form the character structure are not directly visible in the Rorschach psychogram and record, but very often can be ascertained through an interpretation of these, our first effort was to develop a list of psychological categories (traits, qualities, drives, feelings, and the like), the presence or absence of which one could expect to see fairly regularly by means of interpretations of Rorschach records, and which might have significance for the problem studied. The outcome of this effort was a trait list, which could be neither exhaustive nor systematic since this study is not experimental but explorative, not intended to prove or disprove any preconceived hypothesis, but to serve as a basis for developing hypotheses.

"In developing the trait list we included, in the order of their importance:

1. All traits that seemed likely to have a bearing on the problem studied.

2. Some traits that possibly might have some significance for the problem.

3. Some traits that have been related to the problem of delinquency by the literature.

4. Some traits that, according to the Rorschach literature, are typically recognizable on the basis of Rorschach Tests."

The resulting list included traits subsumed under the general headings of Basic Attitudes to Authority and Society; Feelings of Insecurity, Anxiety, Inferiority, and Frustration; Kindliness and Hostility; Some General Qualities of Personality; Dependence and Independence; and Goals of Drives. (See Appendix C-1 for detailed list of traits.)

"These traits, feelings, and strivings," says Dr. Schachtel, "may be either conscious or unconscious. In contrast to Rorschach's original view (Rorschach thought that his test could not be used 'as a means of delving into the unconscious' but later he seems to have modified that view somewhat, especially in so far as movement, color, and abstract responses were concerned. See note 13: Rorschach, *Psychodiagnostics,* pp. 123, 204-213), I believe that unconscious traits and tendencies can be seen on the basis of Rorschach records. But it is more difficult sometimes to see whether and to what extent a person is or is not aware of a particular tendency in himself than it is to recognize the presence of that tendency, be it a conscious or an unconscious one.

"The trait list is not systematic. Hence the sections into which it is divided and their headings have to be understood as convenient, loose groupings of traits which are related to each other. Since all traits in the human personality are interdependent, occasionally also traits in different sections will be closely related to each other (for example, masochistic trends in the section, Goals of Drives, are intimately tied up with attitude toward authority in the section, Basic Attitudes toward Authority and Society). And some of the sections are more closely related to each other than others (for example, the section, Dependence and Independence, is more closely related to the section, Basic Attitudes toward Authority and Society, than to any other section).

"The psychological concepts underlying the trait list are mostly derived from the psychoanalytic theory of personality as developed in the work of Freud, Erich Fromm, Karen Horney, and Harry Stack Sullivan. While the interpretation of Rorschach records, just as the interpretation of any other human behavior, can be undertaken on the basis of any theory or personality, the concept of personality in the mind of the person analyzing a Rorschach record will inevitably influence his interpretation, regardless of whether he is or is not aware of his personality concept and regardless of whether this concept is consistent or contradictory, vague or articulate. The soundness of the interpretation, especially in so far as it goes beyond mere nosological classification and tries to outline the main trends of the personality structure, will depend on the soundness of the psychological concepts used."

In addition to the determination of attitudes, feelings, traits, and drives, we asked the Schachtels whether they could make a mental diagnosis of each boy on the basis of the Rorschach analysis, without having available any data from the social investigation or from the psychological and psychiatric examinations. They agreed that it would be possible to arrive at the following classifications: no conspicuous mental pathology, poorly adjusted, neurotic trends, mild neurotic, marked neurotic, psychopathic, psychotic trends, organic disturbances, and undifferentiated pathology. These were later to be compared with the diagnoses derived from the psychiatric examinations.

In order to supplement the data on intelligence to be derived from the verbal and performance components of the Wechsler-Bellevue Scale and the Stanford Achievement Tests in Reading and Arithmetic, we asked the Schachtels whether they could make any determination from the Rorschach Test regarding the quality of intelligence. This they agreed to do: "We will include in a section on intelligence mostly the qualities that are difficult to see in the Wechsler-Bellevue Test." These qualities or traits are: originality, creativity, banality, power of observation, unrealistic thinking, common sense, intuition, phantasy, oververbalizing intelligence, methodical approach to problems, and potential capacity for objective interests.

PSYCHIATRIC INTERVIEW

By comparing the delinquents and non-delinquents in respect to personality, largely through the Rorschach Test, we sought to determine differences of an emotional and dynamic nature, which are partially instinctual and partially conditioned by the relationship of the child to the parents during the first few years of life. In addition to the Rorschach Test, psychiatric interviews with the delinquents and non-delinquents were included. While, of course, a series of many consecutive interviews with each boy would have elicited more material, one such interview served to supplement and corroborate data from other sources.

The nature and content of the psychiatric interview were limited by the dangers inherent in delving into the conflicts and underlying motivations of behavior and stirring up buried emotional disturbances without carrying out any psychiatric treatment. A distinguished psychiatrist of rich and varied experience, Dr. Bernard Glueck, in assisting us to delimit the scope of the psychiatric examination, emphasized that it should deal essentially with personality and behavior characteristics that do not fall strictly and clearly within the scope of psycho-pathology. We soon realized that it would have to limit itself largely to data predominantly on a behavioral level. We recognized the dangers of overvaluing data gained from one interview with a boy. In determining the content of the interview, therefore, we limited it to those details that we believed a highly experienced psychiatrist would be able to gather in a relatively brief time.

The psychiatric interview was meant not only to supplement and complement the data revealed by the Rorschach Test, but also to round out and supplement information derived from the investigations into the boy's family and personal background. It included some items that should rightfully have been in the social investigation but that could more readily and uniformly be secured by the psychiatrist during the course of his interview—for example, club membership, play places, church attendance, companionships, academic and vocational ambitions, school subject preferences and dislikes, nature of employment experiences, and so on.

The psychiatrist was asked to question the boys in regard to their misbehavior. Although ample information was available on the misconduct of the frankly delinquent boys, the interview with the non-delinquents would be especially helpful in revealing petty misdemeanors, which in some cases resulted in our transferring a presumably non-delinquent boy to the delinquent group or eliminating him entirely. These queries would help the psychiatrist to glimpse a boy's stresses and conflicts, to determine how he resolves his conflicts, and to learn something of his inherent personality traits. They would also provide insights into the reasons for persistent misbehavior in the case of the delinquents, and preventives or deterrents to misbehavior in the case of the non-delinquents. On the basis of all these data the psychiatrist was to make a diagnostic classification of each boy.

The preliminary content of the psychiatric interview was prepared with the assistance of the staff psychiatrist, Dr. Bryant E. Moulton, who for seven years had been an associate of Dr. William Healy and Dr. Augusta Bronner on the staff of the Judge Baker Foundation (now known as the Judge Baker Guidance Center) and who had therefore had many years of contact with young boys, mostly delinquents. It was tested on twenty cases (ten delinquents and ten non-delinquents), and the findings were subjected to critical study. From this analysis the final content of the psychiatric interview was determined. At this stage it was submitted to Dr. Schachtel for his comments, and he agreed that it would effectively supplement and partly overlap the data to be derived from the Rorschach Test.

The psychiatrist proceeded with the utmost caution in his interviews with the boys in order to avoid arousing any deep-seated emotional conflicts that he would be in no position to resolve, since we were not carrying out a treatment program. In one instance, for example, he commented: "This boy certainly has some conflicts in regard to sex that it would not be advisable to bring into consciousness and then do nothing about." In another case: "This boy seems rather apprehensive, shows some evidence of nervous tension; I would make a guess that he has some conflict over masturbation. Would not go into this in one interview with him as it might stir up more conflict and resentment toward the whole procedure."

In the correctional schools, the psychiatrist reported that he found practically no resistance to the interviewing because the boys accepted it as part of the institutional regime. At first they were somewhat relu tant to discuss their delinquencies, especially those that were not already a matter of record; but as time went by and they were convinced that he did not reveal their confidence to the officials, their suspicions vanished.

The interview was found to be most effective if the psychiatrist began by questioning the delinquents about their misbehavior. He then sought to convince them that they did not necessarily know the real causes for their misconduct—an idea which most of them accepted quite readily. The more intelligent were not a little intrigued with the probability that their own particular experiences might eventually throw some light on the whole problem of the causes of crime; the mentally dull accepted the interview without any critical reaction or resistance to it. In some cases the psychiatrist had information from the "cottage parents" in the correctional institutions that he found of great assistance in interpreting a boy's personality difficulties.

In the public schools where the non-delinquents were interviewed, the psychiatrist was eager to know whether they had any delinquent ideation or had been misconducting themselves without the knowledge of school authorities, their parents, or police.

The non-delinquent boys were told that the psychiatrist assumed that each one had misbehaved to some extent but that this did not mean they were delinquents. Thus encouraged, they told of their peccadilloes, such as window-breaking, truck-hopping, occasionally sneaking admission into a movie theatre, or even stealing once or twice from a five-and-ten-cent store. In the initial approach to the non-delinquent boys the fact of their non-delinquency was not stressed too much, since this would have placed some of the real but undetected delinquents on the defensive.

The psychiatrist sometimes had an initial knowledge of the boys gained through his interviews with other delinquents and non-delinquents, who mentioned members of their "gangs" and "crowds."

The emphasis in the interviewing of the non-delinquents was largely on those factors in their mental and physical make-up which had contributed to their social adjustment or their avoidance of delinquent acts. The interview began quite naturally with the school progress and attitudes of the boys. This led to their vocational aspirations, the desirability of continuing school, and parental attitudes toward their ambitions. This, in turn, led easily to a discussion of any specific assets or liabilities, physical, intellectual, or temperamental.

When a boy manifested great curiosity about the results of the inquiry, he was told that by making an appointment with the psychiatrist he might subsequently be given information about some of his tests. Only a handful of boys have taken advantage of this invitation.

Comparison of Rorschach and Psychiatric Findings

Although we realized in designing the research that a diagnosis made by the psychiatrist as the result of one interview with a boy and derived from a behavioristic level of personality structure could not be conclusive, we nevertheless felt that as experienced a child psychologist as Dr. Bryant E. Moulton would be able to make reliable diagnostic classifications for purposes of comparing and supplementing the diagnoses arrived at by the Rorschach analyst.

When the two series of examinations were entirely completed, we ourselves compared the two sets of diagnoses, keeping in mind the somewhat different concepts that were used in making the classifications by each method. Wherever significant differences were found, Dr. Schachtel was asked to resolve them after we had made available to him the full psychiatric report. As Dr. Moulton was at this time no longer connected with the research, the materials were not submitted to him.

We found what seemed to be inconsistencies between the two sets of diagnoses in only 74 cases, and these were examined by Dr. Schachtel in the following manner: "In examining the differences between the psychiatric and Rorschach diagnoses, a distinction has been made between diagnosis proper and personality description. This has been done merely for the sake of presentation and in full awareness of the fact that these two factors are really inseparable and that diagnosis constitutes essentially a very generalized, highly abstract summary of certain aspects of the personality description.

"In comparing the diagnoses the fact must be kept in mind that some of the psychiatrist's categories of diagnostic classification have not been used for the Rorschach diagnoses and some of the Rorschach classifications have not been used by the psychiatrist, and furthermore that the definitions of some of the diagnostic categories (especially of the term neurotic) differ as between the psychiatric and Rorschach materials.

"For these reasons the apparent differences in diagnostic classification often may not be real, but merely differences in terminology. Perhaps the most frequent seeming, but not real, differences arise from the fact that the psychiatrist does not seem to use the concept of character-neurosis and that the Rorschach does not use the concept, constitutionally inferior. Most of the cases classified as neurotic in the Rorschach diagnosis suffer from character-neurosis.

"In view of these differences in diagnostic terminology, in all cases where the diagnoses seem to differ markedly I have primarily compared the personality descriptions and ratings. Where these are not contradictory or markedly different from each other in essential respects, I have generally assumed agreement and noted that the seeming difference in diagnosis is the result of the definition."

The following results were achieved by Dr. Schachtel's study of the 74 cases.

In 20 cases he found that the differences resulted from differences in definitions or in terminology. For example, Case No. 11: Rorschach diagnosis: *marked neurotic*. Psychiatric diagnosis: *no conspicuous mental pathology*. "Psychiatrist mentions the 'distinct impression that this boy has definite conflicts,' is non-confiding, has extreme compensatory tendencies, is stubborn and suspicious. This fits well with the Rorschach description and forms the basis for the Rorschach classification of *neurotic*." Case No. 38: Rorschach diagnosis: *psychopathic*. Psychiatric diagnosis: *no conspicuous mental pathology*. "The material in the psychiatric interview makes it much more likely to my mind, that this boy has marked pathological features than that he has none. The psychiatrist states that he is very suggestible, has marked inferiority feelings, and was rejected or deserted at a very early age by both parents. The last circumstance almost inevitably would lead to serious disturbances and is typical in the life-history of many psychopaths. The boy must have resented this desertion deeply. Also, the final statement of the psychiatrist that even under the most favorable conditions the boy will be a poor risk and will need guidance all his life speaks for the likelihood of the Rorschach diagnosis." Case No. 511: Rorschach diagnosis: *marked neurotic*. Psychiatric diagnosis: *no conspicuous mental pathology*. "Essentially, both the Rorschach materials and the psychiatric materials agree on submissive attitude toward authority and lack of self-confidence. There is disagreement only as to the degree of these traits. According to the Rorschach analysis, they are so marked that they make this boy quite repressed and dependent."

In 43 cases, although the diagnoses were apparently different, the personality description (made by the psychiatrist in the text of his report) was in the direction of substantiating the Rorschach classification. For example, Case No. 108: Rorschach diagnosis: *no conspicuous mental pathology*. Psychiatric diagnosis: *psychoneurotic tendencies*. "I doubt that this is a disagreement. The wording of the psychiatric diagnosis seems to indicate that the psychiatrist does not want to classify him as acutely, out-and-out neurotic, but only as tending in that direction. There are some neurotic trends, as described also in the Rorschach Test. They did not seem sufficiently strong to classify the boy as neurotic. If there is any difference between the psychiatrist and the Rorschach analysts it is a question of estimating degree of trends rather than of assuming or not assuming a characteristic diagnostic picture; difference of degree rather than of kind." Case No. 265: Rorschach diagnosis: *between neurotic and psychopathic*. Psychiatric diagnosis: *no conspicuous mental pathology*. "The psychiatrist mentions unconscious conflict and sense of inadequacy. This would easily be compatible with the assumption of neurosis. The type of stealing, for immediate use, goes well with the assumption of oral-receptive trends." Case No. 624: Rorschach diagnosis: *marked neurotic*. Psychiatric diagnosis: *no conspicuous mental pathology*. "No evidence of definite disagreement. Outstanding in the psychiatric interview is the impression that the boy does not really talk freely and that one does not quite know what he is like and what his motivations are. The psychiatrist also notices indications of compensatory processes. This could very well be compatible with an underlying structure such as the Rorschach analysis points to."

In 4 cases the differences were due to the fact that the particular category used by the psychiatrist could not be derived through the Rorschach Test. This refers especially to epileptic personality. For example, Case No. 328: Rorschach diagnosis: *no conspicuous mental pathology*. Psychiatric diagnosis: *epilepsy*. "Epilepsy is not among the Rorschach categories since quite often it cannot be seen on the basis of the Rorschach record. This boy's Rorschach Test shows none of the outstanding epilepsy symptoms, but this might merely mean that his epilepsy is not apparent in the Rorschach, which happens quite often. His intensive feeling reaction, mentioned by the psychiatrist, also shows in the Rorschach."

In one case the comparison could not be made because the data were not sufficiently clear.

331

Finally, in only 6 cases was there frank disagreement between the Rorschach and the psychiatric diagnoses. We cite them all. Case No. 236: Rorschach diagnosis: *no conspicuous mental pathology*. Psychiatric diagnosis: *abnormal personality, unstable neurotic*. "The Rorschach record does give a less unstable picture than the psychiatric. The life history of this boy would lead one to expect that he is unstable and neurotic. The psychiatrist's diagnosis is the more likely. The two diagnoses agree on the lack of spontaneity and insecurity." Case No. 713: Rorschach diagnosis: *marked neurotic* (?). Psychiatric diagnosis: *no conspicuous mental pathology*. "Disagreement in personality description. According to the psychiatric record, the boy is unattractive, has a stiff knee joint that is the cause of an awkward limp. The psychiatrist feels surprised that the boy does not seem to have any intense conflicts. The Rorschach analysis quite definitely points to an unstable, pathological personality and to destructive-sadistic trends such as often develop on the basis of physical or other handicaps." Case No. 725: Rorschach diagnosis: *psychopathic*. Psychiatric diagnosis: *no conspicuous mental pathology*. "Disagreement. The Rorschach picture is definitely that of a quite egocentric, unstable personality tending toward impulsiveness. The destructive trends, assumed in the Rorschach analysis, may be questionable. The only symptoms mentioned by the psychiatrist that may point to some disturbance are tenseness, a tendency to stutter, and insecurity." Case No. 314: Rorschach diagnosis: *no conspicuous mental pathology*. Psychiatric diagnosis: *unstable—on organic basis*. "The Rorschach record definitely does not indicate any organic disturbance of the central nervous system. Whether there are any other organic disturbances cannot be seen from the Rorschach record. On his unstableness the two diagnoses agree." Case No. 466: Rorschach diagnosis: *psychopathic trends*. Psychiatric diagnosis: *no conspicuous mental pathology*. "The Rorschach analysis stresses impulsiveness and rebellious-destructive trends more than the psychiatrist and gives a more pathological picture. This seems to be more than a difference in emphasis." Case No. 478: Rorschach diagnosis: *marked neurotic*. Psychiatric diagnosis: *no conspicuous mental pathology*. "Disagreement in diagnosis and in personality picture."

Index

Set in Linotype Granjon
Format by Katharine Sitterly
Manufactured by The Haddon Craftsmen, Inc.
Published by HARPER & BROTHERS, *New York*